Citizen Tom Paine

CITIZEN
TOM PAINE

HOWARD FAST

GROVE PRESS, INC., NEW YORK

To Bette

First Evergreen Edition published in 1983
ISBN: 0-394-62464-5
Library of Congress Catalog Card Number: 82-84625

Manufactured in the United States of America

GROVE PRESS, INC., 920 BROADWAY, NEW YORK, N.Y. 10010

10 9 8 7 6 5 4 3 2

CONTENTS

PART ONE: AMERICA

PART TWO: EUROPE

There is nothing more common than to confound the terms of *American Revolution* with those of the *late American War*. The American war is over, but this is far from being the case with the American revolution. On the contrary, nothing but the first act of the great drama is closed.

1787   BENJAMIN RUSH

PART ONE

AMERICA

1

MY NAME IS PAINE

On a cool, pleasant early fall morning, in the year 1774, Dr. Benjamin Franklin was told that Thomas Paine had been waiting to see him for almost an hour. Dr. Franklin, who had lived in England for many years, who was known through all the civilized world as a great scholar, a witty philosopher, a scientist of no mean parts, and altogether a good deal of a man, was acquainted with everyone in England who mattered, and a good many who did not matter, but whose names did. Yet he could not recall ever having heard of Thomas Paine.

The old man who announced visitors said that Mr. Paine was not a gentleman.

It was no novelty for Dr. Franklin to have visitors who were not gentlemen, yet the curl of the old servant's lips defined an extreme. Franklin wrinkled his nose to set his glasses a trifle closer to his eyes, moved his big, shaggy head, and said without looking up from the letter he was writing, "Well, show him in, why don't you?" and then added somewhat testily, "Why didn't you tell me he was waiting? Why didn't you show him in before?"

"He be dirty," the old man said sourly, and went out, and then came back a moment later leading the other, who set himself just inside the door, almost defiantly, and said,

"My name is Paine, sir!"

Dr. Franklin put away his pen, studied his visitor for a moment or two, and then smiled and said, "Mine is Franklin, sir. I'm sorry I kept you waiting," nodding for the servant to leave the room.

"I'm sorry I waited," Paine said belligerently. "You had no other visitors. You can tell me to go to the devil now, and I'll be off. I didn't want to see the King, only Dr. Franklin. And I didn't have anything to do but to sit there."

Dr. Franklin continued to smile and look at his visitor. Paine wasn't handsome; he wasn't prepossessing; somewhere between thirty and forty, the doctor thought, his sharp hooked nose adding years if anything. His chin was sharp, his mouth full, his oddly twisted eyes tight with bitterness and resentment; virtue or evil in that face, but no joy for a long time and no hope either. His whiskers were a week on his face, and he needed washing. He was not tall nor short, but of medium height, with the powerful, sloping shoulders of a workman who has put in long hours at a bench, and his hands were from the bench, meaty and broad. His cheap coat had split under both arms and his breeches were paper thin at the knees; his stockings were a shambles and his toes breathed freely in what were never good shoes.

"How long is it since you've eaten?" Franklin asked.

"That's none of your damn business! I didn't come for charity."

"Sit down, please," Franklin said quietly, and then went out and came back in a few minutes with a loaf of bread, a piece of meat, and a crock of beer. He set it all down on the table, and then went back to his letter writing, nor did he look up again until Paine had finished and was standing up, uncomfortable and somewhat abashed.

"Feel better?" Franklin asked.

Paine nodded; inside of him, something was burning uneasily; his toes tried to draw into the battered shoes, and with a hand in either pocket, he attempted to stare Franklin down. Drawing out of one pocket a handful of dirty bills and silver, he said, "There's thirty guineas. I didn't come for charity."

"I didn't think you did," Franklin answered. "Why don't you sit down? Why don't you let the world roll by, Mr. Paine, instead of trying to hold it on your shoulders? I approve of thrift, and if a man wants thirty guineas in his pocket and not a shilling's worth on his back, it's reasonable enough for me. But a man's bread isn't to be refused, and there's no charity in breaking some of it. Who are you, Mr. Paine, and what do you want of me?"

"I want to go to America," Paine blurted out. "You're an American. I heard you were an easy man, even with nobody, and not to begrudge something that won't cost you a penny. I thought maybe you'd write me a letter for a position."

"I will."

Still holding the money in his hand, Paine nodded slowly, put the money away, tried to say something, and succeeded only in muttering a few words that meant practically nothing. Then he sat down and spread his broad hands to cover his threadbare knees. Then he fingered his week's growth of beard. Franklin didn't watch him; sealing a letter, glancing up only for a moment, he asked Paine's trade.

"Staymaker," Paine answered, and then added, "Yes—for ladies' corsets and men's vests. I was an excise man," he said, "a gauger for fifty pounds a year. I'm a bad carpenter; I cobbled shoes for sixpence a day because I wanted to live, although God knows why. I swept a weaver's booth for half of that and sold ribbons for maybe twice. I write sometimes," he finished.

"What do you write?" Franklin asked quietly.

"What a man can't say because he's got no guts in him to say it!"

They had talked for an hour. Paine had put down a quart of the beer. His twisted eyes glittered and his broad hands clenched and unclenched with almost rhythmical nervousness. He had forgotten his clothes, his beard, his unwashed skin, his memories; and lost himself in the fascination of an old man who was strangely young and vibrant, and wise as men said he was.

"What is America like?" he asked Franklin.

"Like a promise, or like Scotland or Wales or Sussex, or like none of them, or like a yoke around a man's neck, depending on the man, or like a bonnet to set on his head."

"Big?"

"It goes on," Franklin said. "It's not been explored or surveyed—" There was a note of regret in his voice, as if here was one thing he would have liked to do, but had let slip by.

"I thought of it that way."

"Good wages," Franklin said. "Nobody starves if he wants to work."

"Nobody starves," Paine repeated.

"You can burn there." Franklin smiled. "The fire won't singe anybody."

"I've had enough of burning," Paine said stolidly. "I want a coat on my back and a pair of good shoes. I want to be able to walk into a tavern and put down a guinea like I knew what a guinea was instead of just the smell of it, and I don't have to worry about the change."

"Have you any Latin?"

"A little."

"You're Quaker born and bred, aren't you?"

"I was, I don't know what I am now. I tried to bang out, and I hit my head against the wall. I'm a little drunk, Dr. Franklin, and there's no bridle on my tongue, but this isn't a good country; it stinks, it rots like a pile of dung, and I want to go away and get out of it and not see it again, and aside from that I don't want so much, only some food and a place to sleep and some work to do."

"You can have that," Franklin said thoughtfully. "I'll write you a letter, if it will help you. Don't bang against the wall, but put a penny by here and there and find a piece of land in Pennsylvania, where land's cheap, and get your hands into it."

Paine nodded.

"I'll write to my son-in-law, who will do something for you."

Paine kept nodding, trying to say somehow that Franklin was being good to him, very good. Paine was a little drunk and tired, his sharp head rocking forward, his twisted eyes closing, the whole of him, wretched clothes and dirty skin and beard, and curious pointed features making a disturbing enigma that Franklin remembered for long years afterward whenever he thought of Tom Paine. Franklin had a taste for enigmas, yet this was one he would never solve.

"Get thee to America, if thee will not work," Paine's father told him when the boy was thirteen years old, and had had more than enough of schooling and dreaming and wandering in the lush fields of old Thetford and climbing in the ruins of the old castle and building castles of his own and thinking that childhood goes on forever.

"Not stays," he said stubbornly.

"And thee are one to say stays or not stays!"

"Not stays."

"And thee know another trade, thee stubborn, ill-mannered, ill-weaned whelp."

He was apprenticed to the art and shown how an artist works. Mrs. Hardy, who was some sort of quality, on the borderline in those days when quality was not nearly so rigidly defined as twenty-five years later, had come to have her corset fitted. Mrs. Hardy weighed two hundred pounds, and most of it was in midriff and above, a bosom like the heathered hills of Scotland and a belly that had given passage to more ale than the Dog's Head Inn. She hadn't bathed in the fourteen months since she had been to the watering place at Bath, and in his first day as a staymaker he had to ram his head against her belly. He had to go into the mysteries and tug and tug, while she squealed like a pig.

"Get thee onto it, Thomas!" his father commanded.

He hung on the laces, while Mrs. Hardy roared, "Paine, you rascal, you're twelve inches short."

"You're twelve inches long," the thirteen-year-old thought miserably. He braced a hand, and it sank deep into a monstrous huge breast.

"Get thee onto it, Thomas," his father repeated, stony and secure in his shell, then stepping out of the room for a moment. Thomas was lost; he sank deeper and deeper into the ocean of flesh; caught in terror and hot misery, he forgot the laces and the corset snapped open and the flesh rolled out at him. Snickering, "You little rascal, you little rascal," she caught him in her arms. He struggled, sank deeper, fought for his life, then broke loose and ran from the shop, across the fields, panting like a dog until he threw himself down in the shadow of the old ruins.

Twelve of the best laid his behind open and bleeding; he was going to be a staymaker; his father had been a staymaker. Otherwise, get thee to America. Old Paine wasn't a hard man, but there was a way of things, and what you were your son was; the world was a bitter, angry place, and if you earned your honest shilling, that was all God gave you reason to expect. Now Tom Paine was going to America, leaving more broken things behind him than a set of stays, and no man really remembers what was here and what was there at the age of thirteen. He had dozed off, and he looked up now to hear Benjamin Franklin reading the letter he had written so kindly to his son-in-law, Richard Bache, a person of influence in a far-off place called Philadelphia:

"—the bearer, Mr. Thomas Paine (and that was America for you, titled Mr. Paine, this dirty raggle-taggle, and not by nobody or anybody, but by Dr. Benjamin Franklin, the wisest man in the world) is very well recommended to me as an ingenious worthy young man—(and hear that, worthy young man). He goes to Pennsylvania with a view of settling there. I request you to give him your best advice and countenance, as he is quite a stranger there. If you can put him in the way of obtaining employment as a clerk, or assistant tutor in a school, or assistant surveyor, of all of which I think him very capable, so that he may procure a subsistence at least, till he can make acquaintance and obtain a knowledge of the country, you will do well and much oblige your affectionate father—"

"I want to do something," Paine said. "No one was so good to me; I have no friends. If I thought to give you some money, you would laugh at me."

"Give it to someone else," Franklin said evenly. "Stop pitying yourself. Wash and shave off your beard, and don't think the world has knocked you harder than anyone else."

2

AMERICA IS THE PROMISED LAND

THIS was the great crossing,
east to west for nine weeks, and then off the edge of the
world, as the old folks back in Thetford believed, having
never gotten more than a mile or two from their native
heath. But he was Tom Paine the traveler and adventurer,
not the staymaker and weaver's assistant, and he had sailed
for nine weeks on a fever-ridden ship. Now he was dying;
no one knew and no one cared, and the captain was too sick
himself to be bothered. The ship gently rocked in the placid
sunshine that flooded the Delaware River, with the red roofs
of Philadelphia only a stone's throw off, while in the black-
ness of the sick-hold Tom Paine groaned away his life.

He didn't care, he told himself. Franklin had said, "Stop
pitying yourself." He cursed Franklin; well enough for
Franklin, who lived like a fat old toad in England; the
world was good for some, but you could count them on the
fingers of a hand, and for the others it was a pen and a jail
and a desolation. Like a pinned-down fly on a board, a man
struggled for a time and then died, and then there was nothing, as in the beginning there had been nothing. Why should
Tom Paine fight it? Why should he fight disease and hunger
and loneliness and misery?

He wouldn't fight it, now he would die, and his pity was

such an enormous thing that he was thrilled and amazed by the spectacle of himself. He wept for himself, and then wiped away the tears and allowed sunny memories of long ago to creep in. A child in Thetford walked on a flower-decked hillside. May Adams, who had long braids, ran before him into the vine-grown ruins and fell and hurt her knee, and he licked out the dirt and then kissed her. Wrong, she said, and when he asked why, only repeated, wrong, wrong; yet for all that they became lovers and no one knew. She died of the pox when he was not much older and he held the sorrow inside of him, sitting at his bench and making a corset for Jenny Literton, not eating, not stopping, his father saying, "There's a boy with industry, and a change from the rascal he was."

Everything died; now he was dying because Franklin had sent him off to America.

The fever ship held the spotlight at the waterfront, and in the twenty-four hours after she docked almost half the people in Philadelphia came down to have a look at her. It was told how five bodies were dropped overboard during the nine weeks, though you wouldn't know it just to look at her; as the sickly passengers, the convalescing passengers, the tottering passengers came ashore, each told a different version of the lurid story. One of them mentioned a man in the hold who had a letter written by Franklin, and Dr. Kearsley who was trying to set up in the great city of America and having a rather hard time of it, smelled a fee.

"What's his name?"

"Paine, I think."

"Did you see the letter?" Kearsley asked cautiously

"No, I heard about it."

"You?" the doctor asked someone else.

"No."

A fee was a fee, but to go onto the fever ship for nothing at all was not part of a doctor's duty. "Did he come in the bilge?"

"Cabin passenger."

The bilge had been full of indentured servants, among whom the sickness had first started, and already the still tottering captain was discussing their sale with a pair of prosperous Philadelphia merchants.

"Duty's duty," the doctor said, and went on board. He went down into the stinking hold, and stumbling over bodies, cursing and regretting that duty bulked so large, yelled above the groaning for Mr. Paine.

Mr. Paine answered. The doctor had a candle which wavered and flickered in the foul air, but candle and all it was a task to pick out Tom Paine, and the search over, a thankless task it seemed to the doctor. The clothes were the same, the beard worse, the dirt thicker, the whole a disgusting bundle of rags and misery that whispered for the doctor to go away and allow it to die in peace.

"Ah, and die you shall," the doctor said to himself.

"Go away," Paine groaned.

"You have a letter from Franklin?" Kearsley inquired, clutching at one last straw.

"Yes, damn him!"

"Ah—and what money, my good lad?"

"Three pounds seven," Paine whispered.

"Ah! And tomorrow you'll be up and walking! Got the money with you? Got any luggage?"

"Can't you see I'm dying?"

The doctor left and then returned with the boatman, who demanded three shillings before he would step onto the ship. Hand and foot, they took Tom Paine, dragged him out into the air, and then dumped him like a pile of rags into the bottom of the boat.

There was a last spark of defiance and consciousness in Paine, only enough for him to call the doctor and boatman a pair of bastards and ask why he hadn't been left to die. The doctor was equally frank, and as the boatman pulled for shore he leaned over his sweating, suffering patient and explained, "Because three pounds seven are not come by every day, not by a man who's starting in practice. I'm not a thief; I'll earn the money; you'll live, though God only knows why."

"The Lord giveth; the Lord taketh away; blessed be the Lord," said a Quaker lady who brought him a box of cookies and a scent bag to hang under his nose. She had heard that there was a homeless one living with Kearsley, and that he was profane and dirty, and that Kearsley had wagered the great Dr. Japes twenty pounds that the patient wouldn't die. That was blasphemous. Now Paine admitted to her that he had been born and raised a Quaker, while Kearsley snickered at the foot of the bed—which made matters worse.

"Pray," she told Paine. "Beg the Lord's forgiveness and his everlasting mercy."

"He's cured now." Kearsley smiled.

"Pray, pray!" she called back as she fled from the room, and Kearsley leaned over the footboard, shaking with laughter.

"What a filthy devil you are," Paine said.

"Call the kettle black! Didn't I give you your first bath?"

"Get out of here."

"I came to remind you that you owe me ten pounds," the doctor said. "You've been here six weeks, so that's reasonable. I've saved your life, for what that's worth, and altogether it's a small piece of gratitude you've shown. What is a man's life worth?"

"I'm grateful," Paine muttered, "and mine's worth little enough. I'll pay you when I find work."

"Doing what?"

Paine shrugged.

"I could throw you into jail for the debt," the doctor speculated.

"You could," Paine admitted. He was thin and worn with his sickness, white skin into which the twisted brown eyes were sunk like heavy question marks, bones stretching him like old clothes on a dryer. Kearsley said he was well, but he felt too tired to talk or plead.

"I'll give you a month," Kearsley said suddenly. "You can leave here tomorrow." And Paine nodded gratefully and closed his eyes.

He must have slept for a while, and now the doctor had gone, and the little room was mellow with twilight. There was a single dormer window that showed him, from where he lay, a half a dozen of the red-tiled Philadelphia rooftops. Beyond, a church steeple poked up against the gray sky, and as Tom Paine watched, the snow began to fall, clean, white, lazy flakes that drifted down faster and faster until a white curtain closed in the little window. The coals of a fire lay in the grate; Kearsley wasn't a brute, but a man tired of poverty and ignorance, all of which Paine could understand and even sympathize with now; Kearsley had cured him and given him back his life, and ten pounds wasn't such a stone around a man's neck. Less tired now, somewhat uncertain but finding his feet strong enough to hold him, Paine left his bed and went to the window. This was the America he had come to, and he was looking at it for the first time, a church steeple in the distance, some roofs flaked with white, some people walking on the cobbled street, the city of brotherly love, America, the land, the dream, the empire, that and much more that he had thought of once, the sum of it coming back to him as his will to live and be Tom Paine returned to him. There was a sweet quality in this winter evening, almost a nostalgia; the church bells began to toll faintly, and it seemed to Paine that the people in the streets were moving more quickly now.

Now life was a sweet thing, like an old song. He began to tremble with eagerness, and then he went back to his bed, but he couldn't sleep that night.

If the place had a prophet, it was Benjamin Franklin; the letter he had given Paine was mildewed, creased and worn, but Bache, Franklin's son-in-law, spread it out, read it carefully, and said, yes, he would do something for Paine. Nothing big or special, but this America was a good place, Pennsylvania a good country, and Philadelphia a good city, God bless King George. Nobody had to starve, not if a man had any guts in him. He wasn't one to say anything about the old country, but in some ways this place was better than the old country.

"I think so," Paine nodded.

Could Paine do anything? Was he a journeyman?

"In stays," Paine admitted. But rather than make corsets, he could cobble a little, weave a little, good work even if it wasn't journeyman work. But he had been sick, and—his face reddening—if he could use his brain instead of his hands for a time it might be a good thing. Not presumptuously, because he hadn't anything in the way of scholarship. But he could spell and sum and he had a little Greek and a little Latin. Bache's face remained noncommittal, and desperately. Paine quoted,

"Faber est quisque suae fortunae."

Bache, fat, prosperous, Paine's age, but a world above him
in assurance, nodded, patted Paine's shoulder, and said,
"Good enough, I'll find you some sort of place."

With his first few shillings, after two days of near starvation, he went to a coffee house and had rolls and butter and
a whole pot of viscous black fluid. Successful men, men like
Bache, sat around him, and whereas in London the state of
his clothes alone would have prevented him from going into
any respectable eating place, here hardly a second glance
was thrown at him. Hardly a glance—why, in the corner was
a buckskin wildman from the backlands, with leather leggings and a fur cap, and his rifle between his knees as he
ate with his hands, just as if he hadn't seen a fork or knife
before. So what if his work was teaching the two Dolan children that one and one made two, that c-a-t spelled cat, and
Mrs. Dolan came in midday and said, "Won't you have a
cup of tea, mister?" and that tomorrow it would be the
Smith children, two little girls and a boy.

Two months ago, he would have raged and burned, but
this was America and he had been given back his life, and
teaching was better than to be a journeyman staymaker. Or
maybe inside of himself something had burned out, that he
was content not even to look for tomorrow, but only to drift
along, satisfying himself with the knowledge that he was
Tom Paine, and no more.

A man changes; he wasn't old and he wasn't young, but
even Kearsley, who was blunt and hard and could be neatly
cruel, had a streak of pity for Paine, not the man, but the
wreck. As shown so well when Paine came back to renew his
promise on the debt, and Kearsley said, "Forget about it.
I won twenty pounds on you."

"I heard about that," Paine admitted, without anger.

"I don't say you're not worth more," the doctor temporized. "I don't know what a man's worth. I hear you are teaching."

"That's right."

"I hope you do well at it," the doctor said, sincere this time.

Paine shrugged; a shilling a day was enough, and two shillings more than enough, and when Mrs. Cradle gave him her husband's third best pair of breeches, he took it. He didn't work hard, and there were whole days when he did nothing at all but wander around Philadelphia, almost childishly intrigued by the colorful, un-European pageant that passed along the streets. There were red Indians out of the wooded mountains, wrapped in their bright and dirty blankets, clay pipes clenched in their teeth; there were wooden-shoed Dutchmen down on their flatboats from the Jerseys, sharp-nosed Yankees from Boston, tall Swedes from the Delaware country, dirty leather-coated hunters from the back counties, carrying their six-foot-long rifles wherever they went, silk-and-satin Tidewater gentlemen up from the south with their slaves, black and white and red and brown, and gray-clad Quakers of the inner circle, Penns and Darleys and Rodmonts. Up First Street, down Spruce, round about the Square, along Broad, he could walk slowly and lazily, divorced from the world in a murky way, his past severed, his future non-existent, a shilling teacher, the butt of smutty stories, his home sometimes a room in one tavern and sometimes in another if the weather was bad, if it snowed and rained and the wind lashed; but if the day was good enough he wasn't averse to bedding into a pile of hay in some Quaker's stable, thereby saving sixpence, which was about the price of the cheapest room a tavern sold.

If he thought of himself at all, it was with pity; when he could afford a bottle of wine it went down in such self-sympathy that he would usually wind up a mass of maudlin tears. And he didn't have to drink alone, since there was usually a tavern drunk to keep him company. Look at his own life, he would point out. Had he a chance? Staymaker when he was still a boy, finding a woman he loved and then losing her, grinding through what lower-middle-class England called life, drunk two weeks, a month on bad gin, the whole world like a fluttering pinwheel, groping in a haze for a little beauty, himself ugly and raw and unkempt.

He wasn't a fool; often he told himself, passively, that the mere fact he had wanted so many things proved it; and never acceptance, since he had hated with such ferocity kings, noblemen, ladies and gentlemen of quality, beggars and thieves and fat, prosperous merchants, sluts and whores and decent women too—and whom had he loved?

There was once a woman he loved, he knew.

Now he didn't love and he didn't hate; he had accomplished one great thing, his passage to the thin fringe of colonies on the American mainland; thereupon he rested. No one gave him shoes, and his shoes wore out; his stockings were a blunt deception; he had been given an old coat that flapped threadbare about his shoulders, and he meandered through the streets with his head down against the cold blasts of wind, his appearance unusual enough for people to begin to know him in such a small city as Philadelphia was then.

"There goes Tom Paine," they said.

A committee of Quaker ladies called on him. They brought him a new coat and a vest. "Thee are a shame to us," they pointed out. "Thee will go on this way until God will turn away his face."

He had been drinking, and he said, smiling foolishly, "I lick God's belly."

That got around the city, and he lost half his tutoring jobs.

That month, January, in the year 1775, was the beginning of a year that would change the destiny of mankind, yet it was such a January as we often have in the midlands, rain sometimes, snow sometimes, sleet sometimes, and sometimes a clear warm day that might very well be June. It was the beginning of a year that was the beginning of an era, and Christ himself might have walked on earth to raise so fierce yet so gentle a voice from long speechless mankind. Yet men for the most part didn't know and didn't care, what with one and a hundred things to be done, buying and selling and providing, loving and hating, profiting and losing.

In Philadelphia, it promised to be a good year. The town was rapidly becoming a city, and situated as a keystone among the nations of America, Virginia, Maryland, Pennsylvania, New York, Massachusetts and the rest, the city gave promise of being one of the great urban centers of the earth. Through its streets, its centers of commerce, which were the coffee houses, its warehouses and its wharves, teemed the trade of all the English colonies in America and of several European nations. It is true that already in the past year a somewhat incoherent body called the First Continental Congress had met in Philadelphia, but they had accomplished nothing, and solid citizens did not believe that the Congress was any menace to the security and prosperity of the colonies. There were disturbances and mutterings, in Boston for the most part and in other Yankee towns to the north; but when was there a time without disturbances? There was unrest in the back counties of the South, but what more could you

expect of wild woodsmen who tramped around free as Huns
with their six-foot-long rifles?

On the other hand, there was more than adequate com-
pensation. In the highlands, the beavers were thick as rabbits, and shepherded by lean Scotsmen and black-bearded
Jews a steady stream of glossy pelts poured into the city. The
Tidewater tobacco crop was better than good; the Jerseys
were bursting with food; and raft after raft of good white
pine floated down the Delaware. Never had the pigs in the
German counties been so fat and never had the sheep, graz-
ing in the rolling pastures north of the city, been so heavy
with wool. In the wild woods, the Allegheny reaches, the
lake country and the Fincastle Highlands, the deer ran thick
as flies; venison in Philadelphia sold for fourpence a pound
and bear meat could hardly be given away. The deer hides
by the thousands piled up in stinking bales on the wharves,
ready to change men's fashions in all of Europe. Master
carpenters were fighting the fad for Chippendale and Shera-
ton and other English cabinet makers; with a loop, a claw,
and a turn, a slim back, a graceful leg, they were not merely
imitating but creating a truly American furniture. The
working men of the city were strong and their hands itched
to make. Houses were going up, and sometimes the bricks
were native as well as the cement.

There were stirrings and murmurings, but there was also
an abundance of good things. There was discontent, yet
there was enough content. War was in the air, albeit vaguely,
but people did not want war; freedom was in the air, too,
but most people didn't give two damns about freedom.

The city was a good one, carefully laid out, bought by
Penn, not plundered from the red men, full of rich Quakers
and poor Quakers, and rich and poor who were not Quakers;

but altogether with such a determined air of middle-class prosperity as you would not find in any European city. The houses were solid structures, mostly brick, some half-timber, some frame. Many of the streets were cobbled, named not for men in an ungodly fashion, but for trees, or descriptively, or numbered. There was a good fire department, a good guard, a good library. There was a philosopher, Ben Franklin, come out of the city. There was more good glass, linen, silver, and furniture than anywhere else in America; and after a fashion there was more freedom of religion and thought. Here in the promised land, Philadelphia was the promised city.

Paine went to a slave sale, not because he wanted to buy or had the money to buy, but because it was on an afternoon when he had nothing else to do, and because he was curious to know what it was like to see human beings bought and sold. The auction was held in a big old barn, with the doors locked, and there were a dozen merchants present. It was a sale of breeding wenches, which meant that only women would be put on the auction block, that they would be either virgin or pregnant, and that the bidding would be very brisk. Not only that, but from what Paine had heard it would partake of other aspects than mere buying and selling.

He was hardly drunk today, only rosy, only enough to say to himself, "Why shouldn't they buy them and sell them? White, too, why only black?" Yet he was neither angry nor offended, but rather pleased with himself that he had persuaded the good merchants to let him in. They were good enough to call him a scrivener instead of a shilling-tutor, and he had a half-formed thought that he might write something about this and try to sell it to a magazine.

In the half hour before the bidding started, the merchants

sat around, perched comfortably on bales of hay, smoking, taking snuff, talking a commercial brand of filth, yet at the same time nervous and shy as adolescents in a bawdy house. For a while, Paine couldn't understand, and then it came to him that they would show the Negroes naked. His throat constricted; he was hot and cold and ashamed and eager, and for the first time in months he despised himself.

He saw that he was unshaven, unkempt and ragged; his fingernails were black crescents and his stockings like ladders; his pity for himself was a wet sop, a lie and a delusion, and if no one could offer proof of any kind for man's nobility, they could at least exhibit Tom Paine as satisfactory evidence of man's debasement.

The auction started. Miles Hennisy, one of the greatest slave callers of his day, came out of the little pen behind the barn where the Negroes were herded, prodding a sixteen-year-old girl in front of him with his silver-headed stick. Hennisy, from his powdered, beautifully curled wig to his polished pumps, was a glorious vision of sartorial splendor; the stockings were silk, the knee breeches black satin, the vest a brocade of silver and gold thread; at his neck and at his throat was bunched lace, five pounds' worth, perhaps; he wore a coat of black Portuguese broadcloth and a three-cornered hat of soft and lovely felt. Such was Hennisy, who was a legend, who sailed to Africa with his own slave ships, who had sold a black emperor, four black kings, and at least a hundred royal fledglings, who prided himself on the fact that when he sold a pregnant Negress, she was pregnant by him. He was a devil and a murderer—and the darling of Tidewater society; he had a long, handsome brown face and tiny blue eyes, and he spoke seven west-coast dialects.

He smiled now, and poked the girl up onto the wooden platform. She was wrapped in a blanket, with only her woolly, frightened head protruding; sweat and terror gave her strange round face a sheen like black marble. Hennisy said, "This, gentlemen, my good friends, is sixteen years old, soft as a lamb, strong as an ox, virgin and beautiful to look on, and old Solomon himself would have given a jewel of his crown to possess her. Her blood is royal, and as for her mind, already she speaks enough of the King's tongue to make herself understood. Her breasts are like two Concord grapes, her behind like the succulent hams of a suckling pig. I start the bidding at fifty pounds to give her away; and, gentlemen, make it a hundred and call out stout and strong; gentlemen, take her home, or to bed, or into the hayloft; make it sixty, gentlemen, make it seventy-five, make it eighty. The blanket goes off at eighty!"

"Eighty pounds!" someone called.

Hennisy ripped off the blanket; she was a little girl, frightened and shivering. She cowered back as Hennisy called, "Virgin, gentlemen, virgin, come up and see for yourselves!"

Paine stumbled through the snow. He had wanted to kill a man, and he had been afraid; he had roamed the streets of Philadelphia for three hours; his feet were soaking wet and cold. As darkness approached, he went into a tavern and sat down in front of the fire, and for half the night he sat there without speaking or moving.

Robert Aitken was one of those lonely, unsmiling Scotsmen who had been drifting into America by ones and twos ever since it had been opened for colonization. They were curious people, utterly beyond stamp or index, likely to settle down and become rich and satisfied, or just as likely to go off and trade for a lifetime with the Indians, never seeing a white face. Perversely, out of their Calvinism came as much broad tolerance as close stubbornness, and it was

a common thing for a Scotsman and a Jew to become life-
long partners in the fur trade. Considered a foreigner by the
bulk of Americans, who were of English descent, the Scotsman nevertheless put his finger on the soul of the little nation and kept it there.

Aitken was long and narrow, with a tight face that told
people who never talked to him that he was dull and without imagination. He had a store where he bought and sold
books; he had a box of upper-case type, a box of lower-case,
and a straight up-and-down press. Now and then he published a small book or a pamphlet. He had in his mind
bigger things, but he was obstinate in going about them and
perverse in approaching Paine. It was the day after the slave
sale, and Paine had come into his store.

"What can I do for ye?" Aitken asked.

Paine explained, stammeringly, that he was a writer of
sorts, that in England he had written a pamphlet or two, and
that here he had been a shilling teacher.

"And a mighty drinker," Aitken said sourly.

Paine nodded.

"I hold toward temperance," Aitken said. "Look at the
image of yerself, dirty, filthy, wretched—and a mighty nerve
you got to come in here and ask me for an honest living!"

"Give me a chance," Paine said.

"And why should I do that? The talk is that you came off
the boat with a letter from Franklin, and sure you did the
good man false. You're walking around the city like a man
daft and wanting his own soul. Sure as God, you're a bad
penny!"

Paine turned toward the door, but with his hand on the
knob, heard the Scotsman's sharp voice calling him back.

"Would you work for a pound a week?" Aitken demanded.

Paine's big, ugly head nodded; his twisted brown eyes fixed themselves upon Aitken as if the skinny bookseller were the sole arbiter of his fate.

"Seen it hard and lonely," Aitken said more softly. "I don't look at a man, but underneath him. You're in no way a fool, and neither am I, although a lot of fat bellies in the town here would think us both so. I put a shilling by, but I spend a shilling when I have to, and I mark a good investment." He went to his till and took out a handful of silver. "Here's a pound, and if you drink it down, don't let me see your dirty face again. Go to a barber, and then buy some decent clothes and put a coat on your back, and then come back here."

Paine nodded, took the money, and went out; he couldn't trust himself to speak, not to think even; as if he had been released from jail, starving, he felt a sudden sickening hunger—he wanted the whole world; he could have it—he wanted the Negro maid, trembling on the auction block; he wanted to take her in his arms and tell her that it would be all right; his sense of power was only the result of the simple fact that he still lived, that he still wanted and hungered and hoped.

He came back in brown homespun, with his face shaven and his hair powdered and his nails clean. Aitken gave him dinner, and then they sat down and talked. The bookseller was an extraordinary man, not brilliant, but filled with a detailed material knowledge about the colonies. He told Paine, frankly, "I have faith in ye because you come cheap. That's the Scotsman in me, and maybe the fool."

They talked all evening, and by midnight, the Pennsylvania Magazine was born. That night, Paine stayed over at Aitken's house, not sleeping, but lying on his back and staring into the darkness.

3

THE RAT TRAP

PAINE was a bad one; a boy or a man should know his place, but Paine beat his head against the wall. At fourteen he was mute, but his silence was dark and sullen, and that revealed to people clearly enough that there was a devil inside of him. Once the Squire whipped him half to death for trespass, and Paine screamed out through his agony, "God help you and your kind! God help you! God damn you! God damn you!"

"A bad one, and take the rod to him before he does murder," the Squire told Paine's father.

Tom said, "He's a fat swine." There was truth in that; two hundred and thirty-five pounds, the Squire was a prime and ruddy English gentleman, hounds in the morning, roast beef and port for dinner, hounds in the afternoon, roast beef and port for supper, hunting talk and whisky until midnight —"By Gawd, he's a fair fine gentleman, God bless him," his tenants said. He was all that, and it was a wonder he put up with the devilishness of the staymaker's son.

The Squire had his own son in Eton, a tall, strong, handsome young man of fifteen, a pleasure to look at, and so well set out that there wasn't a villager but was delighted to pull a forelock and give young master Harry Good Morning. Young Harry, during his last term at school, had lost eight

hundred pounds at cards, and the Squire, hearing about it.
slapped his knee and roared with laughter: "Damned young
devil! Damned young devil!"

Home from school with three other young bloods, Harry
found country life boring. Necessity spurred him to a certain
degree of inventiveness, and he and his friends decided to do
a bit of lessoning on Tom Paine. However, they preserved
an air of legitimacy, waiting for him to trespass, a circum
stance not at all rare considering the amount of land the
Squire owned. They caught the boy, beat him insensible
with birch rods, and then hanged him by his foot from an
oak tree. They cut him down only when it seemed that he
was dead, and then, slightly disappointed to find him still
breathing, they stripped him naked and rolled him in a bog
They gave him some whisky to revive him, and then whipped
him home naked. Altogether, it was such a game go as they
hadn't even dared to hope for that summer, and it would
provide them with an endless stream of conversation at
school the following year. The Squire himself told and re
told the tale, and whenever he related it went into such
paroxysms that his wife feared he would have a stroke.

At his bench, fastening stays under his father's eye, Tom
said quietly, "Thee were a staymaker, and I—and if thee
were a beggar, that way I, and if thee were a thief, that way
I, kneel down to the Squire, live in poverty and dirt, jump
from the path when the hounds come running, pull a forelock when the lady comes, go to church and pray to God—"

"Shut thee!" his father roared.

"I'm a man!" the boy cried hoarsely. "I tell thee, I'm a
man, a man, a man!"

"Shut thee!" his father yelled. "Shut thee, or I'll break
thee sinful head!"

"You are a staymaker, and I am a staymaker," the boy sobbed.

"Thee! Thee, thee sinful devil! With the brain of Gentiles and the speech of Gentiles, God help thee!"

The devil was in him, roaring, buzzing in his ears, prodding him on. A month later, he ran off to sea, shipping aboard a privateer as a cabin boy. The captain, grinning, said to him, "What do I want with a Quaker?"

"Take me, try me."

"Will you fight?"

"I'll fight," Tom said eagerly. "I'll fight, I swear I'll fight." Here was a vision of freedom broad and dazzling; on the sea, a man was his own master; riches meant freedom, and there were no heights to which a man might not rise. The captain caught him across the ear and flung him full length on the deck.

"Come along, little one, come along," he smiled.

The captain was drunk constantly and a beast about it; the mate was drunk only half the time and only half a beast about it; but both of them took it out on the cabin boy, and by the time they had coasted around and into the Thames, Tom Paine was a livid mass of bruises. There was only one relief, and that was to get at the captain's rum and swill it down. And for that, the beatings were doubled. Anchored outside of London, the boy slipped over the side and swam to shore. For the next two weeks he lived in the hut of a half-witted garbage collector, and in that time he ate what he could pick out of the buckets.

They had warned him in Thetford that London was a sinful city, but as he wandered wide-eyed among the sewer-

like streets, he began to understand the difference between
those who sin and those whose life is a sin. The lower-class
Londoner of that time, the beast whose forest was a maze of
alleyways, lived on cheap gin, cheap sin, and cheap robbery.
For the first, the punishment was slow death, for the second
horrible death, and for the last death by hanging or stoning
or quartering. For a tupenny piece a man could get roaring,
crazy drunk, and since drunkenness was the only way for the
poor to forget that hell was now and not in the hereafter,
gin had during the course of years come to replace almost
every other food. Three-year-olds drank gin by the glassful,
nursing mothers lived on gin and quieted their babies with
it, working men took for their supper a can of gin, old folks
hastened death with it, and adolescents made themselves in-
sane with it. In some streets, at certain times of the day, the
whole population would be screaming drunk with gin. Pros-
titutes lost their livelihood when any female from a child to
a mother would sell herself for a penny to grind in the gin-
mill.

In this, Tom Paine lived and drank and ran like a rat,
and stole and cursed and fought, and slept in alleys and sheds
and slimy basements. Until one day he took hold of himself,
left Gin Row, and apprenticed himself to a staymaker.

There was no hope, he knew, no escape, no salvation.

Sixteen, a staymaker's assistant, he hadn't touched gin in
over a year. His clothes were clean, if not good, and he read
books. Night after night, he read books, all the books he
could lay hands on—Swift and Addison and Pope and Defoe
and Congreve and Fielding and Richardson, even Spenser,
and sometimes Shakespeare; most of what he read he did not
understand; Defoe and Fielding were somewhat plain to

him, yet he rather resented that they should write of what he knew so well, instead of the dream world he fancied in print. He was a man, making his own way; it took him only a little while to completely expunge the Quaker "thee" from his speech. He swaggered through London, and with a rosy haze before his eyes, he would stand for hours before White's, the great Tory gambling house, or Brooks's, the Whig equivalent, and watch the bloods come to lay their thousands and their tens of thousands on the turn of a card. "That for me," he would say to himself, "that for me, by God!"

He made two friends, Alec Stivvens. a draper's assistant, a thin, tubercular boy of fifteen, and Johnny Coot, apprentice chimney sweep, twenty-two, but with the body of a twelve-year-old. The three of them would go to a tavern and drink bitters until their heads felt like mighty lumps of lead, and then hanging onto each other, they would go reeling home, singing at the top of their lungs. These drinking bouts meant beatings for two of the apprentices, but for Tom there was always the intercession of Mistress Morris, his master's wife.

It had started the time Master Morris, a wasted little man of sixty, went off to Nottingham on a matter of business. His wife, twenty years younger, plump, pretty, considering that smallpox had marked her whole face, called Tom in to fix a split corset.

She said to Tom afterwards, "You're a sly devil, the way of you Quakers. But don't you go to talk on me or I'll put a knife in your back." Still she couldn't harm a flea, and it made him feel like a man afterwards, boasting to Stivvens and Coot. She was good to him, and she brought him cakes and cookies and kept impressing Morris with what a fine boy Tom was. But Stivvens, inflamed by Paine's stories, tried the same thing on his mistress; a rolling pin put an inch-high lump on his head.

Stivvens wanted to be a highwayman; he talked of almost nothing else, and he said a hundred times if he said it once that as soon as he was sixteen he would go off and join Red Gallant's band on the Dover Road. That was in the time when highwaymen still wielded great power, when bands of forty and fifty cutthroats roamed over the King's Roads and fought pitched battles with the redcoat troops.

"'E's a prince, that Red Gallant is," Stivvens would say.

"Fair enough, but it's a short life. Me to live to ninety," Coot remarked cautiously.

Tom said there was only one way of life, and that among the bloods. If you weren't blood in England, you were dirt. He was minding the bloods and watching their ways.

"Be one yerself, eh?"

"Maybe," Tom said.

"And 'ow?"

"There are ways. I ain't saying it comes easy, but there are ways."

Stivvens was impressed. "You got a way, Tom?" he inquired.

"Ah—"

"Lum!" Coot snorted. "Out a dirt ye come; dirt breeds dirt! Don't I know? Down it's easy, but no goin' up."

"I ain't saying," Tom nodded.

"Lum!"

But Stivvens afterwards told Tom that he had faith; a man didn't have a head on his shoulders for nothing, and he himself was making for a take, a small take, nothing impressive, but as Stivvens put it, "Enough shillings for an eve-

ning full a noxies. Pretty ones too. Four shillings a poke, I
intends to pay."

Tom saw the intent and warned the boy, "They can hang
you for stealing."

"If they catch me."

Tom dreamed that night, slept fitfully, had nightmares,
woke and slept, and the next day begged Stivvens, "Don't
do it, Alec, don't."

They caught Stivvens; he had broken into the till of a
weaver next door to his master's shop and made off with
two pounds eight. Like a fool, he put the money into his
shoes, and while he overslept in the morning, his master
took the shoes to cobble, thinking he would take the cost
out of the boy's pay. The weaver came in to tell his tale, and
the sum of the money fitted in too nicely. They beat the
boy, and it took only thirty of the best to make him confess.

For the next few weeks, Coot talked of nothing else but
Stivvens in Old Bailey. "Fancy," he would say to Tom, "little
Stivvens."

"It don't seem possible," Tom agreed.

"They'll try him with the great ones," Stivvens decided.

"Hanging?"

"Don't see what else."

"They can't hang him, he's a baby, a little fool. He never
had sense. His wits were addled."

"Lum, open and shut. 'E broke in, now it's a rope around
'is neck. Open and shut."

Open and shut it was. Tom and Coot managed to see him
once after the judge had done the sentencing. It was the first
time Tom had been in jail, but Coot was an old hand at
such things, having been in debtors' prison twice, and it
was he who suggested that they bring along a loaf of bread

and a bottle of gin. They each brought a quart, and Coot assured Tom it was a handy thing to make the rope stretch easy. At the jail, Stivvens couldn't say a word, but just sat and stared and stared, the tears making little designs on his dirty cheeks.

"A tight lip," Coot said. "You're in with the great ones now—on the same scaffold as Johnny Hasbrook of Watling Street was stretched, all the time laughing. By God, 'e was a great un, murderous mean an' having twice the men as Red Gallant ever did."

But there wasn't a sparkle from Stivvens, only the tears running down his emaciated cheeks.

"Save the gin and drink it tomorrow," Tom forced himself to say.

"Save it, save it," Coot agreed. "Lum, get heated, and you won't feel the rope, but by God you'll spit in the hangman's eye."

They both went to the procession the following day, their masters giving them the afternoon off; and they would have gone, even if they hadn't known Stivvens, for when there was a great hanging procession, starting out at Newgate, and proceeding in such a magnificent manner two miles to Tyburn, all of London took a holiday. All along the two-mile line of the march, the mob made a sea of human faces, a raggle taggle that swayed and shifted and screamed and cursed and hooted and shouted and whistled and shrieked, men, women and children, old gaffers, babies, almost everyone with bread and cheese and pickles, wine for the sturdy tradesman or journeyman, gin and bitters for the working folk, pickpockets, ruffians, sluts, noblemen, scholars, and in carriages and chairs the great gentlemen and ladies of the land. For when a human being went to die, it was drama, high and glorious, such as the stage or the bedroom could never provide; and what did it matter so near to the gates of heaven or hell whether the condemned person was high-born or low-born?

Coot groaned and whimpered at his lack of size; he charged the crowd, worming his way through like an eel; he was indefatigable, and he wore Tom out. And once he got through and caught a glimpse of Stivvens, swaying in the cart, his peaked little face hardly able to comprehend that he himself was the author of this glorious fete, the cart would pass on, and the plunging and squirming would have to start over again.

"It ain't no way to treat his friends," Coot complained. "It ain't no way."

For an hour the chimney sweep and the staymaker's apprentice battled their way along the line to the gallows, and during that hour Tom Paine noticed a change come over Stivvens. Either the gin was taking effect, or else the glory of the occasion had driven the fear from his heart. Stivvens was posturing and bowing and posing; he even did a little dance in the cart; he waved his hands; he grimaced like a little ape.

" 'Igh and mighty, 'e is," Coot crowed. " 'Igh and mighty."

And the crowd cheered him. Not even Johnny Hasbrook of Watling Street had gone to his death in that fashion.

And even on the scaffold Stivvens stood and smiled foolishly.

That night, Paine left Morris; he ran away; he beat his head blindly against the walls of the cage; he wandered for two days in the streets of London, and then he fed himself into the gin mill. He holed up in a haunt of beggars and thieves and heard things that are not good for human ears;

but he was not human, and the beggars and thieves were not human.

For two months he dragged himself through hell, and then, because part of his stubbornness was a will to live, he apprenticed himself to a cobbler. He was able to hold onto the simple belief that it was better to make shoes than stays.

4

THE NINETEENTH OF APRIL AND 'SEVENTY-FIVE

Lᴏɴɢ afterward, he would remember the day; for while it meant nothing to some, and something to a few, to him it was the beginning and always would be the beginning, the break between two periods in his life and two periods in the life of mankind, the time when he discovered that Tom Paine was made of stuff strange and terrible—and he didn't cry for himself again.

He had been many things, and now he was an editor, a man with a job, a little money in his pocket, shaven, a good suit of clothes on his back, a good pair of shoes, stockings without holes, a person of some standing in the community, respected by some, liked by some, disliked by some, but truly and actually a person of standing. Walking down Front Street and having them say, "Good morning to you, Mr. Paine," or "Have you heard the latest from Europe, Mr. Paine?" or "I've read your latest issue and it's brisk, Mr. Paine, brisk, I repeat," he had to shake his head and concentrate on his identity, nor could he pass a beggar nor a loafer nor some poor wretched devil without thinking, "There, but by the grace of God, goes Thomas Paine."

Yet with his position, with the value Aitken placed upon him, with issue after issue of the Pennsylvania Magazine emerging under his hand, he still could not shake off his terror of life. Life was a beast, and when this holiday was over, the beast would tear at him again. A man was a fool to struggle or fight back, since in the end a man was grooved in his place, and in the world there was neither pity nor justice.

That was until something happened on the nineteenth of April, in seventeen seventy-five. Then, for Paine, there was a beginning; a crack showed in the wall against which he had been battering his head, and sunlight came through. The devil reared up on his hind legs and bared his teeth, and twenty angels blew a mighty chorus upon their trumpets. But otherwise the world was mighty little disturbed; in places the sun shone, and in other places it rained, and the sound of musketry was heard no farther than a man may hear those things. No shot fired was heard round the world, and up and down the American coast line, where a motley arrangement of three million people were settled, life went on in the placid, bucolic way it had gone on before.

But not in Lexington. On the evening of the eighteenth, a whooping, shouting, over-excited horseman drove into this pretty little New England village, and roaring at the top of his lungs woke everyone who was not already awake. From the white clapboard houses, the tavern, the manse, and even from a farm or two not properly in the village, the good Massachusetts householders came pouring, clad in their long white nightshirts and their tasseled white night caps, their clumsy firelocks in hand, their wives chattering behind them, their children poking heads out of upstairs windows.

"What's to pay?" they demanded of the rider, whose name was Paul Revere.

"Hell's to pay!" he shouted.

From the house of the Reverend Jonah Clark came two
gentlemen for whom his statement had deadly pertinence.
They rubbed their necks feelingly and drew their nightshirts
closer about them. Their names were Adams and Hancock;
the first was a politician, the second a smuggler, and together
they shared a stubborn resentment of foreign rule of the
little seaboard colony wherein they lived. Their resentment
had taken the form of meetings, congresses, incitements to
riot, and wholesale parading of every grievance their com-
patriots might have; they were dealing with good material
for their purpose, stubborn, stiff-necked farmers who had
come from a fertile, pleasant land to scratch at this rocky
coast simply because they had odd notions about religious
and personal freedom. Now, albeit gingerly, the British king,
the British prime minister, and the British government were
hacking at these liberties of theirs, nibbling the edges, clip-
ping away a right here, a privilege there, adding a tax here,
a duty there; nothing really to make a man's life less pleasant, less easy, but enough to set him to thinking if he was
of this stiff-necked, stubborn breed.

The hot-headed rider was brought down to earth by Pastor
Clark, who wheedled detail after detail out of him, while
the nightshirted farmers, angry to be thus routed from their
sleep, crowded closer.

"The British are coming," he kept insisting.

"From where? On foot?"

He nodded and said from Boston. Then there was time.
Pastor Clark assured everyone that there was time enough
to think out things, and that there never was a Christian soul
saved by hot-headedness, and that they might as well go back
and get their sleep.

"There's time for sleep and time for other things," someone snorted.

"And time for sleep now," the reverend said quietly. "God's in his heaven by night as well as by day. But night was made for slumber."

"Now, pastor," said a tall, hook-nosed husbandman, "will you be telling that to the redcoats?"

"I will if I can herd them into my church," Clark pronounced, and this sally fetched a laugh all around, easing the tension considerably. Someone dragged out a huge, turnip-shaped silver watch, stared at the face, and pronounced solemnly, "Two hours past midnight."

"Lord a mercy!" a woman squealed, and began to shout at her children to get their faces inside the window and go to bed, or she'd take a stick to them right this minute. A group of giggling girls managed to attract the attention of three nightshirted boys, weighted down by the immense firelocks they carried. Abner Green told his little sister to scat, and then he himself was dragged away by his mother, who had taken a firm grip on his ear. "Fine state of things," she said. "Men acting like children and children acting like men."

The night was cool, the pastor's words cooler, and the men, under the influence of both, drifted away, a few back to their beds, but most to the Buckman Tavern, where already a great fire was roaring in the hearth. The husbandmen leaned their guns against the kitchen wall, sent children and wives for their breeches, so loath were they to leave the excitement and warm comradeship of the group for even a moment, and then brewed pitcher after pitcher of hot flip, a concoction of rum, molasses, and beer—which they drank with a heady instinct that sometime before dawn destiny would come seeking them.

But back at Clark's house, Hancock and Adams still felt gingerly at their necks and wondered what was this strange devil of revolt they had raised. The pastor nodded, and agreed sagely that if the British caught them, they would no doubt hang them.

"I hate to run away," Hancock muttered.

"This is only the beginning," Clark said seriously. "Do you know what you've raised up? Men will fight and die, and there will be more than one running away."

"Don't condemn me," Hancock said. "I did what was right."

"We all do what is right," the pastor nodded, "and I condemn no one. For me, tomorrow, I will take the Book under one arm and the gun under the other, and God forgive me. I never killed a man; I never thought I would, but there are times when a man puts God behind him and turns away his face. I'll have horses brought for you, gentlemen."

It was curious how quickly the memories of the other world, England, Thetford, London, Dover, faded after Paine, with the dour blessing of Aitken, undertook the publication of the Pennsylvania Magazine. For the first time in his life, he had work he loved, work that did not demean him, work that allowed him the simple dignity of hope and intelligence. In the attic which the Scotsman had given him for an office, he sat and labored, in the beginning from dawn through to midnight. He had never been an editor; he had to learn typography, spelling, punctuation; he read the colonial magazines until his eyes ached to get the style, the taste, and, most of all, the political and economic feel of the colonies.

He shed his Britishness as a duck sheds water. He had no time to travel now, but in the taverns and coffee houses, he buttonholed everyone who had been to the far-off countries, or who lived there and was passing through Philadelphia:

New Yorkers, Vermont men, Virginians, men from the Deep South, Carolina, Georgia, drawling backwoodsmen, boatmen from the Ohio, soft-voiced Creoles from New Orleans, rangers who had crossed over the mountains into the wild cane-brake of Kentucky, leathery-skinned fishermen from Maine.

Philadelphia was the place for that, and if you waited long enough the whole of America passed along Broad Street. Paine pumped them, and for the first time in his life he found many men, men from every walk of life, who treated him with respect.

Out of this, out of the town itself, out of Aitken, out of the things he read, he was beginning to form a picture of America—a picture detailed by the fringe of tidewater colonization. Here was a land of no one people, of no one prejudice, of no one thought, a country so big that all England could be tucked away in a corner and forgotten, a country so youthful that half the people one met were foreigners or the first generation of foreigners, a country so inevitable that it was calmly, even lazily, stirring itself to revolt against the greatest power on earth.

It was the inevitability of America that stirred him most; here was a new breed of men, not out of blood nor class nor birth, but out of a promise pure and simple; and the promise when summed up, when whittled down, when made positive and negative, shorn of all the great frame of mountains, rivers, and valleys, was freedom, and no more and no less than that.

He was not blind; he had been in the rat cage too long to ever be blinded, and he saw the bad with the good. It was flung in his face, for directly across the street from the print shop in which he worked was the chief public slave market of Philadelphia. There was brought the run of Pennsylvania, Maryland, and Jersey human merchandise, the

black to be sold body and soul and forever, the white to be
auctioned off for bond, for debt, for punishment. Morning
and afternoon, the auctioneer would be singing out: "Here's
a buck, here's a buck, here's a choice fat black buck, strong
as iron, ripe as an apple, as full of juice as a rip-snorting
stallion, feel him, come in back, gentlemen, come in back
and see his virility, he's been whipped fine, he's been broken
and trained—" Oh, it was the city of brotherly love, all right,
but who ever went through it without stopping for an hour
at the slave mart?

The open shed where the selling took place fronted on
the swank London Coffee House where the young fops, gotten out in laces and ribbons and silks and satins, a credible
imitation of the bloods and macaronis in the old country,
sipped their drinks and enjoyed the show.

And there was not only the slave market; there were the
stocks, the whipping posts, the gallows, the incredibly foul
jails where debtors and murderers, men, women, and children were thrown together in a tight pen of death and disease.

There was the bad with the good in Philadelphia, but
there was no rat cage. If a man had guts or brains—or a little
of each, he made his own way. Look at Franklin!

But Aitken would say, when Paine paused at his work to
stare at the shed across the road, "Keep a tight lip, Thomas,
that be no part a yer business."

Sometimes Paine wondered what was his business.

"Ye'll no' be writing slavery in the magazine," the Scotsman said. "There's slaver and non-slaver pay their shilling.
Ye'll no' be writing rift and rebellion and incite to riot. I
hold no brief for the fat king in London, but his way is a
way of peace and prosperity, and I dinna hold with them
that scream so loud for liberty." Aitken was never quite sure

what lay behind Paine's rough, hook-nosed face, his twisted eyes that seemed to be turned inward more than outward. The magazine which had started off as a venture was rapidly becoming a success, six hundred for the first issue, fifteen hundred for the second—and, at a shilling a copy, Aitken could see a fortune just over the horizon.

"I have a debt to you," Paine murmured. "But the magazine is my making. Remember that."

"And yer my making, remember that," Aitken said. "Ye were a dirty wretch when I picked you up. Show yer ingratitude to others, not to me."

A few months before Tom Paine arrived in America, a number of men on horseback had converged toward this same town of Philadelphia. They came from a good many of the countries that made up the fringe of settlements, and some were rich and some were poor; some were brilliant and some not so brilliant, and some were known in their day and others long afterward. There were the two cousins from Massachusetts, Sam and John Adams, Cushing from the same state, strange and burning those Yankee men were, Randolph from Virginia, Patrick Henry also from Virginia— and a big, quiet planter from the Potomac country—his name was Washington—Middleton from the Deep South, and many more, dandies, tradesmen, farmers, hunters, and philosophers.

In Philadelphia they roamed all over the streets, mainly because many of them had never seen a good-sized city before; they ate too much, drank too much, talked too much. They called themselves the Continental Congress. They had a long list of grievances against the British way of government, taxes in which they had no say, repression of trade, heavy duties, import monopolies held by Britain, restrictions

on manufacture, redcoat troops quartered on colonists, en-
couragement for the Indians on the frontier to kill and loot—
but with all those grievances, they didn't know what to do
and hadn't thought too deeply about what they could do.

Not only that, but among themselves, they were strangers.
The Yankees didn't like slavery and made no bones about
it, and the Tidewater and Deep South people didn't like
Yankees and made no bones about that either. Sam Adams,
the rabble rouser from Boston, whom many of them thought
just a wee bit mad, ventured to talk of complete independence; he was shut up and marked down for a fool and a
dangerous fanatic. But he captured the imagination of a
rawboned, bespectacled Virginian, Patrick Henry by name,
who roared out, "By God, I am not a Virginian; I'm American!" Then, while the Congress was in session, Massachusetts
reared up back at home and declared her independence from
British authority. Paul Revere rode down from Boston to
Philadelphia with the news, and the Congress wrote a Declaration of Rights. Then the bleak, terrible prospect of what
they had done broke on them.

"If it means war—" they said softly to one another.

But, of course, it wouldn't mean war; it simply couldn't;
they talked down any suggestion of danger; they talked and
talked and talked, and all the words made them certain that
everything would come out in the best way possible. They
drank that peculiar, vile American concoction, flip, by the
hundreds of gallons, and on October 27, 1774, they disbanded, saddled their horses, and started on the long ride
home.

Some months afterwards, the London, Dover, and Thetford staymaker, Tom Paine, devoured the record of all they
had said and didn't think it too wordy. "Words pile up," he

said, "and afterwards men do things. First the words." He was holding out at the Ridgeway Coffee Shop with Clare Benton, the printer, Judah Perez, the Jewish fur trader, Anthony Bent, a smith, and Captain Isaac Lee of the Philadelphia militia.

"This is a new thing here," Paine said. "That's why no one knows what to do."

"When the time comes to fight, we'll know what to do," Captain Lee insisted, giving stubborn emphasis to a theme he had repeated over and over.

"No, we have to know what to do first. It's no use to fight if you don't know what you're fighting for. Even if you win, it's no good."

"And I think," Perez put in, "that if you know what you're fighting for, it doesn't make too much difference if you win or lose."

"You don't lose," Paine said heatedly. "This is like no other thing the world has seen; it's new; it's a beginning, and it has to be explained. We have something here, and yet we haven't got it, and suppose we lose it and it slips through our fingers?"

"Then we're as well off," Bent grinned.

"Are we? You don't know; you're American! I came from back there!"

"What does that mean?" Benton demanded. "You shook the king's hand?"

"I didn't even spit in his face," Paine said sourly.

"That kind of talk is still treason."

"Is it? Treason's a word for a lot of things."

"Easy, easy," the smith said.

"I go easy," Paine said. "Believe me, I hate no man for what he is, not even that fat German bastard, George the Third. But I've seen man nailed to a cross, nailed there for

God knows how many thousands of years, nailed with lies, oppression, gunpowder, swords. Now someone puts an ax in my hand, and I have a chance to help cut down that cross. I don't pass that chance by." Paine's voice was loud; his words rang out, and by the time he had finished speaking, half the men in the coffee house were gathered about the table. Someone put in, "Is it Independence you're talking?"

"Independence is a word."

"You seem almighty fond of words."

"And not afraid of them!" Paine roared. "I come into a land of free men and find them afraid of the one word that would bind their freedom! This is a land of promise, and there is no other on earth!"

He was quieter on paper than vocally. All his life he had wanted to write, and now he had a whole magazine at his disposal. The more writing he did on his pound a week, the better pleased Aitken was, and Paine could see a good deal of reason in his desire to keep the magazine on the fence. His writing wasn't good, but he poured it onto paper—essays, bad poems, scientific research, even a letter or two to the great Benjamin Franklin. Fortunately for him, the literary taste of the Pennsylvania people was sufficiently untutored for them to accept Paine and the magazine and the dozen pen names he used—and even to be somewhat enthralled by the breathless pace of his energy. All at once Paine was a theologian, a historian, and a scientist, and he brought into the magazine the wide knowledge of a staymaker, a cobbler, a weaver, and an exciseman. The combination was good, and the circulation went up steadily.

But Paine couldn't stay quiet; he had too many memories, too many sleepless nights, too many dreams. Looking out of his windows, he would see the white chattel slaves being sold in the market. And there were other things he would see as, pen poised, he remembered all the years before now.

"I'll be raising yer wages," Aitken said to him one day.

He had respectability, position, a job—and yet he had nothing. His torments drove him to the brothels where were kept the limp-eyed, half-foolish bondwomen, brought over from England and Scotland by regular firms of dealers, selling their poor peasant graces to all comers for three shillings, sixpence of which was supposed to go for their freedom. Yet somehow none of them got their freedom, but became hard, painted, vile-tongued tarts. For Paine, there was no relief in those places, and even when he bought freedom for two of the girls, his conscience was not eased.

Rum was a way out. He went back to the bottle, and was drunk more and more frequently. Deep in his cups, he had a run-in with Ben Frady, the Tory mouthpiece, and they were both dragged off before the magistrate.

Aitken said, "Yer dirt, and back to the dirt ye go."

"God damn you, shut up!"

"Be none too certain with yer damn Whiggish way. That pound more will no' go on yer salary."

"Go to hell!" Paine yelled.

Then, one night, he sat in front of his candles and wrote and wrote. It came from the heart and now he had no trouble with words. All his hatred for slavery poured onto the paper, all his pent-up fury. And not able to print it himself, he went out in the morning and posted it to a rival magazine. A week later it was printed, and that same day Aitken rushed in holding it in his hand.

"Be this yours?" he cried.

"That it is," Paine nodded.

"Then out ye go and back to the dirt!"

"Do you have another editor for a pound a week?" Paine smiled.

"I give ye a month's notice!"

"Make it two months," Paine said, "or by God, I'll make it two weeks."

And that night, for the first time in a long while, Tom Paine slept quietly and easily without the benefit of drink.

It was the twenty-fourth of April, seventeen seventy-five, the slow end of a cool, bright spring afternoon. Long, rich shadows lay over the cobbled streets, and on the air, blowing from the inland hills, was the tangy smell of growing things, new leaves, turned dirt. On that quiet afternoon, the streets of Philadelphia rang with hard-driven hoofbeats, and a lathered rider on a lathered horse drove to a halt in front of the City Tavern. He yelled that he had news, big news, mighty news, and from every side people came running. Then the rider refused to talk until he had finished off a mug of beer, and as a good horseman should, seen his horse wiped and watered. While he drank, the word spread like wildfire, and the crowd became larger and larger. Paine, who was at his shop, heard men shouting, and ran along with the rest.

"It's war," the rider said, wiping his lips. "It's bloody damn war!"

Someone gave him a pinch of snuff; others kept back the crowd.

"Of course, they knew that Hancock and Adams were at Lexington," he said.

Coherency was asked for: dates, details, background.

"That was April eighteenth," he said.

There was a sudden hush; news went slowly, but events

moved fast, and with startled, pale faces the men and women in the crowd looked at each other.

"They were at Pastor Clark's house," the messenger went on. "That was all right. Men went out of Boston to warn them, and there was time enough, since the redcoats went on foot and our boys rode like hell. And Pastor Clark kept a cool head; he sent them away."

"They weren't captured, Hancock and Adams?"

"They got away."

Again the hush; the journalists scribbled furiously, but the rest waited, and the only sound was the shrieking of children who scurried like hares on the outside of the crowd. The rider called for another mug of beer, and it was rushed through the crowd.

"He couldn't send the whole town away," the messenger said. "They were all awake, and most of them stayed awake—" There was more talk, more beer, more questions. Bit by bit the whole story came out, haltingly some of it, some with a rush, sometimes a long break when the rider just stared and attempted to comprehend the events he was narrating.

That night of the eighteenth, few of the Lexington villagers slept. Most of those who were dragged home by their wives dressed themselves and slipped away, taking gun, powderhorn, and bullet pouch with them, to join the group at the tavern. The devil walked tonight, but angels were behind him; there was never such a night before, and there wouldn't be one again. The men at the tavern talked in whispers, although they could have shouted and not found a sleeping body to be wakened, and they fingered their guns nervously, counted their bullets, and wondered whether to shoot a man was any different from shooting squirrels and rabbits. Captain Parker, their commander, who had seen guns go off during the French War, was none too easy himself, and found it difficult to answer all the questions flung at him.

A while before dawn, out of a need to do something, Parker sent Zeke Sudberry over to the church to set the bells ringing. Zeke rang until everyone in the village was thoroughly awake, the women with their heads out the windows crying, "Shame, shame that a lot of grown men don't know any better!"

Parker told his men to fall in, which they did rather self-consciously, grinning at each other, whispering back and forth:

"Fine soldier you are, Isaac."

"Click your heels. Jed. Act like you got a real fancy waistcoat on."

And to fourteen-year-old Jerry Hicks, "Now, Jerry, why don't you go home and study your lessons."

"Forward march!" Parker shouted, and they stamped over to the lawn in front of the Congregational Church. Once there, Parker scratched his head, seemingly unable to think of a further movement. The pastor, a light fowling piece in his hand, came out and said, "Bless my soul, and it isn't Sunday."

It was nice having him there, and everyone became easier and began to talk a great deal. The gray of the dawn was now changing to pastel pink and peach and taupe, and across the fields the crows screamed angrily, "Caw, caw, caw!" Joshua Lang's dog, who was a fool for any sort of bird noise, ran toward the crows, barking at the top of his lungs.

Then the talk stopped; they stiffened; they looked at one another. There was another sound in the world. Faintly, thinly at first, and then more clearly, and then sharp and hard came the beating of drums, the shrilling of pipes, a mocking swinging cadence, an invitation to glory, death— and God only knows what else.

No one had to say who it was; they knew, and no one spoke. Leaning on their guns in that cheerful April morning, tense, frightened most of them, knowing for the first time in their lives an overpowering desire to run away, men, boys, old gaffers, children, the simple folk of a simple New England farming community, they kept their appointment with destiny.

At the City Tavern in Philadelphia, the rider had his fourth glass of beer and said, "They stood, by God!"

"A fight?" someone asked.

"Hell, man! I said they stood. Boy and man, they faced up and goddamned the redcoats all to hell."

"And then?"

"You never saw a bloody lobster turn his back on a gun," the messenger snorted.

The redcoat troops marched to within a dozen yards of the villagers before their officer commanded them to halt, and then they stood in their precise files, in their precise and colorful uniforms, in their great shakos, in their white wigs and white belting, men of London, of Suffolk and Norfolk, of Devon and Wales and Scotland and Ireland, staring so curiously at the gawky farmers, who, having come from the same places that bred them, were now outlanders, incredible rustics. For long moments the two groups faced one another; it was a moment the redcoats were trained for, but the farmers' hands were wet on their guns.

Then Major Pitcairn, commanding the British, made up his mind, spurred to the front and roared, "Disperse!"

The farmers growled.

"God damn you bloody rebels, lay down your guns!"

It was there, hot and terrible; they were rebels. This idea that they had conceived, that they should be free men with the right to live their lives in their own way, this tenuous, dream-like idea of liberty that men of good will had played with for thousands of years had suddenly come to its brutish head on a village green in Lexington. The farmers growled and didn't lay down their arms; instead one of them fired, and in the moment of stillness after the roar of the big musket had echoed and re-echoed, a redcoat clutched at his tunic, knelt, and then rolled over on the ground.

After that, there was no order, no memory even. The redcoat files fired a volley; the farmers fired their guns singly, by twos and threes. The women screamed and came running from their houses. Children began to cry and dogs barked madly. Then the firing died away and there was no sound except the moans of the wounded and the shrill pleading of the women.

A fifth glass of beer in front of the City Tavern in Philadelphia, and the rider told how the redcoats had marched away. "They were not after Lexington, but after Concord," he explained. "That's where the stores were."

"They took the farmers?" someone asked.

"No, they did not take them! Do you take a mad dog? They left well enough alone and went to Concord and walked into the town and stayed there maybe four, five hours. Then they set out back with never a thing done, like their wits were addled. And when they came to the bridge, the folk was waiting for them, not a few now, but over four hundred.

" 'You dirty bastards!' the major yells, 'you dirty peasant bastards! Clear out and back to home!'

"They didn't move," the rider said.

"God damn you bastards, clear the bridge!" the major roared.

They were solemn and they didn't move; their jaws worked evenly; their guns crept to level and their lips tightened, yet they didn't move. And then the British attacked and hell broke loose. Cannon roared, and there was crash after crash of musketry. With bayonets fixed, the British charged the bridge, and with clubbed muskets the farmers drove them back. Yelling, screaming, cursing, praying, the Yankees forced the redcoats off the bridge back on the Concord side of the stream. But the effort couldn't be sustained; they were farmers, not soldiers, and after the first heat of rage had passed, they gave back and allowed the redcoats to re-form, cross the bridge, and resume their march toward Lexington.

It was only then, after they had laid out their dead and tended their wounded, that the farmers realized a victory had slipped through their fingers. A cold New England bitterness took the place of their hot-headed fury. They picked up their guns and began to run—down the road to Lexington.

It was six miles to Lexington, six miles of perdition for the redcoats. The whole countryside blazed, and that April afternoon every stone wall, every fence, every house, every bush, every tree roared defiance. Sick men crawled to their windows to fire at the invaders, boys crept through the grass and picked their targets, women behind barn doors loaded guns for their husbands, farmers ran the length of New England stone walls, firing again and again. A boy climbed into a tree with a brace of horse pistols, killed a redcoat subaltern passing underneath, and himself was shot. But on the whole, the redcoat volleys were useless against this stabbing, hacking, hidden warfare.

There was no leadership, no direction, no command; the farmers fought instinctively, desperately, more brilliantly than they were ever to fight again, as if they knew that here, today, the poor, suffering simple folk had finally felt their power.

Six miles to Lexington before the British had any surcease. The town was a place of homes, and in the town were women and children, and therefore the men waited out in the fields and the woods. At Lexington, reinforcements met the redcoats, but at the same time hundreds and hundreds of farmers, drawn by the noise of the firing, by the swiftly spread news, were converging on the village.

Reinforced, the British set out once more on their retreat to Boston—and this time the hell was worse. Stabbed, hacked, bleeding, they staggered along—

"They got to Charlestown," the rider said, "what was left of them."

5

THE MAKING OF A REVOLUTIONIST

Out of it, the noise, the tumult, the strange story that the rider brought down from New England, was coming something new, something colossal and beyond understanding, something that could be translated into movement and action, but not into plan and reason. So Tom Paine thought the next day, standing as one of the surging mob in front of the State House, the biggest mob in all the history of Philadelphia, almost eight thousand people. The mob was a mob and no more; it yelled, shouted, flurried, eddied, and quieted partially now and again to listen to various speakers who climbed up to denounce tyrants and oppression, both very general and very safe terms. Predominantly, the mob was pro-Boston in sentiment, but here and there a Tory stood, smiling the way Tories were prone to smile these past several months.

For all that speakers were addressing the whole mob, smaller fry competed in their own particular circle, and Jackson Earle, a journeyman wheelwright, who was delivering a furious indictment of kings and tyrants in general, and one king in particular, called upon Paine to be his witness.

"Tom," he demanded, "do we have over us a German or an Englishman?"

Paine shrugged. Yesterday had excited and terrified him, but today he was cold, and the old lassitude was returning. He had dreamed one brief, bright vision, and he didn't know now why this crowd was helping it to dissipate. Yet he knew one thing, that he was outside of it; he was Paine, the editor, he had been Paine, the beggar, but in both stages, he had nothing. He could hate and squirm and protest, but how could he dream?

"George, I mean," Earle persisted.

"German, I suppose."

"German! And what manner of a German?" Earle asked the crowd. "A slaving Hanoverian, a fat, guzzling swine—and his is the divine right! From God? Now listen, my good friends, and I'll tell you! Put me in God's place—"

The speaker, Quincy Lee, perched on an impromptu platform of boxes, was begging for quiet. Arnold, who was a Quaker, had just proposed a militia, armed. "And what of it?" Lee yelled at the top of his lungs, a tall, gangling, cross-eyed man, hopping with excitement. "What have the people to say?"

The crowd roared.

"Who will be the first to step up and offer, as I offer, my life, my arms, my sword for this sacred thing called freedom—"

How the crowd roared!

"As they died at Lexington and Concord—"

As Paine pushed out of the crowd, Arnold was crying, "As Englishmen have always fought for the rights of Englishmen—"

"Drinking?" Aitken said to him as he came in out of the cool, starlit night.

"Drinking," Paine nodded.

"Yer liver will be so rotten ye'll no' have it in you long."

Paine grinned and nodded again.

"Were ye at the square today?"

"I was there," Paine said, dropping into a chair and staring at his feet.

"And were ye happy now that ye got yer blood and thunder?"

"I was not happy," Paine said. "I was afraid."

"Then ye're drunk. My little man, ye're good on paper, but bad with a clenched fist."

"I wasn't afraid of that."

"Ye should no' be." The Scotsman had settled his long form back against the counter, and now was taking a savage delight in prodding his editor. "Ye should no' be, I tell ye, for what is yer life worth?"

"Nothing."

"Ah, then—and ye admit it?"

"I know it," Paine said savagely.

"But ye're afraid."

Someone knocked at the door, and Aitken broke off his attack to answer. It was an old man whom Paine knew by sight, Isaac de Heroz, the beadle of the Jewish congregation. Under his arm he carried a tattered prayer book, which, after bowing in slow greeting to both Paine and the Scotsman, he spread on the counter, handling the loose pages gently and lovingly.

"Can you print one like it?" he asked Aitken.

Both Paine and Aitken bent over the book, Paine looking curiously at the first Hebrew writing he had ever seen, Aitken squinting at the old type.

"I have no' the letters nor the skill."

"I have some type, not all. The rest you can cast. You set as they are set."

"And what is the meaning? I will no' set a devil's concoction."

"They are prayers," the old man smiled.

"I would no' set a Papish prayer," Aitken said doggedly.
"I would no' set a heathen prayer. Yet ye ask me to break
my neck contriving the letters."

"They are simple prayers that anyone could understand,"
the old man said softly.

"Read that in English," Aitken said, turning the pages
and pointing at random.

The old man read,

> *"These things I do remember: O I pour*
> *my soul out for them. All the ages long*
> *hatred pursueth us; through all the years*
> *ignorance like a monster hath devoured*
> *our martyrs as in one long day of blood.*
> *Rulers have risen through the endless years,*
> *oppressive, savage in their witless power,*
> *filled with a futile thought: to make an end*
> *of that which God hath cherished. There was once*
> *a tyrant searching in the Book of God*
> *For some word there to serve him as a sword*
> *to slay us; and he found the line which spake:*
> *'He that doth steal a man and selleth him,*
> *he shall be surely put to death—' "*

Paine stopped him, putting a hand on the old man's arm.
"That's enough, father, we'll print it."

Aitken, who was going to say something, looked at Paine
and stayed quiet, and Paine asked the old man, "Were you
at the State House today?"

"I was there."

"And what did you think?"

"I thought that this is the beginning of something long and hard."

That night, past midnight, hours after the old man had gone, Paine sat and watched Aitken wrestle with the Hebrew characters and curse under his breath.

"Go to bed," Aitken told him for the fifth time.

"I'm in no mood for sleep."

"I ought to give ye notice, getting me into this hell's broth."

Paine wanted desperately to talk; he wanted a human being to sound to his thoughts; he wanted to hear laughter and tears, song and music.

"Have you ever loved a woman?" he asked Aitken.

"Are ye daft?"

He wanted to find a part of his past he could take something from, and then give it to another before it vanished like smoke.

Paine had been a staymaker in Thetford, in London, in Dover, in Sandwich, in Portsmouth and Brighton in the south, at Bath, at Winchester, at Bristol—no place could hold him. Always when he tried another trade, it was back to stays, from weaving, cobbling, carving, sewing, digging, plowing, planting, it was back to stays, which was his place. And it was at Sandwich that he saw Mary Lambert.

She was plump, saucy, pretty in a way; she had a dimple in either cheek, brown eyes, round arms, and she was a few years younger than he. At that time, he was twenty-one.

She was in service, and the first time he saw her, she was out buying chops. She wasn't the kind to be content with looking at her meat; she felt it, pinched it, and then spoke up to the shopkeeper, "Now, mind you, not all fat. I won't be cheated."

"They're as pretty chops as you ever seen," the butcher said.

"Coo! I should have a shilling for all I seen better!"

"One dozen."

"And cut the fat, mind you."

All this time Paine was staring at her, and she knew it, staring and forgetting why he had come into the shop, whether to buy a piece of meat for his supper, or a bone for the dog he had at that time, or because he had known that she would be there and then nothing on earth could keep him away.

As she left, he followed her, not hearkening to the butcher's, " 'Ere you, what do you want?" walking after her some twenty feet before she turned and faced him and told him,

"Be on your way."

Paine stood foolishly and dumbly.

"Now get on! I want nothing of your sort."

"I meant no harm," Paine said.

"Coo!" she snapped, and turned on her heels and strode along, Paine after her, Paine catching up and begging, "Please, tell me your name."

"Tell you my name! And what else should I tell you?"

"Let me carry your bundles, please."

"I'm well enough able. And get along and keep a clean nose, or I'll have a word to my master about you."

He saw her again; it was impossible not to in a little place like Sandwich. He asked about her, and discovered that her name was Mary Lambert. Of course, she knew; he couldn't keep away from her, but followed her, stalked her, even managed to say a word to her now and again. When she smiled at him, as she sometimes did, he would be in an ecstasy of delight. His master at that time, John Greeg, took to winking at him, poking him in the ribs, and putting a tongue in his cheek.

"Eh, Tom, you be a sly un, but I know."

He was hopelessly, madly in love, and at something like that would only smile foolishly.

"Eee—un got an arm around 'er yet? I'll be putting ye up a shilling."

Sometimes she let him walk with her. He had taken to buying her things because he found she was more tractable toward him when he gave her a gift. He had asked her to walk down toward the stream with him one quiet evening, to which she said, "Coo, it's softy, dirty marsh!"

"It's pretty there. And you're so beautiful—"

"You're a funny un, you are, Master Paine. Ain't you not had a girl before?"

He screwed up his courage and said, "Not one I loved."

She shrugged her shoulders and tossed her head.

"Mary—"

"I like to walk in town," she said. "A maid shouldn't be off alone "

"Mary, don't you care for me, a little?"

"Maybe."

"Mary!"

She began to ramble on about the house, her mistress, the second housemaid, the cook, the footman who was quite crazy about her. "Bussed me yesterday, 'e did," she said.

"Mary, I love you!"

"Coo!" she smiled.

He asked her once about being in service.

"I always been with quality," she said.

"But did you like it, being a servant?"

She bristled. "It's better than some I knows ain't got the graces to go in service."

"I didn't mean any wrong," he apologized. "Only I don't like to think of you as a servant."

"Think what you please."

"I love you."

She tossed her head.

"Doesn't that mean anything? I tell you I love you, I tell you I'd be willing to die for you—I'm not just a staymaker. I want to do things and be things; I want the whole world and I want to give it to you!"

"Cool!"

"I can give it to you," he said fiercely.

She placed her hands on her hips and dropped a curtsey. "Master Duke!"

He tried to kiss her, and she slapped his face with all her might. He stood there and stared at her and rubbed his cheek and thought of the footman.

"High and mighty," she snapped. "Just a corsetmaker, but them in service ain't fit to be with you."

"You hate me, don't you?"

"Maybe."

Then he made up his mind that he would never look at her again, and for two weeks he managed not to see her, muttering at his work, black and hopeless.

"Get an arm around un," Master Greeg advised him.

"Shut up and go to the devil."

"I'll dock ye that shilling."

The black mood passed, and he had a fit of tremendous resolve. He would set up for himself. Carefully, he had laid by nineteen pounds, and now he left Greeg, took an old shop, and moved his tools and bench in. Morning until night he worked, putting by every penny he could save, denying himself food, denying himself every little bit of comfort a man could have, drink, things to read, dreaming only of the day when he could afford to marry the woman he loved. And then he sought her out and asked her.

"I knew ye'd come back," she said smugly.

"Yes, I had to."

"Then mind you behave."

"I want to marry you," he said desperately.

"Coo!"

"I love you, I'll do anything for you, I'll make you happy—"

"Go on." But she was weakening; this was better than the footman, who had never proposed marriage, better than the butcher's way, better than her master who would catch her in the pantry; for a moment the twisted, burning eyes of the staymaker captured and held her, and in her small, fluttering mind she formed one glimpse of half-born dreams. She smiled and dropped a curtsey, and Tom Paine's soul reeled with gorgeous triumph.

"Kiss me, go on," she said.

He held her in his arms and the world was his.

"And mind, no nonsense about being in service."

"No, no, you're the whole world for me! Do I care what you've been. You'll be Tom Paine's wife now and I'll put you high as a duchess—higher!"

"Go on."

"I'll be rich. I won't always be a staymaker!"

"High and mighty for you— Eee, you're a strange one."

"You care a little," he begged her.

"Mind you, marriage."

"Yes, yes, my love, my darling."

"You are a chap for words," she said admiringly.

"They don't mean much; they're cheap. We'll have more, we'll have children."

"Mouths to feed. Things come high," she pointed out, making a face.

"If only you love me—"

"Maybe," she pouted.

He thought afterward that if certain things had not been, if certain things had gone otherwise, it might have been different. What she was, she couldn't help, and knowing that only made it worse for him. Long after, he would think of how he had tried to teach her to read and write, and how after ten or fifteen minutes of struggling with an idea, she would turn on him with childish fury. Sometimes he was sure she hated him, and sometimes, holding her in his arms, he would have a brief moment in which he knew she loved him. She was what she was, beaten into shape by her tiny world, a tribal creature laid over and over with a thousand taboos. Sometimes, probing as gently as he could, uncovering layer after layer, he would be at the point of finding her frightened little soul, and she would burst out at him, "Coo! High and mighty and fine you are, making fun of me again, you with your fine airs!"

"I have no airs, Mary darling."

"Acting like a duke, and you a corsetmaker."

He would shrug and nod and tell her that he was sorry.

"Scornful of service you are, and I was that comfortable there, with gentlefolk too, not your dirty pigpen quality!" Or if she really became enraged, she would tell him details concerning the footman, her master, others, pouring it on to see him squirm and twist.

Nothing went right with his business. Staymaking was a long-term trade, and unless you had quality on your list you could just as well give up. There was not enough business in Sandwich to support two staymakers, and when Paine could no longer pay his rent, when he was down to his last crown piece, he went back to Greeg.

"You be na a steady un," Greeg said stolidly, and that was the end of it.

They were given their eviction notice, and Paine said, "We'll try another town."

"And I was to be higher than a duchess," she mimicked him.

"Things go up and down," Paine said quietly. "I'm not beaten." But for the first time in his life he felt old, he at twenty-two, longing for a childhood he had never known, caught in the cage and racing round and round, like a squirrel on a treadmill. This time he expected her to go back into service, but she stuck with him, berating herself for it, giving him worse, yet caught by the glimpse of a dream she once had known, hating him for his ugliness, for his gangling insufficiency, for his hopelessness as a man of any practical affairs, but at the same time in awe of him.

The other town was no better, and then it was a third, the two of them trudging along the dusty highroad, Paine with his tools on his back, Mary with everything else they owned tied together in a kerchief. For Paine there was only a deep and abiding sense of guilt, and if Mary screamed at him, "It's your fault, your fault, I was that comfortable and that well," he could only nod his head. "Not even able to keep a roof over my head!" Yes, that was true. "Fine ideas, fine ideas, fine ideas! Looking down your big nose at me in service! Going to change the world, you are, coo, Master Tom Paine—ye dirty, lazy lout!"

They would lie behind a hedge at night, with the cool mist of evening settling on them, with all the sweet, late smells of the English countryside riding the dark winds, and if it was quite cool she would move close to him, and for a brief time there would be peace. He could hold her and say to himself, I am in my castle, my home, and she would be sleepy enough to give in and hold her tongue. His love was so fierce and desperate, challenging God—you gave me

this, she's mine and beautiful and lovely, and I can make her
into what I desire, that every movement of hers, every whimper, every twitch of fright struck a deep chord of pain in
him. He didn't blame her, but only himself; something deep
and terrible inside of him gave him the power to look at
the world and know, to see justice and injustice, and feel in
his own soul the whip laid on the backs of millions. He was
twenty-two and he was old, and what wasn't broken inside of
him was being forged into a hard core of steel; but she was
just a child, and at night when she was asleep, he would
croon softly over her, "My baby, my little one, my darling."

He stole that they might eat, and that gave her a stronger
club to hold over his head, so that in her fury she would
scream, "I'll give you to the sheriff, ye dirty poacher!" The
penalty was death. He crept into a barn and took a sack of
turnips. The penalty was to be drawn apart by two teams
of horses. He killed a rabbit, and for that the penalty was to
have his ears and nose removed. But he would have murdered, killed in cold blood, his bitterness was such a growing, grinding thing; only toward her did he display any
sweetness and mercy.

In Margate, where they finally arrived, footsore and weary,
he talked his way into the lease of a shop. Mary was pregnant, and Paine's desperation became almost a form of madness. All day he toiled over his bench, and at night hired
himself out for whatever work there was. She was ailing so
that the bitterness went out of her, and she whimpered and
fretted like a hurt child. He didn't eat, and one by one sold
his precious tools to give her cream and fowl and now and
then a piece of beefsteak with pudding; half starved, he
could think of only one thing, to keep a roof over her head,
a fire in the grate, and a little food in the pot. His trade,
what there was of it, barely paid the rent, and his efforts to

obtain other necessities became a sort of frenzy. He remembered Gin Row, put a patch over one eye, bound and twisted a limb, and begged through the streets. He was sure a leech could help his wife, and finally, with many threats and coaxings, got one to come to the shop for a shilling.

"Festering fever," the leech said, while Mary looked at him, wide-eyed and frightened.

"What can you do?" Paine asked him, afterward and away from the bed.

"One performs and expects a certain amount of bloodletting," the doctor remarked. "Docendo discimus of the evil vapors, the spirits that distend her veins. Haud longis intervallis the blood must flow—"

Paine shook his head wearily. "I don't have Latin."

"Ah, but medical terms, medical trade, medical mystery. Keep doors and windows close locked. When sickness comes, the devils dance like noxies. . . ."

That night she said, "Tommy, Tommy, I'm going for to die—"

"No, no, the doctor said you would be all right."

All her spleen was gone, and she held onto his hand as if it was the last real thing on earth. And that night, white and wax-like from all the bleeding, she closed her eyes and turned her face away from Paine.

He sat all the next day, wide-eyed, silent, while the curious thronged the house, while the neighbors who had never taken any notice of them, poured in and out. He had no grief now, only a blazing anger that would burn within him forever.

West of the town of Philadelphia lay a green and rolling meadow called the Commons, and there Tom Paine made his way to watch the militia drill. He had thought of a mob before coming to the meadow on this placid, sunny spring afternoon, but this he saw was no mob. Neither was it an army, even in promise; neither was it anything the world had ever seen before, this group of men and boys, apprentices, journeymen, masters, clerks and students, smiths and millers, carpenters, weavers, barbers, printers, potters, men in aprons with the stain of their trade on their hands. These were the citizens of Philadelphia, yet not all the citizenry. The distinction eluded him, though it was there. Not that they were workingmen all, for there were masters and rich men as well as those who worked for hire; there was one banker, two mercers, a journalist, Tom Jaffers, who was rich enough to do nothing at all, three pastors, a grain speculator, and a fur buyer, to add to those who worked with their hands. There were Quakers, who were pacifists, Methodists, Puritans, Baptists, Roman Catholics, Presbyterians, Jews, Congregationalists, Dissenters, Diests, Agnostics, and Atheists. There were free blacks along with the whites, Negro slaves along with their masters.

What moved them? Paine wondered. What distinguished them? What had brought them together?

Slowly, he walked around the field, his heart racing with excitement, apprehension, fear too, withal a hopefulness he had never known before. He watched them drill with their own weapons, this awkward, stumbling, self-conscious first citizen army the world had ever known; firelocks they bore, great old muskets, bell-mouthed matchlocks that had come into the country more than a century ago, a few long, graceful rifles from the back counties, halberds, axes, pikes, cutlasses rapiers, two-handed museum-piece swords, and those who had no weapon, not even a horse pistol, just sticks which they carried with dead seriousness. Some of them, those who had a shilling to spend strutting, already had uniforms, fantastically colored outfits with mighty cartridge boxes upon which was painted either "Liberty," or "Freedom," or "Death to Tyrants," or some other slogan calculated to impress the world with their state of mind. Officers they had too, fat old Fritz van Goort for a colonel, little Jimmy Gainsway a captain, Captain Jacob Rust, the miller, and that only the beginning, for the officers' list was near a mile long, with all of them shouting orders at once with no attempt at synchronization, left face, about face, forward march, halt, forward march, men poking into each other, being bowled over, stumbling, tripping, whole lines of men going over like tenpins, shouting, a musket firing by accident—of course, they all had them loaded, with shot, too.

Paine continued on his rounds, and there he was not alone, for a good half of the city had turned out to watch the militia in its first drill. The women stood in colorful clusters, umbrellas open to keep off the sun, the children ran back and forth screaming, and the old gaffers smoked their pipes and asked what the world was coming to. And the militiamen who saw their wives, sweethearts, or sisters, stopped their drill to wave or whistle. Sir Arnold Fitzhugh was the center of the Tory crowd, polite sneers and many silver snuff-boxes, and now and then a guffaw when the citizen soldiers did a particularly stupid thing. And when Paine approached them, Fitzhugh called merrily, "Well, scrivener, what do you think of our rebels?"

"I haven't been able to think yet."

"Blast me, hear that, he hasn't been able to think yet."

Pastor Blane, the Quaker, said, "I see thee are not with them, Tom."

"No—"

"Scruples."

"Doubts, I think," Paine answered slowly, thinking that

if he went ahead now, there would be no turning back, ever.

"Thee see what has happened to their scruples," the pastor said, half sadly, half bitterly. "Eighteen of my flock in there. The Lord said, thou shalt not kill, but a Roman holiday is not to be turned aside from that easily, and now they are marching with sticks, as if the one worthy possession for a man were a gun."

"The strangest part of America," Paine said softly, "is that men have guns. When they shoot them off—"

"I don't follow thee?"

"I don't follow myself," Paine shrugged.

Jacob Rust came to the print shop and said, "I want you in my company, Thomas, my boy." He was a little fat man with a great booming voice.

"Yes?"

"A damned fine little force we're going to have."

"I'll think about it," Paine nodded.

"Is it something to think about?"

"Yes. There's a devil of a lot to think about these days."

"Now look, Master Thomas, you're over from England these few months. People are going to ask, is he England or is he Pennsylvania? Does he smell sweet or does he stink?"

"I don't mind my smell," Paine grinned.

"But we do!"

"I don't go the way the wind blows," Paine said evenly. "I know what I have to do, or I am beginning to. I wonder whether you do, Rust? I wonder whether you know what all this is?"

"It's standing up for our rights as free Englishmen, by God!"

"Is it?"

"And we mean to fight for them!"

Paine shrugged and turned away.

And for some, nothing at all had changed. Paine went to a ball given by the Fairviews, wealthy importers of Tory leanings. They had him because he represented the Pennsylvania Magazine; Paine went because he had to have answers, many answers and coming from all sides, answers to his doubts, his longings, his prayers, his hatreds. Four pounds bought a coat of fine, brown broadcloth, a better garment than any he had ever put on his back. He wore a ruffle at his throat, a new white wig, and good leather breeches, a gentleman right enough with a stick and a three-cornered hat, invited to the best, stepping into quality on his own, into a hall lit by four hundred candles, where a Negro slave called melodiously, "Mister Thomas Paine!"

Four hundred candles, and heaven was never lighted brighter. Black servants walking with silver trays and silver punch bowls, mounds of dainty cookies and cakes, cold meat from twelve different kinds of game and enough Claret, Madeira and Port to float the British Navy. The women were in heavy, brocaded gowns, gilded, silvered, the men in lace and satin and velvet, and he was Mr. Thomas Paine, his opinion asked on everything.

"This Lexington business—of course, a rustic rabble, but here in town, did you see the beggars trying to drill?" They had all been to Europe at one time and another.

"And for one who's seen the King Guards!"

"But, Mr. Paine, what line does an editor take, I mean, a man with a head on his shoulders?"

"I don't fancy a rebellion—I don't fancy anything more than a lot of noise and shouting."

Mr. Paine said practically nothing.

"It doesn't help trade."

"On the other hand it does. People get frightened, and then they buy like mad."

"Really, a straw in the wind. I fancy Lord North will take his sails in after he gives them a sound drubbing."

"I read your magazine faithfully, Mr. Paine," said a young woman, well-gowned, lovely, looking at him with admiration, he, Paine, the staymaker. "I read your poems," she said. "I think they're beautiful and that a man who writes poetry cannot help but have a soul, don't you think?"

"I think many people have souls."

"Do you? Now isn't that frightfully clever. I can't say clever things, but that's frightfully clever."

They had punch, cakes, and they walked in the gardens. There was a moon and stars, and finally she said how strange it was that he had never married.

"I was married." After a moment or so, he said his wife had died.

"What a terrible tragedy!"

"Yes."

"But don't you think it made you a better, a broader man, Mr. Paine?"

"What?"

"You're not listening to me at all, Mr. Paine."

"I am sorry," he said. "What were you saying?"

He wrote a piece for the magazine called *Reflections on Titles*. He was restrained. Again and again, he told himself, what happened to me does not matter. I must write as I think and know and reason and believe, so people will listen. They must listen.

He had it out with Aitken. *Reflections on Titles* struck at the privileged class and struck at them hard. He was not one of the mob, not one of the militia drilling on the Commons, not even one of the Congress party. Instead, alone, he groped in the dark and sought for direction, desperately and sometimes wildly. All the times before he had failed; now he must not fail.

"You will not print that," Aitken said.

"But I will!"

"Then ye part from me!"

"If you want to let me go, let me go. No halfway measures," Paine said.

He became persuasive. "Thomas, have we not always got together on one thing an' another, notwithstanding the arguments?"

"Yes?"

"An' why will ye be stirring in that devil's broth of rebellion?"

"Do I print it?"

"Print it an' be damned, an' have yer notice!"

Paine shrugged. He had been given his notice before, and he no longer cared. He still worked with the Pennsylvania Magazine, and finally he had kicked it off the fence and bent it to his own purposes; but as a part of his life, it was over. What the next part of his life would be, he didn't know, any more than he knew what would be here in America. It was not that he was animated by resolve so much as tension, and all that he could hope for was both nameless and formless.

On May the fifth, Benjamin Franklin returned to America, his mission in Europe over, all the long years there, considered politically, coming to nothing, an old man come home to a boiling country. He took up his residence at Market Street with the Baches, and there, after a few days, Paine managed to see him. Franklin had a half hour for Paine, no more; there were too many threads he had to pick up in America, too much to be done in too short a space of time. But he remembered Paine and shook his hand and said that he had been looking through the Pennsylvania Magazine; it was good; it was clever and it made bright reading.

"Do you like America?" Franklin asked.

Paine nodded; there was much he wanted to say, yet he didn't know how to say it. Having thought to himself for so long that of all the men he had known, Franklin was the wisest, the deepest, and the best, he was now strangely dissatisfied, almost antagonistic.

"You've found yourself," Franklin said.

That was trite, Paine thought, foolish almost. He had found nothing. "What is going to happen?" he asked Franklin. "Will there be war?"

"War? If fighting is war, yes. There has been fighting; there will be more."

"But what does it come to?" Paine demanded, almost fiercely. His next thought was that it was cruel to badger this old man, this very tired old man. "Where are we going—?" For the first time, Paine felt and realized in himself a hard, driving cruelty. He didn't have to ask where they were going; for himself, he was going only one way, and each day it shaped itself more clearly.

Franklin said, "We have to be strong, that's the main thing, isn't it? Once we are strong enough, the ministry will see reason. There's no need for war, never any need for it. War is bad."

"As one would say salt is salty," Paine thought.

"We want our rights," Franklin went on. "We want our freedoms, we want our decencies, our privilege to live a full and good life—that makes good men, the chance to work and put a shilling by, to have a piece of land and a roof overhead. We are not owned part and parcel by England; they must realize that partnership and conciliation—"

"And what of independence?" Paine asked.

"Do we want that?"

"I don't know," Paine said tiredly. "When I was a little boy, even then, I felt that certain things should not be. And when everyone else accepted those things, I thought I was mad, that the devil rode on my shoulders. Can you build anything good on a rotten foundation?"

"Old men don't make revolutions."

"My God, sir," Paine said, "you're not old! You gave me back my youth!"

The next week, a second Continental Congress convened at Philadelphia.

Once more men from all the colonies converged toward Philadelphia. The militia put on a show, and welcomed and welcomed, as if to prove that all their drilling was not for nothing. Back and forth they marched, until their feet ached, and those of them who could afford horses made a cavalry troop to ride out and meet the delegates. "God and Jesus," men said to one another, "that we should live to see this, the port of Boston under siege by the British, the Congress back here in town, and old Ben Franklin still alive and here again." They were back again, the Adams cousins, Hancock, Randolph of Virginia, Jefferson, this time with another Virginian, a big man who like a stage performer wore a magnificent uniform of buff and blue—he was a colonel of the Virginia militia and his face wasn't familiar in Philadelphia; Washington was his name; he walked with long, gangling steps and hardly ever opened his mouth, shy, stupid perhaps. Paine was introduced to him by young Tom Jefferson, "Col-

onel George Washington of Virginia," and Paine squinted
at him.

"I'm glad to meet you, sir. Delegate?"

"I'm a writer," Paine said, as if to justify himself. "I edit
the Pennsylvania Magazine."

"Yes, of course." But obviously, he had never heard of the
Pennsylvania Magazine. He stood silently, looking at Paine,
as if he could think of nothing to say, and afterwards Jefferson explained, apologetically, "He's very wealthy."

"Yes?"

"Perhaps the wealthiest man in America, but land poor,
like many of us Virginians. Not clever, but he has guts."

"He wants to fight, and he doesn't have to talk about it.
People talk so damned much."

"What makes you think he wants to fight?"

"The uniform. He's not a clown."

"I didn't think of it that way," Jefferson said. "He's an
enigma to me."

Paine spent two days in his room, struggling to put down
on paper what he thought. Then he went to listen to the
Congress proclaim to the world that Americans had taken
up arms for protection of their lives and property. Then he
had beer with Sam Adams and Michael Closky, the expatri-
ate Pole. Adams was violently furious, fanatically against
compromise. Knowing he was despised by both the intellec-
tuals and the gentlemen of the Congress, even by his cousin,
John, he turned to these two whose violence, if not obvious,
at least took strange directions.

"You know what you don't want," Paine said quietly, after
listening to a half hour of Adams' denunciation. "That's
only anarchy. What's positive? There is fire burning in a
dozen parts of this country, but what does the fire mean?"

It meant nothing, the Pole said. In his country it had

been the same. Was this the first time the common man lifted up his head to revolt? Yet always it came to nothing.

"The halfway measures," Paine said. "The fence sitters. I'll go so far and no further—"

"How far will you go?" Adams asked him, peering curiously at this British staymaker, this broad, hulking, hooknosed man with his slab-like peasant hands.

"All the way," Paine said softly.

A little drunk, his stubble-covered face wavering in the light of the candle between them, Adams grinned like an imp and asked how far was all the way.

"I want a new world!"

"Utopia?" Adams said.

"God damn it, no! What we have here, a way of life, a way for children to smile, some freedom, some liberty, and hope for the future, men with rights, decent courts, decent laws. Men not afraid of poverty and women not afraid of childbirth—"

The Pole roared with laughter, but Adams' face was suddenly serious. "Independence," he said.

"For a beginning," Paine agreed, sleepy suddenly, tired before and not after the act, seeing his whole life arranged and frightening in its clarity. Now doubt was almost gone. Doubt, built up so slowly and painfully, had resolved itself. He knew some of the answers, and in a little while, he would know the rest.

6

HOW TOM PAINE WROTE A SMALL BOOK

His PARTING from Aitken was curiously mild, and for the first time Paine realized that the Scotsman held him in some esteem and regarded him with a certain affection. Aitken, whom Paine had considered as far removed from emotion as a human being can be, shook his head stubbornly, and at first, when he gave Paine his hand, was able to say nothing at all. Paine knew it was not entirely the impending doom of the Pennsylvania Magazine that moved him; the publication was doomed, not only through its loss of its editor, but because the rising upheaval in the colonies made it already an antique of some vaguely remembered epoch. This whole peaceful land, which went on without much appearance of change—as lands do even when the world begins to burn—was inwardly bubbling and boiling and preparing to explode. Paine thought that Aitken knew it, not as a Tory, nor even as a rebel, but as one who losing security would lose all reason to live. Paine pitied him.

"Ye will no' change yer mind?" he asked.

That was not the question, as Paine knew. A pound a week was good pay and more than enough to keep him comfortably, and what with things he had written for other publications he had some twenty pounds to fall back on. Perhaps he was a fool to give it up, the more so since the course he planned was very vague.

"It is bread and butter," Aitken pressed him.

"No, I'm sorry."

"Think it over, Thomas. Ye'll be sucked in with the madmen, an' it's no' Christian, Thomas. Let well enough alone." But when Aitken saw he couldn't persuade him, the Scotsman said gruffly, "Ye'll no' hold a grudge, Thomas?"

"Why should I?"

"There are mean men an' there are sweet men, but ye no go in a category, Thomas."

"I never held a grudge," Paine said, "except against myself."

Tall, slim, fair as a girl and as comely as Paine was ugly, Tom Jefferson won him heart and soul. Jefferson was a gentleman in Paine's memory of the sharp division of things in England, and the Thetford staymaker's first reaction was one of sullen hostility. Jefferson was graceful and handsome and accomplished and clever, all that Paine was not, and in his first advances Paine saw only some petty need for the favor of the magazine. The gall in his soul poured acid on Jefferson, and admiring the man, thrilling with pleasure if Jefferson so much as nodded at him, Paine's outward reaction was only to try and turn the Virginian into an enemy. Jefferson wouldn't become an enemy; God only knows what he saw in the graceless staymaker, whose hands always had dirt under their nails; but whatever it was made him want to find the man beneath the crust. He pretended not to see the point in Paine's caustic remarks, and met the editor on such a basis of easy equality that bit by bit Paine's reserve disappeared. Being one of the inner circle of the Congress, Jefferson knew everything, met everyone, and was able to

smooth things considerably for Paine. A few years younger
than Paine, he combined fresh youthfulness and maturity in
a manner that was, for Paine at least, completely charming.

To share a pot of coffee with him was something that
Paine looked forward to; dinner with him was sheer delight,
and after an evening spent with him in front of a fire, Paine
glowed with a warm happiness he had never known before.
Slowly and deliberately, Jefferson drew from him as much
as any man could of the story of his life; he had a wonderful
knack of taking the confused memory and assembling it with
meaning. He once said to Paine, "All in all, as it was, with
the dirt, the privation, the misery, the gin and the utter
hopelessness in the way you and those around you lived, that
alone, terrible as it was, could have been endured—" The
sentence hung in the air, and Paine tried to see what he was
driving at.

"Poverty is a degree of things," Jefferson said. "I have seen
people here in America whose poverty was complete and absolute, yet they retained—"

"Dignity," Paine said.

"Dignity."

"Then that's all we live for," Paine reflected. "If there's
any meaning in human life, then it's there, in the dignity of
a human being."

"I think so."

"I never realized that before; I began to feel it here, but
I didn't know until I spoke of it tonight. It's true though;
all through ten thousand years men have been corrupted by
having their dignity taken from them. When my wife died
and the neighbors poured in to look at her poor, tired body,
the little, evil thrill of it the only excitement in their lives,
each bringing a scrap of food for admission, I could think,

God help me, only of how comical it was. If we were made in the image of God, how rotten that image has become!"

Another time, Jefferson was giving a small dinner for George Washington and he asked Paine to come. Randolph was to be there, too, and at first Paine refused; he was frightened; he valued his relationship with Jefferson too much, and he was afraid he would make a fool of himself in front of the three Virginians whose culture, quality, and wealth were almost beyond his imagination. He had heard of Mount Vernon, Washington living there like a great feudal baron, with packs of hunting dogs, strings of horses, countless black slaves, rivers of wine, the "quality" coming and going endlessly, a coach that had cost two thousand pounds; he had heard of the Randolphs; certain Quakers of Philadelphia never tired telling tales of these three godless agnostics, and Paine had little basis upon which to separate the true from the false. What meaning for him or for any common man could a rebellion have if their kind were at the bottom of it? Wasn't it all a clever cover for their desire to be freed from the dictatorship of the British tobacco agents, and weren't they, as all their class, ruthless enough to spill a hundred thousand quarts of blood to see their great plantations thrive?

But at last he gave in to Jefferson's urging, forswore himself to sullen silence, put on his best suit, his best wig, and came to the dinner. He was surprised at how eagerly they shook hands with him; they knew of him; they read the Pennsylvania Magazine, even Washington who, Paine had presumed, read nothing at all. Peyton Randolph, the eldest of the three, had an eager, inquiring air, as if he had looked forward to nothing so much as meeting Paine. Washington said little; he sat and listened with his chin on his hand when he wasn't eating, his long face intent upon what was being said, his brow furrowed with a shade of annoyance now and again, perhaps most of it an impatience with his own lack of understanding. Jefferson took up the conversation and did most of the talking. Paine noticed that of the four, Washington drank the most and seemed least affected by what he drank.

Jefferson toyed with the idea of independence; as an intellectual concept it appealed to him, for it was filled with limitless and entrancing possibilities, but his manner of treating it was entirely objective, and Paine saw that he never considered it as any more than a dream. When he made a simile of a child being forced out of a house by his father, the child in this case being the colonies and the father England, Washington smiled, showing his bad teeth and said, "But he remains in the family."

"Only by name."

"Yet we are Englishmen, Virginians true enough, but Englishmen nevertheless," nodding generously at Paine, their provincialism polite as it was narrow.

"Oh, damn it, we're at war," Randolph said impatiently. "Why don't people realize that?"

"For our rights."

"Rights! Rights! What are rights? Where do they begin and end?"

Jefferson laughed and said, "What do you think of rights, Mr. Paine?"

"I think there are no such things. I think that by right of birth all things belong to all men. You can take away rights, but you can't give what belongs to all."

"You make no exceptions, Mr. Paine?" Randolph asked. "None!"

"Then you would reform England as well as America?"

"It's not reform for men to claim what is theirs."

"But it's dangerous. You sound bloodthirsty, Mr. Paine."

"I hate war," Paine said slowly. "Of all ways to hold man in contempt and make a beast of him, war is the worst. There is nothing on earth I hate more than war."

Paine wasn't surprised when the Congress made Washington commander in chief of the rabble of Yankee farmers who lay like hungry wolves around Boston. There was something about the tall, dry-faced Virginian that made people trust him. "As they always trust stupidity," the Philadelphia wits said. But Paine wasn't certain of that, and on the day when Washington rode through the streets, cheered wildly, Paine stood in the crowd and tried to understand what dull, curious force in the man could draw out the admiration of these shouting fools.

Although a state of actual war was beginning to exist that summer of 1775, the people of Philadelphia could not take it quite seriously. For one thing, Massachusetts was so far away; for another, business was good. Even when news came to town that there had been a terrible, bloody battle fought in Boston, at a place called Breed's Hill, and that the redcoat dead lay like pigs in a slaughtering pen, it did not seem quite real to Philadelphia. After their first rush of enthusiasm, the militia enlistments fell off sharply; the wags did caricatures of the citizen soldiers. The drills became sloppy affairs; the men came to resent their officers, and the whole scheme of a citizen army showed signs of going to pieces.

For Paine, those early summer days were leisurely and almost carefree. He had money enough for the first time in his life; his lodgings cost little, and a few shillings a day more than provided for him. His reputation with the magazine gave him enough of a name for him to sell an article here and there, and his reaction from the restrictions laid down on him by Aitken was to write quickly, purposefully, and better than ever before. He read a good deal, talked a good deal, and took to long, rambling walks along the river front. The Pennsylvania countryside, so like yet so different from England, fascinated him, and he would wander out into the hills, put up for the night at the stone house of some Dutch farmer, smoke a pipe, drink good homemade beer, and argue about everything from crops to government. With working-men he was able to drop the chip from his shoulder, and he, to whom good speech came with such difficulty, lapsed with ease into the broad Pennsylvania country drawl.

One day, hot and tired, he climbed over a stile into a farm-yard where a buxom, fair-haired girl of twenty or twenty-one was drawing the buttermilk off her churn. "Could I have some?" Paine asked, and she poured some into a wooden mug and laughed at the way it ran from the corners of his mouth.

"Ah, you're a dry one," she said.

"Can I pay you?"

She laughed again and asked him whether he had come up out of Philadelphia.

"All the way," he said proudly. It was a good twelve miles, and only here in America had he learned the deep pleasure of walking.

"You don't look like a walker."

"No—"

"What do you do?"

He told her he was a writer, and she smiled at him quizzi-cally, as if a writer were the strangest thing that had ever come her way. Then, as easily and inoffensively as she had made his acquaintance, she dropped it and went back to her butter-making as if he had never existed, running off the milk and lifting the rich white butter out of the churn, molding it like clay in her strong freckled hands. Paine, comfortable, quite rested now, sprawled in the shade of a tree, entranced by the wonderful pattern the sun and the leaves made on his dusty clothes, stretched out his legs, drank his milk, and watched her beat the butter on the board. The farm was evidently a prosperous one, the fieldstone house square and solid as a fortress, the barn half stone, half timber, strong hand-hewn beams jutting from under the eaves. They had had their first haying, and the sweet-smelling stuff was piled in great heaps out on the fields and, beyond, the corn and oats were coming up as if they could not hasten from the earth soon enough. There was a pen full of rooting black and whites, and the chickens ran loose and aimless. Out in the fields, a half mile or so away, two men were working a team, and a fat pile of smoke ran from the chimney to show that things were doing inside.

When the girl had finished her butter, she lifted the board in her arms and said to Paine over her shoulder, "You may come in if you wish." Her recollection of his presence was so casual and good-natured that he couldn't help but follow her, and they went into a long, low-ceilinged kitchen where another woman, evidently the girl's mother, was mixing a batter of dough.

At one side of the kitchen, there was a great hearth, full eight feet long, with a Dutch oven on either end. The floor of the kitchen was red brick, swept so clean you could eat off it, and down the center was a long sawbuck table. Two handmade benches flanked the fireplace; there was a wide sideboard, loaded to the shaking point with pewter and crockery. Those and several straight chairs made up the furnishings of the room, but from the ceiling hung smokings of ham and bacon and jerked venison and beef. And from one of the benches four tow-headed children, three boys and a girl, regarded Paine with a wide-eyed but reticent curiosity.

The girl said, "Mother, this here's a writing man, walked up out of Philadelphia."

Paine bowed and said, "My name is Thomas Paine, madam. I was hot and thirsty, and your daughter was good enough to give me a glass of buttermilk."

"We have plenty of that," the woman smiled, not leaving her work. She was past middle age, but broad-shouldered and strong, her sleeves rolled up, her large arms white with powder past the elbows. Her face, lined with work, was pleas- ant in its big, regular features. "Our name's Rumpel," she said. "That's Sarah." She pointed to the boys and called off, "Ephraim, Gideon, Samuel." The little girl was Rachel. Then she went on with her work, and Paine sat down in a cool corner.

At noon, the long table was set. The farmer, Jacob Rum- pel, clumped in with his hired man, shook hands with Paine, and sat down at the table. Without words, they had made it evident that he would stay and eat, and he had no desire to leave. Sarah set a place for him next to her father; when she looked at him there was a twinkle in her eyes, and now and again Paine had a feeling she was laughing at him. The chil- dren raced to the board, never taking their eyes off Paine, and the farmer, who had been turning the name over in his mind, said finally, "You be with that Pennsylvania Maga- zine."

Paine nodded, somewhat pleased that they should know him here.

"I don't hold with it!" Jacob snapped.

"Neither do I."

"Then why are you not man enough to throw down your pen?"

"Father," Sarah said, "your food will be cold."

"I did."

"Ah—"

"That's why I can walk in the country," Paine smiled.

Turning to him suddenly, the farmer demanded, "Were you thrown out or did you quit them?"

"Some of each."

"I know Aitken, a tight man with a rope around his soul. He waves this way and that but lacks the guts to fall. Paine, there's good men in writing and bad. I read Ben Franklin and Jim Hall. I read MacCullough and Tom Jefferson. I like a man with gall. I like a man—"

"Pay no attention to father," Sarah said quietly.

"—who can look at a thing and say right or wrong. Right is right and wrong is wrong. I don't hold with in-between. I reckon I side with the Boston men, what's mine is mine so long as I got powder for my gun—" He was a tall, lean, brown-faced man, with a bobbing apple in his throat and tiny blue eyes.

"Go an' eat, Jacob," his wife said.

For Paine, the Rumpels were a new and wonderful experience. There was nothing like them in England, and he was sure there was nothing quite like them anywhere else in the world. In wealth and possessions they were richer than many a squire at home, yet Jacob Rumpel worked with his hands and Hester Rumpel, his wife, did the cooking for the whole huge family. They were not peasants, yet they could not be put in the class of the English yeomen farmers. Their hired man sat down with them at the table as an equal, not as a servant, and the children shared in the chores as if they took pleasure in the mere act of labor.

Jacob Rumpel plowed his own fields, yet at night he read not only the Pennsylvania Magazine but Voltaire and Defoe. His wit was the wit of Poor Richard; Ben Franklin was his

god and the greatest intellectual influence upon his life; and
he could only philosophize in terms of action. He made his
own candles, his own soap, his own cloth for which he raised
his own flax and wool. The farm was his, but a younger
brother had packed his possessions in a wagon and gone west
into the lonely hills of Fincastle, and Rumpel took it for
granted that some of his sons would do the same. His wife
came of Puritan stock, but he himself was comfortably ag-
nostic, not out of reason, but rather out of unbounded confidence in things that are. He and God walked the earth on
even terms; he did what was right, and he was content with
his doubts. He hated slave-holders, and he drank no tea out
of principle, but his admiration for the Boston men, whom
he considered in other ways a bloodless and intolerant breed,
would not be translated into action until the redcoats
marched on Pennsylvania soil. When Paine asked him what
he would do then, he said, matter of factly, "Take my gun."

"And the farm?"

"I reckon the farm'll limp along."

But after he had gone back to the farm half a dozen times,
welcomed by Rumpel who was just naive enough to con-
sider Paine a great figure in the intellectual life of Philadelphia, a favorite with the children to whom he told endless
stories of highwaymen and privateers, Paine no longer denied to himself what brought him there so constantly. He
was not in love with Sarah, not as love goes; inside he was
dry and empty, and the memory of the serving girl who died
in the shack in Margate hung like a stone around his neck.

But being with Sarah was compounded of peace and rest-
fulness, and a content such as he had not known before. In-
dolence was something very new to him; unemployment he
knew and starvation he knew, just as he knew poverty and

drunkenness and squalor and all the shambling wrecks who did nothing because there was nothing for them to do. But the pleasure of sheer laziness, the sweet satisfaction of dawdling in a Pennsylvania summertime was as strange for him as was this curious family in their stone house with its foot-thick walls.

He would sit in the barnyard and watch the girl, or else in the kitchen where he told endless stories both to the children and Hester Rumpel. He found in himself a gift for a mild sort of fun-making; he found he could say things that would make them laugh. And as often as he could, he would help Sarah. That was difficult, for her own strength was a very matter-of-fact thing, while few people realized the layers of broad peasant muscle in Tom Paine's sloping shoulders. But in carrying buckets of water or sacks of feed, he was permitted to have his own way now and again, and it gave him a strange pleasure when his strength dragged from her a grudging smile of admiration.

She spoke little, as if taking it for granted that he knew how much she could convey with a smile and a word, or simply with a movement of her fair head. When Paine confided to her the work he was doing, he half doubted whether she understood more than a part of it.

"I'm writing a small book to make things clear," he said once.

"You mean the Boston men?"

"That and yourself."

She smiled and nodded and didn't ask him what he meant by that.

"It's like having lived for one thing," he tried to explain. "This book is the one thing. I want it to sweep everything out of the way, so men and women can start fresh."

"Father will enjoy reading it," she said.

There were never any words of love, he never kissed her. If he stayed of an evening after the children were put to bed, they might walk down the lane while Jacob smoked his pipe on the porch. There was a moon, waxing and waning through the nights; there were the birds courting in the darkness and competing with the crickets; there was the far-off barking of dogs. Yet it was no surprise to him when she said, on one of those evenings, "Will you be asking for my hand, Tom?" And then added, as if he had asked a question, "Mother says there's a mighty difference of age, but I don't hold with that. I've a great favor for you, Tom, and I think I love you with all my heart."

She was simple, he decided, simple and no more, but the rush of pain in his heart, searing, hopeless pain told him that never in his life had he wanted anything more than this fair-haired girl. Whether he loved her or not was suddenly unimportant; she was his first and last good hope; she was all that makes a man human, and after this he would not be human; after this he would walk silently and alone.

They went on a while further and then sat down on a stone fence, and he told her, "I was married twice before."

She looked at him without reproach, and he told her who his first wife was and how she had died.

"That was a sorrowful thing," she said, still without reproach, but he knew it was over and done with, that Sarah was alive again, freed from this strange, hook-nosed wanderer. He should have gone then, but he wanted to tell her; he wanted to justify himself where no justification was needed. He tried to make her understand how a man might be broken and go to shelter as an animal goes to ground; but in her way of life and thinking there was a dignity that could not be broken but only destroyed. The story came out haltingly; it was nine years after his first wife had died, and he was at the bottom; but what did she know of the bottom with her health and her bountiful vitality? He tried to tell her of the things he had done in those nine years, of the hell that was London for the poor, of his pent-up savage desire to be free, of the trades he had followed, the degradation, the misery, the brief surges of hope when he preached in the meadows with the Methodists—"Cast off sin and come ye into the arms of the Lord"—and then the hope gone, the bottom rungs of the ladder, and then finally the very bottom, the deepest bottom, the complete hopelessness where there was nothing but death.

"And then this man took me in," he said. "He was a good man. He kept a little tobacco shop and he had almost nothing at all, but he took me in. Like Christ, he knew not the evil from the good, but only the weak from the strong. God help me, I was weak, I was dying."

"But what was his life worth?" she might have thought from that brief picture of inferno.

"I had a debt to him?" he asked her.

"Yes."

"Then he died. He had a wife and daughter. I wanted to care for them, I stayed with them. And then there was talk, and for the mother's sake I married the girl whom I didn't love—"

She could see that.

He tried to tell how the business had broken up, it was such a poor little trade, the way his wife began to hate, how he tried to help others, to work some good. His words were no use any more. He couldn't tell how his wife despised him, how she left him, his dread of the debtors' prison, how he fled. He didn't want to make himself out to be anything, but the more he tore off in abasement, the less Sarah comprehended. This half-world, this dreadful twilight land of hopelessness, was as far away and as unreal to her as the sandy wastes of Egypt. For her, human beings were compounded flesh and blood, not pain and terror and wretchedness.

When he said goodnight, he knew he would never come back, and as he walked away she looked after him, neither happy nor sorrowful, but thinking of how he wanted to write a small book to make things clear.

Things were quieter in Philadelphia. Members of the Second Continental Congress, after they had said all they possibly could say and accomplished practically nothing at all, remembered their farms and estates, their mills, shops, and distilleries, and by ones and twos they trickled away from Philadelphia. The new commander in chief, General George Washington of Virginia, started his leisurely ride northward to Boston to take command of the several thousand Yankees who now sprawled around that city in a sort of siege. The bloody battle which afterwards came to be known as Bunker Hill but was then called Breed's Hill, was still fresh enough in the minds of the British to make them move very cautiously, and as things were now both sides waited for the other to make the next move.

In Philadelphia, a hot, slow summer set in. Prudent shopkeepers, feeling that this was another storm blown on its way, took down the shutters from their shop windows; and as a whole, the citizens of the town were quite satisfied things had not come to a head.

Meanwhile, Paine stayed close to the city, lived with it, and felt its pulse. He never went back to the Rumpels after that last evening there, yet he took a certain grim pride in the fact that the incident had not set him back on his heels. Slowly and painfully, out of all the broken, dirty pieces of his life, he was building a plan, a course, and a method. Now he was content to walk alone; he quite knew what he wanted to do, and he felt an ominous certainty that as time passed it would become even more clear. In the life on the peaceful, prosperous farm he saw something good and peaceful and sweet, yet he was half grateful that it was denied to him.

He had a little room, a bed, a bolster, chest, coat-rack, and table, two fairly good suits of clothes, ink and paper. That was enough, a man should want no more. He needed a few pennies for candles, something for food, something for drink. During this time he no longer allowed himself to be drunk, yet he saw no reason to do without liquor. Rum helped him; caring little for himself or for what became of him, he was ready to use anything that might make his pen move more easily on the paper. He was writing stuff out of thought and making something out of nothing, and after he had worked steadily for five, six, or seven hours, the little room closed in on him. Rum helped; as he drank, his movements would become slow and painful, but the quill would continue to scratch, which was all that mattered. He had no delusions; what he wrote might never be read by more than a dozen persons, but it was all he could do and what he had to do. Men don't make new worlds in an afternoon; brick has to be placed on brick, and the process is long and incredibly painful.

Without realizing it, he neglected his appearance, sometimes spending twenty-four hours in his room, shaving less often, hoarding his small store of money, allowing his stockings to wear out and his clothes to become shabby. Those citizens of Philadelphia who noticed the change remarked that Aitken was wise to fire him. "Good riddance to bad rubbish," they said. His money low, Paine spent a night writing a poem and took it to Aitken, who gave him a pound, certainly more than it was worth. But somewhere in his flint-like, Scotch shell, Aitken nursed a fondness for this plodding, almost bullish man, who childishly believed that the world wanted to hear his solution to its woes.

"How goes the masterpiece?" Aitken asked him.

"It's no masterpiece. It's an attempt at common sense, of which I have little enough, God knows."

"I will no' print it, so don't come asking me."

Paine grinned.

"Will ye have supper?"

"I will at that," Paine nodded. He hadn't eaten a good cooked meal in God knows how long, and he felt a sudden longing to be with people he knew. At Aitken's table was Joshua Craige, a linen merchant recently come over from England, full of news of how London was taking the revolt. "There's more for the colonies than against them," Craige said. "You would think the revolt is coming there, not here."

"And perhaps it is," Paine said thoughtfully.

"And how do you make that out, mister?"

Paine shrugged and avoided the question. Only vaguely defined in his mind was a picture of the whole world renewing itself, dreams of a brotherhood so vast, so complete that the half-drawn conception was overpowering and beyond words.

Jefferson would not call attention to Paine's poverty, his failings in matters of dress; Jefferson was in the process of adoring the common man, and being only thirty-two he was still young enough to attach reality to his conception. Himself the immaculate aristocrat, it astonished him—though it shouldn't have—to find that Paine arrived at much the same conclusions out of experience that he, Jefferson, had gathered out of philosophy and reading. But whereas Jefferson had dreamed enough democracy to make it real, he could never quite grasp the concept of revolution. For Paine it was the other way around, and his thoughts and ideas were closer to those of the average working man than Jefferson's ever could be. Listening to Paine read something of what he had written, Jefferson wondered whether Paine knew what devils he was loosing upon the quiet eighteenth-century world wherein they lived.

Paine read hoarsely and self-consciously, ashamed before Jefferson:

"The sun never shined on a cause of greater worth. 'Tis not the affair of a City, a County, a Province or a Kingdom; but of a continent—at least one-eighth part of the habitable globe. 'Tis not the concern of a day, a year, or an age; posterity are virtually involved in the contest, and will be more or less affected even to the end of time, by the proceedings now. Now is the seed-time of Continental union, faith and honor. The least fracture now will be like a name engraved with the point of a pin on the tender rind of a young oak; the wound would enlarge with the tree, and posterity read it in full grown characters. . . ."

There was no style; it came forth as raucously as the preaching of a Methodist minister, and it struck with frantic hammer blows. A man could memorize words like those and drive his plow or hammer to the rhythm—

"O! Ye that love mankind! Ye that dare oppose not only the tyranny but the tyrant, stand forth! Every spot of the old world is overrun with oppression. Freedom hath been hunted round the Globe. Asia and Africa have long expelled her. Europe regards her like a stranger, and England hath given her warning to depart. O! receive the fugitive, and prepare in time an asylum for mankind."

Jefferson didn't smile; a working man who cribbed from

the Bible all he knew of style, who in the terms of a backwoods preacher roared a new creed for mankind, nevertheless said something no one else dared to say outright.

"What are you going to call it?" Jefferson asked.

"I think, common sense. That's all it is."

Word of Paine's project got around, and people would say,
"That's common sense." They would say, "He is preaching
dissolution and hatred and revolt. Separation from the
mother country." Or, "Another common sense," when someone spoke a word for the independence of the thirteen colonies.

A little book to show men what to think.

"Of course, separation in time," old Ben Franklin said to
him one day. "But be careful, Paine, be careful."

He carried the manuscript around with him, crumpled,
ink-stained paper, and sitting in a tavern with a mug of rum,
he would write, correct, write again, smudge and blot and
scrape together the future of America.

"Is it still common sense?" he'd be asked.

He wove the Bible into what he was writing. To the devil
with the sophisticates of the city, he told himself. The man
with the plow is the man with the gun, and the man with
the plow reads and believes only one book. So he took from
the Bible whatever he could whenever he could, and wove
it into the rest. One night in a coffee house, having had a
little too much, he read aloud. Of course, it was common
sense, and he could draw a crowd, and it was very well put
that the devil can quote scripture.

"To hell with all of you and all of you be damned!" he
roared at the well-dressed, well-paunched Philadelphia merchants. And then, going home that night, he was set upon
by half a dozen young toughs, his manuscript torn to shreds,

himself rolled in the mud and beaten, his pants removed and a lash laid twenty or thirty times over his behind.

He kept his lips tight about it, and when Aitken came to him and said he might have a hint as to who the assailants were, Paine simply shook his head.

"It doesn't matter. The few pages they tore up I know by heart."

"But you, man, you!"

"I'll live," Paine said briefly.

The Reverend Jared Heath of the Society of Friends put it to Paine in a different fashion.

Heath, a small, moist-eyed man, said to Paine with utter sincerity, "Thomas, thee know not what thee do."

"And exactly what am I doing that I don't know?" Paine demanded.

"Thee are setting brother against brother and father against son and workman against employer with this writing of independence. Who, Thomas, speaks for independence? Thee should know that not the good people, not the considerate, not the gentle, but the discontented, those who make mock of God, the foreigners among us. Thee are one of us, yet thee write to plunge us into bloodshed."

"I am one of many things," Paine said wearily, not wanting to hurt this little man who evoked memories of his father, his uncles, of the old meeting house at Thetford.

"Come to us and pray and thee will see light."

The summer past, the leaves turning red and brown and yellow as they rustled over the cobbled streets of Philadelphia, the cold clean winds blowing from the northwest, Paine still scraped at his paper. The thing was done or never done; he didn't know. He had written a little book to make men see the thing clearly, and it asked for independence. With deliberate hatred, he had torn apart the whole conception of monarchy. He had pointed out how long man had been nailed to the cross, and in words a farmer could understand begged for a good new world in this good new land. He had even tried his hand at a form of government. But always he harped on a single fact, that regardless of the pain, the torment, and the bloodshed, here must be a new and independent country.

He wrote on the first page, as if purging himself, "Common Sense, written by an Englishman."

And then it was done, a heap of scribbled-over paper. No one would read it and probably no one would print it, but it was for the doing that Paine worked.

He was tired and listless, not left even with a desire to be drunk. Fascinated by the cool change of season, he wandered lazily through the narrow streets of Old Philadelphia, sniffing the winds that blew from the wide and grave and mysterious west. Never in England came such a change of season, sharp and clean, the air washing over a whole continent to thunder at the tidewater wanderers fled from the old world.

He discovered, so short was the memory of men, even for a ribald jest, that few now remembered he was Common Sense, and fewer poked fun at him. He was left alone, and often he said to himself that was just as well.

He let Aitken read his finished manuscript; no animosity was left between them, and Aitken, glasses perched on his nose, followed the scrawl carefully and considerately. Finally he said, "It's no' a bad thing, Thomas, but, my lad, it's muckle dangerous."

"If anyone reads it," Paine said.

"I will no' publish it, but why na' take it to Bobby Bell, who's a fool for such matters."

"If you think so," Paine nodded.

Bell was a Scotsman too, hatchet-faced, with ink-grimed hands. He said a good morning to Paine, and then took the manuscript, leaned against his counter and began to read. Paine dropped to a chair, closed his eyes, dozed a little, opened his eyes to see that the Scotsman had started over at the front page. His face never moved, never changed expression as he went through the manuscript again. Then he folded it carefully, laid it down on the counter, and placed a paperweight on it to hold it in place.

"You don't want it," Paine said.

"No-o—"

Paine began to rise but the Scotsman said, "Be in no hurry. I canna guarantee a profit, but I will set type and make a book of it. A man canna say will sell or will no' sell, but I lean to standing up to what's mine. They're good, clear sentiments."

"I don't want any money," Paine said. "I wrote this because I had to, that's all. If you make money, you can have it; I don't want it."

"I have no argument with a man who desires to throw a penny in my lap."

"Then you'll print it."

"That I will," Bell said somberly.

And then Paine rose and left the shop as casually as he had entered.

7

COMMON SENSE

D<small>R. BENJAMIN RUSH</small>, a young Philadelphia physician who had some time since decided that more than physical ills ailed mankind, told Ben Franklin how Bell had cooled toward the idea of Paine's book. "I think he was afraid," Rush said. "I don't blame him. Like a hundred thousand others, he doesn't know on what side his bread is buttered; he has other things to think about, all men have, I suppose.

"But, God, the more I think of it, the more I wonder how those farmers at Lexington had the guts to stand up to it."

"Did you read the book?" Franklin asked.

"Yes."

"And did you like it?"

"It's not something a man likes or dislikes. Neither is gunpowder, nor bleeding."

"Of course, you got Bell to go ahead?" Franklin said quietly.

"Was that wrong? He owes me, and I suppose I put my finger on him where it hurt a little."

"Things are not right and wrong any more," Franklin reflected, almost sadly. "We go ahead, and that's all."

"Of course, they're right and wrong!"

"Of course," Franklin shrugged. "It was right for kings

to rule the world for a thousand years. It was right for little
people to suffer and die. It was so right for men to be slaves
that there was never a need for chains." He added, after a
moment's hesitation, "I'm sorry I am an old man. I would
like to see—"

"If you want to read the book," Rush said, "it will be off
the presses in a few days. You've probably seen parts of it in
manuscript. That man Paine certainly isn't reticent."

"Bring me a copy," Franklin nodded, reflecting that he
had had a hand in opening Pandora's box, almost boyishly
eager to see what Paine, who would shake the world apart,
had to say.

From the press and just sewn together, it still smelled of
ink and smudged as Paine held it in his hands, a thin book
called "Common Sense, written by an Englishman," with
big block letters on the cover, sticky as Paine opened it.

"Done," Bell said.

Paine told him, "I don't want you to suffer for this," and
Bell shrugged. "I'll want to buy a few copies," said Paine.

Bell nodded.

"To show them to my friends."

"Ye may."

"You'll give it to me a little cheaper than the regular
price?" Paine remarked, not able to keep a note of anxiety
out of his voice, his hand in his pocket holding all the money
he had in the world.

"I may."

"It makes a pretty book," said Paine.

Consigned to Baltimore by stage, the package had neither
the sender's name nor the contents marked on it, only the
destination, the shop of Marcus Leed, a small bookseller. But

Bell, to purchase the driver's silence, had given him a dozen copies to sell himself at two shillings to whoever would buy. In the coach, the passengers took one to share among them and while away the hours with—fat, bespectacled Parson Amos Culwoodie, Methodist free preacher, reading sonorously:

"There is something exceedingly ridiculous in the composition of Monarchy."—The parson had always felt as much. —"It first excludes a man from the means of information, yet empowers him to act in cases where the highest judgment is required—" Jacob Stutz, the miller, sitting alongside the parson, knew that if man doesn't live by bread alone, bread at least is as necessary as anything else, and now wondered what king on earth could do a simple grading of flour.

A long journey and a noisy one. The parson reaffirmed his position as God's right hand man when he read, "How came the king by a power the people are afraid to trust, and always obliged to check?"

"How indeed?" Mrs. Roderick Clewes asked.

The parson took off his hat in deference to a lady. "There is no divine right in man," he stated decisively.

"None?"

"None, I tell you, madam. For a minister, a call perhaps, an inspiration, an unfolding of the darkness, a nearness to God. But divine right—that, madam, I assure you, is dispensed by Satan."

In the old Brackmeyer Coffee House by Dr. Rush's arrangement were met David Rittenhouse, James Cannon, Christopher Marshall, Ludwig Rees, and Amberton St. Allen, a strange company of the high and the low, united by a desperate feeling that now there was no turning back. It gave them a feeling of romance, a feeling of living high and swiftly and gloriously, to know that when the redcoats came to Philadelphia they would be among the first hanged. Withal, theirs was an intellectual approach, and their god was Ben Franklin, not the Adams cousins. When Rush told them he had called them together to read a pamphlet, they nodded, called for drinks, and set themselves to listen.

"Never mind who wrote this," Rush said, and then he read slowly and meticulously for almost three hours, stopping now and then to answer a brief question, but toward the latter part of his reading holding his listeners in a rapt silence.

"It's called *Common Sense*," he said when he had finished.

"Of course, it's Paine's thing," Rittenhouse nodded.

"That's right."

"If this be treason—" someone paraphrased.

"You don't realize—it's so damned insidious."

"How much?"

"Two shillings."

"Well, it ought to be less."

"You think people will buy it?"

"Is there anyone who won't? The man's a devil and a genius."

"No, he's a peasant. Have you ever seen his hands, like slabs of beef. He's a peasant, and that's why he understands us, because we're a nation of peasants and shopkeepers and mechanics. He comes here a year ago and he knows what's in our guts. He's not writing for you and me, but for the man at the plow and the bench, and, God, how he flatters them, crawls inside of them, tickles them, seduces them, talks their own language, says to them: Isn't this reasonable? Isn't this common sense? Why haven't you done this long ago? Bathe the world in the blood of tyrants! You and I and all the rest, why are we slaves when we can be free?

Is he Christ or the devil? I don't know. I know, after hearing that thing read, there will be no peace for a long time."

"For how long?"

"Not ten years—maybe a hundred, two hundred. Maybe
never—I don't know if men were made to be slaves or free."

Abraham Marah was a trader with the Indians, a lonely
man, a strong man but black-eyed and black-visaged. His
name when he came to the country as a little boy had been
Abraham ben Asher, but they called him Marah because he
was bitter, and as he came of age and lived more and more
in the dark forests he called himself Abraham Marah, after
the new fashion. He was a Jew, but at the synagogue he was
known as a rebel. "I'm a free man," he would say, "and God
has done nothing for me."

But he wasn't slow with money when they asked for con-
tributions. As they said, What use had he for money? With
no home, no wife, no possessions but the pack on his back
and his long Pennsylvania squirrel gun, he would roam on
for months at a time. He knew the Indians—the Shawnee,
the Miami, the Wyandot, and the Huron—and they knew
him. Fur hunters they all were, and he could come back
from six months in the dark forest with a fortune in pelts on
his donkeys. Now, starting out again, he came to Bell and
bought twenty copies of Paine's book.

"Why, Abraham?" Bell asked him.

"Because I read it, because where I go, others think twice,
and then in the end stay home."

He brought the first copy to Fort Pitt. John Neville and
his Virginia militia had already taken the post, and now
they were sitting around, drinking more than was good for
them, wondering whether to go home, wondering why they
had taken up guns when there was neither purpose nor rea-

son nor goal. They were long, hard men in dirty hunting shirts, and many of them had not deciphered a written word these ten years past. But, as Lieutenant Cap Heady said, when a Jew gives away something, there's a reason. Heady read out loud in the light of a campfire:

"In England a king hath little more to do than to make war and give away places; which, in plain terms, is to impoverish the nation and set it together by the ears. A pretty business indeed for a man to be allowed eight hundred thousand sterling a year for, and worshiped into the bargain! Of more worth is one honest man to society, and in the sight of God, than all the crowned ruffians that ever lived."

It was the sort of thing the Virginians enjoyed hearing. "Go on," they told Heady.

Marah's way was long and rambling. A copy stayed in a Kentucky stockade, another in an Ohio stockade, one in a lake cabin with the promise to pass it on and on. Three copies were saved for the French Canadians, the voyageurs whom Marah loved better than all other Americans, and one copy was unfolded, page by page, in an Iroquois longhouse as Marah painfully translated *Common Sense* into the Indian tongue.

General George Washington of Virginia was a troubled man; come up from his Mount Vernon, from his beloved Virginia, his broad and stately Potomac, from all the good, earthy things of his life, the lush fields, the fruit trees, the many bottles of good wine, he was now bogged down outside of Boston, in command of several thousand sprawling, lazy, totally undisciplined New England Yankees. The war, for all apparent purposes, had come to a halt; but the doubts of intelligent men, who had little idea of what it all meant or where it was taking them, went on. For Washington, who had come into this without any clear idea of means or end, but simply with a fierce love of the land he tilled, a decent respect for the dignity of himself and his friends, and a hatred of the English method of conducting the tobacco business, doubt mounted steadily and surely. The word "independence" was too frequently spoken; it had a quality of terror, burn, pillage, and kill—remake the world! Washington loved the world he lived in; the earth was good, and better were the fruits of the earth. But to remake this good-enough world into some uncertain horror of the future—

It was in such a mood that he sat down and read a book brought from Philadelphia by express messenger. It was called *Common Sense*. Jefferson wrote him, ". . . you will want to know that this is Paine's work; you remember him, I think. He has sound ideas for building a strong and united nation, and considers that already we are a people at war for our freedom. . . ."

They were a strange people in Vermont. "A mortal, sinful people," a pastor from Virginia said. "A presumptuous people. They build their fence posts of carved stone, as to say a man's days on earth are not numbered." A silent people too, and a cold people who covered their bridges and never spent a penny until after they had earned it. The saying went that Maine men were hard, but Vermont men harder, Maine men mean, but Vermont men meaner. People not so delicate in their speech said, Court a Vermont lass with gloves.

They liked figures, they liked to know that two and two made four, and they had little patience for ideals. Independence was all very well for Vermont, but they were not going to be hasty and pick up their guns for foreigners in New York and New Jersey. And in the green hills it was bruited about that the middle countries were more or less Dutch provinces where a man could walk for weeks and never hear a word of English spoken.

They took *Common Sense* at arm's length. A few weeks after publication Hiram Jackson, the leather dealer, brought a dozen copies over the New Hampshire border into Vermont and handed them out to the farmers who sold him hides.

"Boston stuff," he said, which was his term for anything even mildly incendiary.

They were read carefully; where Paine pointed out that less than a third of the inhabitants of Pennsylvania were of English descent, they felt confirmed in something they had always suspected; when Paine said that it would be good business sense to break from the Empire, they read on. A copy came into the hands of Jeremiah Cornish, the Bennington printer. He approved of it after three days' discussion with his neighbors, and considering that Pennsylvania was a good distance off, certainly too far for an apology or a royalty payment, set it up himself. The first run was a thousand copies that went like fire for a shilling-fourpence, and Jeremiah seeing a small but respectable profit in the offing, did another run of five hundred which he sent across into New Hampshire. Ichabod Lewes, a New Hampshire printer, knew enough of Vermont people to suspect Cornish had wildcatted the edition, and accordingly set it himself, ran three thousand, of which he sent twelve hundred to Maine. The Maine men were frugal, but they liked the pamphlet; it made sense; somehow, it echoed what they had been thinking, just as it curiously echoed what men had been thinking in Vermont, New Hampshire, Massachusetts, New York, and other colonies down into the Deep South. It was the kind of thing that was good for an evening of raging debate; it was the kind of thing a man could chew on while he did his work.

They didn't reprint in Maine, but passed the things from hand to hand until they were falling to pieces.

Allen Johnson had a farm seven miles outside of Trenton, a wife and three children, and eleven Bibles. He didn't need eleven; in fact, four or five of them had never been opened, and now and then in a moment of heresy he would say to himself, "What on God's earth does a man want with more than one Bible?" But the Bible man came through every November, regular as the frost, his cart bulging with Scriptures and almanacs.

Johnson didn't have the almanac habit, but it was a mortal sin to refuse a Bible offered for sale, like denying the word of God, and that being the case the row of Bibles became longer by one each year. Nor did Johnson blame the Bible man, who called himself Pastor Ames; one man's living was another man's backache, and that was the way things were. This year, Pastor Ames was almost a month late, and when he did show up, the almanacs were missing from his cart; instead he had about a hundred and fifty copies of a little book called *Common Sense*.

"Come with the word of God," he said to Johnson.

Doing his best not to hear, Johnson made a point of inspecting the stock. "No almanacs?" he questioned, as if this year he had just come around to buying one.

"Politics," the pastor said. "Lord bless us, it's a mighty year for politics."

Johnson picked up a copy of *Common Sense* and turned over the pages.

"Two shillings," Pastor Ames said.

The Bibles were four.

"I'll take one," Johnson said.

It was only afterwards that Johnson recalled that a purchase of the Bible relieved him from the arduous duty of reading it, a task that was taken from his shoulders every Sunday morning at church. On this little book, he had an investment of two shillings, and determined not to throw his money away, he sat down that same evening to read it. When his wife asked him what on earth he was reading, he said:

"For the Lord's sake, Mandy, leave a body alone!" He knit his brows and read on, and slowly what was a task turned into a most amazing discovery.

The printer, Bell, was astonished, almost frightened; this had never happened to him before; indeed it had never happened to anyone in the country of Pennsylvania before. After he had set type on Paine's book, he had started the printing with a moderate run in the hundreds, and that was as it should be according to all his experience. Almanacs, which were in great favor with the country folk, sold well, and sometimes, as was the case with Franklin's almanacs, in the tens of thousands; but in the country political pamphlets had never been in great favor, and even in town, unless they were throwaways, they had only a limited demand. Even with popular English novels, a run of fifteen hundred was considered most successful, while two thousand was distinctly out of the ordinary. Paine's book was overpriced; he had known that; two shillings put it out of the class of apprentices, most workmen and small farmers; but Bell had laid on the heavy price to protect himself in what he was quite certain would be a complete publishing failure. Paine had friends in Philadelphia, and what with the friends, the cu-

rious, and the opposition, Bell had felt confident of a sale
of at least five hundred copies.

He had already, a week after publication, sold more than
two thousand.

He ran a full thousand for New York, then another thousand; he took on a journeyman printer and two apprentices.
They labored all one night getting out an edition of three
thousand in demand here in Philadelphia. Franklin Grey,
a local bookseller, asked for a thousand at a shilling-two-
pence, wholesale, and Bell agreed to supply him. Then, by
post from Charleston, came an order for two thousand. Hart-
ford wanted seven hundred; the little village of Concord in
Massachusetts a hundred; a place he had never heard of,
Brackton, fifty.

Angus MacGrae, a roving book jobber whose wide terri-
tory included Maryland, Virginia, and Carolina, and who
sold as many books straight from his lumbering, canvas-
covered wagon as he did to various small shopkeepers, was
a regular customer of Bell's, as he was of the many other
Philadelphia printers, publishers, and book dealers. He had
picked up a copy of *Common Sense* in Maryland, and for
the hundred lazy miles between Baltimore and Philadelphia,
he had let the reins hang and had read it and reread it as
his two old drays ambled along. If ever a man knew the
pulse, the fever, the beating tempo of America, that man was
MacGrae; he loved the written word only less than the
spoken one, and if he had not given a good deal more effort
to talking about books than selling them, he might have
been a very rich man.

When he left a copy of Defoe in a backwoods log cabin,
he glowed with pride, and it was he who talked several hundred good Presbyterians into believing that lush hours spent
with Fielding would not destroy their immortal souls. He

had sold Swift and Pope to buckskin-clad hill men as well
as cultured plantation owners, and he had arranged for his
own translation of *Candide*. His love for America was compounded of its literacy; European-born, he never ceased to
wonder at this strange, hard-muscled motley conglomeration
of people who had so tender and shy a love for the written
word.

When he finished Paine's book, parts of it read over three
and four times and committed to memory, he made up his
mind to meet the writer, and when he did, said quietly,

"Mon, mon, but it is glorious."

Paine, still tired, still unable to comprehend what was
happening with the small thing he had written, was able to
say nothing, only nod foolishly.

"It must be read widely," MacGrae stated.

"I hope so."

"Be no' afraid of that. I have made other writers, such
as the Frenchman Voltaire and the Englishman Swift, a reputation a mon need no' be ashamed of."

To Bell, MacGrae said, "I want five thousand copies."

"And are you entirely out of your head?"

"Almighty sane. I pay one shilling, and I will no' bargain
with ye, Bell."

"I canna do it. I have no' the presses nor the paper nor
the labor."

"Mon, I give ye two hundred pounds—what are ye afraid
of?"

And Bell, all this beyond his understanding, sighed and
agreed.

When old Ben Franklin came to Bell's shop for fifty copies
to add to the fifty Franklin had already mailed here and
there, Bell tried incoherently to explain what had happened.

The Scotsman looked haggard, red-eyed from lack of sleep, grimed all over with printer's ink.

"It's no miracle," Franklin said. "A book sells because people want to read it, or because it answers things they've been asking."

Bell showed Franklin two wildcat editions, one from New England and another from Rhode Island.

"I wouldn't be angry at that," Franklin said.

"And I am not. I am a small man, and night and day my presses are not idle. God knows how many I've printed, not I. Over a hundred thousand, sir, I assure you. I weep for paper, I sob for ink, and I have moved out my family to make room for the apprentices. I dream nightmares, and it's *Common Sense*."

"Others will dream nightmares," Franklin smiled.

Outside of Boston, the sprawling, bickering, discontented Yankee army that had been besieging the British for so long now, fell avidly on *Common Sense*. The long, dreary hours in winter quarters had set them to wondering why they were fighting. In a fashion, Paine's book told them; they dreamed out the new world. At first, it was a copy read monotonously to a brigade, then argument, then a few more copies to set a man in his reasoning, then a hundred, then a thousand copies, then a dog-eared, dirty copy of *Common Sense* in every haversack, good to wipe a razor on, good to start fires with, good for a man's soul and his body, good to copy into apologetic letters sent home:

"My dear and Affectionate kept wife,

"Always in my memory, I think of you night and day, but do not entirely berate me for selfishness, as things are to be done and there is not a way to live Quietly and Happily without doing them. A man who is an Englishman not an

American writes Sundry and Sound reasons in a book called as COMMON SENSE. He says and I agree with him, O ye that love mankind! Ye that dare oppose not only the tyranny but the tyrant, stand forth! Every spot of the old world is over-run with oppression. Freedom hath been hunted round the Globe. I agree with him and you will when you read the Book I send you. Have Jamie stay with Jenny night and Day when she comes to Calf. . . ."

Out of a prisoner's rucksack, a copy came into the hands of Colonel Bently, who read it and brought it to General Howe of His Majesty's Army. Howe read it, too, and de-cided:

"My word, but the beggar's devilishly clever." He told Bently, "I want a point made of taking this *Common Sense.* I want him hanged, do you understand?"

8

THE TIMES THAT TRIED MEN'S SOULS

Iₙ ₒₙₑ way you are a fool," Franklin told him. "Not a brave man, but a fool."

"How is that, sir?"

"Have you ever shot a musket?"

"No."

"Or loaded one?"

"No."

"And wouldn't any farmer boy from the backwoods make a better soldier than you?"

"I suppose so," Paine admitted.

"What do you believe in? Did this war come out of the mouth of a gun or the mind of a man?"

"That's done," Paine said. "I wrote a little book because I wanted men to see what they were shooting at. I didn't know what would happen. Now would you want me to stay here and let others die for what I said?"

"So you could keep saying it," Franklin pointed out.

"No—"

Franklin shrugged.

"I'm happy," Paine said. "I've never been happy before. I suppose I could have a better musket, but suddenly they've become so scarce that I ought to be satisfied with what I've got. I know what I'm made for; I am not a fool nor a martyr, but just a man who has discovered what work he can do."

"When will you be leaving?" Franklin asked.

"Tomorrow."

"Good luck then," Franklin said.

"Thank you, sir—"

"And don't try to die. Don't doubt your own courage. Remember that this is only the beginning."

He was no longer Tom Paine; suddenly and curiously, he had become Common Sense. He had written a little book, a hope or a suggestion; he was a stranger in a tidewater colony that had defied the world. He was nobody, yet out of that he became everybody, for he had seen, with the candid eyes of a peasant, the hope of mankind.

Yet they never knew what to do. The farmers stood at Concord and Lexington. The militia roved through the forest to the backwoods posts and ripped them from their small British garrisons. New York and Philadelphia belonged to the radicals, although they had been driven, cursing, fighting, bleeding from Boston. It was much as if a wave of sudden, furious fire had burned through America, brightly at first, then with less intensity, then just a simmer of revolt that promised to die.

Now he was Common Sense.

One night, walking alone in the cool evening, trying one street of Philadelphia and then another, wanting nothing at the moment, not the warmth and companionship of a coffee house, not the hot sustenance of drink, not a woman or a man, but only himself in a proper perspective, Tom Paine turned over in his mind what he had done.

Not abruptly can a small man reach for the stars. Christ was a carpenter, and he, Paine, was only a staymaker, an ex-

ciseman, a cobbler, a weaver. "Paine, Paine, be humble," he
told himself, and in his thoughts going back to the speech
of his childhood:

"Thee are nothing, dirt thee are, dirt, dirt, and both
cheeks have been slapped. Thee have been humbled, thee
face in the filth—" And he found himself laughing and praying, "God, O my God, how thou hast exalted me." Love inside of him was without measure, and his strength too without measure. Again and again, he clenched and unclenched
his hands. Men were brothers. "Oh, my brothers, my brothers," he whispered.

He said, "No, I'm not going mad—"

Benjamin Rush had pointed out to him, "Revolution,
Paine, is a technique which we must learn with no history.
We are the first, and that's why we blunder so. We have no
precedent, but only a theory, and that theory is that strength
lies in the hands of the armed masses. I am not speaking of
ideals, of right and wrong, of good and bad, not even of a
morality, for in the last analysis all those things are catch-
words and the only implement is strength."

Paine nodded. Slowly and painfully, he had been coming
around to the same point of view. "The strength was always
with the people," he said.

"Of course—firearms don't change that. But there was
never, in this world, a technique for revolution. There was
a technique for tyranny and strength implemented it, but
always the strength of a few. The strength of many is revolution, but curiously enough mankind has gone through several thousand years of slavery without realizing that fact.
The little men have pleaded, but when before have they
stood up with arms in their hands and said, This is mine!"

"There were never the circumstances before."

"Perhaps. It's true that we have here a nation of armed men who know how to use their arms; we have a Protestant tradition of discussion as opposed to autocracy; we have some notion of the dignity of man; and above all we have land, land enough for everyone. Those are fortunate circumstances, but now we must learn technique. The man with the iron glove has held this world for God knows how many thousands of years, and in how short a time do you suppose we can take it back from him—not to mention holding it?"

"I don't like to think about that."

"You must. We are learning a bloody, dreadful business, this technique of revolution, but we must learn it well. You wrote a little book, and because of that men will know why they fight. You wanted independence, and we're going to have it, mark my word. Six months ago you were rolled in the dirt because people knew what you were writing; two weeks ago a man in New York was almost tarred and feathered because he planned to publish an answer to *Common Sense*. That's not morality; that's strength, the same kind of strength the tyrants used, only a thousand times more powerful. Now we must learn how to use that strength, how to control it. We need leaders, a program, a purpose, but above all we need revolutionists."

Paine nodded.

"What are you going to do?"

"Join Washington," Paine said.

"I think you're right. Keep your eyes open, and don't be discouraged. We are a free people, but we are only a few generations away from the slaves. We will whimper and cry and groan, and we will want to give up. We are not an orderly people, Paine, and I don't think we will make good soldiers. In a little while we may forget what we are fighting for and throw away our muskets. Remember that—always remember that."

Fame sat uneasily on his shoulders, and suddenly Philadelphia was repugnant to him, a fat, satisfied town that talked eternally, criticized vehemently, and did almost nothing at all. On the streets and in the coffee houses, where Paine's book was fast becoming another Bible, talk of independence was free and easy, but in the Assembly the eastern delegates still held out against it. The frontier delegates stalked the streets with black faces, but there was nothing they could do.

A banquet was given for Paine; he did not have the money for a new coat, for lace cuffs, and he would neither beg nor borrow. He came as he was, shabby, without even a wig, sitting glumly at the table, thinking, "I told Franklin I was going, I told Rush—why don't I go?" But it didn't matter so much; the armies were sitting idle. Of course, give a thing a chance and it will blow over. On the table, as a centerpiece, was a monster pasteboard replica of *Common Sense*.

"Oh, the glory that this stranger has given our cause!" said Thaddeus Green, the toastmaster. "Oh, words of his that are fire, live forever!" Green had come in his militia uniform, blue and yellow. "Will not freemen lay down their lives gladly?" he cried.

Paine was getting drunk. He drank thirty-two toasts, and lay with his head in his plate, his mouth drooling. Almost everyone else was drunk, snoring, telling dirty stories, pawing the waitresses, dirtying their fine and fanciful uniforms, their lace and silk, shouting suddenly:

"God damn King George!"

"Liberty forever."

"Like this," Paine muttered. "Here the glory of free men."

Jefferson had asked him to come. He sat there in a corner of the room, feeling like a fool, his hands on his knees, while Jefferson explained how Washington had reacted toward reading the book.

"You've done a great thing for your country—" Jefferson said.

Paine could not help thinking how empty and stupid words were. What was his country? What was he to these suave, aristocratic, lace-draped intellectual democrats? Why did he always feel like a fool?

"Naturally, you said what we've all been thinking," Jefferson went on. "What we've been saying too. Yet you have to say a thing so men will understand it and comprehend it, even a man like Washington, and he's no fool, you understand. Your book says it—and to everyone. Now we're committed to independence."

"I was waiting," Paine said. "I was never really certain."

"And what will you do now that you are satisfied—and I trust you are?"

"Join the army."

"Is that wise?"

Paine shrugged; to have his decision weighed so, back and forth, with the supercilious attitude that no man could serve this movement by taking a gun in his hand, but only by sitting here in Philadelphia and mouthing words, was breaking down both his nerve and his determination. Slowly, he was becoming aware that these great and important men of the colonies, even Jefferson, whose reason was a creed and a religion, looked upon him as a sort of performing animal, a peasant to represent the numberless peasants who would make up the army of rebellion, a clever rabble rouser to be used for their purposes.

When in the newspapers someone attacked the revolutionary movement, the conception of an independent America, and Paine answered hoarsely and vehemently, there was a chorus of polite handclapping.

"We're in committee now," Jefferson said, "Franklin, Adams, Sherman, Livingston—I am making the draft of the declaration, purely and simply for Independence. I want you to know that I am using *Common Sense*, that I am proud to."

"But not proud enough to include me in committee," Paine thought, yet with a sort of satisfaction that he was out of that, that he could use himself according to his own desires. And he said, "When do you expect to have a vote on it?"

"In July, perhaps."

"And then it will be the United States of America?"

This time Jefferson smiled and shrugged. "We owe a great deal to you," he nodded.

"Nothing."

Handling the future with assurance, Jefferson said easily, "Remember, Paine, if out of this comes something real and concrete, a republican state, you will not find it ungrateful."

Then it was done, and the bright new world was made, and in the teeming, excited city of Philadelphia there were few who doubted that the people would rise to support this grandiloquent, rhetorical, generalized declaration of independence. Glory is born in July, 1776, they told each other. They paraded, singing that fantastic bit of doggerel that had attached itself to the army of the revolution, Yankee Doodle went to London Town—and who knew but that they would all be there? Invade Canada? Why not? And why not England? And why not the world, to make this the new Christianity? Of course, when Jefferson's first draft of the declaration had been submitted to the Continental Congress, Benjamin Harrison leaped up and roared, "There is but one word in this paper which I approve, and that is the word Congress." But on the other hand, hadn't Caesar Rodney ridden eighty miles in twelve hours, killing horses, just to be on the floor of the house on July fourth and sign the document?

Paine was honored; hurt and honored, when a few days before the presentation of the document Jefferson had come to him with a sudden tenderness and said:

"Let me read you this."

"Read it if you want to," Paine said.

"It's at the end, the summing up, and you did it. My God, Thomas, we don't know our debt to you. History is like bad housekeeping entered into an account book."

"Why don't you get on with it?" Paine thought.

"We, therefore," Jefferson read, "the representatives of the United States of America—" He glanced up at the slope-shouldered, unkempt man who had given him that phrase. "How does it sound?"

"Read it!"

"—in general Congress assembled, appealing to the Supreme Judge of the world for the rectitude of our intentions, do, in the name and by the authority of the good people of these colonies, solemnly publish and declare that these united colonies are, and of good right ought to be, free and independent States; that they are absolved from all allegiance to the British crown, and that all political connection between them and the states of Great Britain is, and ought to be, totally dissolved; and that, as free and independent States, they have full power to levy war, conclude peace, contract alliances, establish commerce, and to do all other acts and things which independent states may of right do. And for the support of this declaration, with a firm reliance on the protection of Divine Providence, we mutually pledge to each other our lives, our fortunes, and our sacred honor. . . ."

"Well, it's done," Paine said.

"Yes—"

Paine was thinking that now there was nothing left to keep him here, he could go away.

Roberdeau, general of Pennsylvania militia, was a portly man with a face as red as a beet, a huge pair of haunches, and a glorious uniform of blue and yellow. A successful merchant, he was quite sure he would be an even more successful soldier, and once he had decided to lead a detachment to Amboy, south and west of Staten Island, he was satisfied that General Washington's troubles were over. He offered Paine the post as his personal secretary. The Associators, as the militia called themselves, had drilled for a good many months now, and Roberdeau pointed out to Paine that to be with this brigade was something of a signal honor.

"I'll come," Paine said. "I don't want any commission. If I can serve you as a secretary, well enough."

"Such things as commissions can be arranged. I would, personally, prefer to see you as a major. More dignity in such a post than as a captain or a lieutenant. Aside from that, have you a uniform?"

Paine confessed that he hadn't.

"Important, my boy, important. Only with uniformity can we inject into the ranks a certain military tradition, such as gleamed like a halo around the great Marlborough and Frederick of Prussia."

"I'll do without one," Paine said, thinking of how those who had seen Washington's army reported that there was not a uniform to a brigade.

"If it's a matter of money . . ."

"It's not a matter of money," Paine said.

Bell had given him fifty copies of *Common Sense;* that, with his rusty old musket, powder, shot, a water bottle, and a bag of cornmeal, made up Paine's luggage. He trudged with the rest, partly out of desire, partly because he could not afford a horse. Roberdeau, who took Paine's abasement as a personal affront, did not talk to him for hours at a time; Paine hardly noticed that. Nothing else mattered but that now, after long last, he was marching shoulder to shoulder with his own kind, the shopkeepers, the clerks and mechanics, the weavers, carpenters, craftsmen. For the time, it was entirely emotional; they had met no enemy, seen nothing of war. And they knew nothing of it except what they had heard from New England. And in Massachusetts, hadn't American losses been fantastically small?

The night of the first bivouac, Paine sat at the fire, heating his corn gruel, tensely aware of himself, unable to speak, tears of joy in his eyes. The voices of the militiamen were loud, somewhat self-conscious, bright. It was:

"Comrade, a light!"

"Share my gruel—porridge for bacon?"

"The devil with that, comrade, I have enough for both of us."

"Citizen, how about a toast?"

There was a wagon full of rum in iron-bound casks. Roberdeau, patting his huge paunch, had one broken open. They toasted the Congress, Washington, Lee, Jefferson, who had written it all down so prettily, old Ben Franklin. A clear, youthful tenor began to sing:

"Oh, the pretty skies of Pennsylvania,
Oh, the meadows sylvan green,
Oh, the bluebird and the nightingale,
Oh, the countries, 'mong the countries,
Our sylvania is the Queen."

Paine could hardly carry a tune, but he sang with the rest. The artillery men sat on their brace of cannon, swaying back and forth, keeping time with their ramrods. The fires trailed a curtain of sparks toward the sky, and a sweet, cool wind blew from the west. This was all Paine had ever thought of or dreamed of, the common men of the world marching together, shoulder to shoulder, guns in their hands, love in their hearts.

For Paine, it was an almost mystical fulfillment, and he said to himself, "Who can measure the forces started here? Men of good will march together and know their own strength. With the power we have, what can stop us, or even slow us? What can't we achieve, what new worlds, what glories, what promises!"

But on the next day, their sublimity began to be more commonplace. A comrade is a comrade, but a blister on one's heel is not to be sneezed at. The glorious cause of independence remained a cause glorious, but the muskets grew no lighter. Most of the firelocks they carried were brand-new, the product of Anson Schmidt, a Front Street gunsmith whose theories were violently opposed to those of the back-country craftsmen. In the Pennsylvania hinterland, a slim, light, long-barreled rifle had been developed. It threw a lead slug the size of a large green pea with amazing accuracy and out-ranged by at least a hundred yards any other weapon known at the time. But Schmidt reasoned, and rightly, what was the use of such a rifle to a man who was not a marksman?

He developed his own gun, the Patriot Lady, he called it, wide of bore, bound with iron, and heavy as a small cannon. It could be loaded with anything, shot, nails, glass, wire, stones, and at thirty yards it was brutally effective. Its great drawback was that it required a strong man to carry it.

The militia were not strong. For several hours they carried their muskets, and then someone got the idea of heaving his weapon into a supply wagon. Soon the supply wagons were groaning with the weight of a hundred muskets, and Roberdeau, blue with rage, screamed what kind of an army was this marching without arms?

"Well enough for you on your horse, fatty," a private told the general.

"God damn you, you'll have a hundred lashes for that!"

"And who'll lay them on?"

Roberdeau backed down, but assured the man that he would write a charge to the Continental Congress. The men were tired, begrimed with sweat, surly; and it was too early in the campaign to look for trouble. Since Paine was the secretary, Roberdeau put it to him, instructing him to write the following to the military committee:

"Whereas one, Alexander Hartson, indulged in treasonable talk—"

"I wouldn't say that," Paine interrupted.

"No?"

"His talk wasn't treasonable. It would be better to have him whipped."

"I think I know how to order my brigade," Roberdeau said. "Write what I tell you to; that's why you're here. I don't need instructions in military ethics from any twopence scrivener."

"Very well," Paine nodded.

There was a tall, loose-limbed man who took to walking

alongside Paine. His name was Jacob Morrison, and he came from the wild and beautiful Wyoming Valley. His wife and child had died of smallpox, and he, sick of living alone in the dark woods, had come to Philadelphia, taken work as a hand in a flour mill, and there joined the Associators. Armed with a long rifle, clad in buckskin leggings and a hunting shirt, he almost alone in that motley group of militia appeared fitted for the business on which they were embarked. He took a liking to Paine, if for no other reason than that Paine continued to carry his own musket. He said to him once, in his slow, back-country drawl:

"Citizen, what do you think of our little war?"

"Things start slowly," Paine said.

"Yes, but I reckon I seldom seen a seedier lot of fighting men."

"Well, give them time—you don't make soldiers over night. And you don't make a new world in one day."

"You're English, aren't you?" Morrison said. "What got you into this?"

Paine shrugged.

"For me, I don't give a damn," the backwoodsman drawled. "I got nothing to lose. But, Lord, there's troubled times coming—"

That night Roberdeau took a new tack, changing from bullying to cajoling. He broke open an extra cask of rum, and announced to the men:

"We have with us here, citizens, a most illustrious patriot, the man who with words of fire wrote *Common Sense*. He has consented to say a few words to us concerning the cause for which we are determined to give our lives. Citizen Thomas Paine!"

Paine wasn't prepared. He stood up sheepishly, stumbled into the light of a fire, and began to talk, very haltingly at

first—"We are embarked on a deed of small men, and that's
what we are, small men, citizens, common people. We are
going to find it hard, and grumble and complain, and some
of us will go home. I think that's how a revolution starts—"

Their permanent bivouac was at Amboy, close to where
the Raritan River flows into lower New York Bay. Across
the river were the hills of Staten Island, and beyond, on
Manhattan, a terrible drama was being enacted. Washington's orders were to hold New York with the rabble of militia he had under his command, twenty thousand in number,
but none of them trained soldiers—New England Yankee
farmers for the most part, some Pennsylvanians, some Jersey
troops, a good many Virginians, and several brigades of
Maryland troops, the latter the best of the lot. But to hold
New York with that raggle-taggle mob was as absurd as it
was impossible. Each day, more British transports and ships
of the line sailed into the harbor, disgorging thousands and
thousands of trained regulars and Hessians onto Staten
Island. Meanwhile, Washington had split his army, placing
half his men in Brooklyn to stave off a flank attack that
might isolate him on the slim ridge of Manhattan. To counter this move, the British shifted part of their army to Long
Island, and on the night of August 27, General Howe
launched his attack. They found a weak spot in the American lines, captured a few sleeping sentries, flanked half of
Washington's army, and then, holding it in pincer jaws,
proceeded methodically to destroy it.

Only through his own cool courage and the aid of a brigade of Marblehead fishermen was Washington able to evac-
uate what was left of his shattered army to New York. And
there, almost before he had time to reorganize, the British

attacked again, this time determined to destroy what was left
of the colonial army.

They came near to accomplishing that purpose. Landing
on Manhattan both from the East River and the Upper Bay,
they again attempted to close the pincers, driving the routed,
panic-stricken colonials before them. It became a wild foot-
race, in which an utterly demoralized mob of militia threw
away their weapons and ran like rabbits for the fortified line
which the Americans still held where One Hundred and
Twenty-fifth Street is today. Whole brigades were cut off by
the Hessians, ripped to pieces with cold steel, made prisoner;
men cowered in barns, haylofts, thickets; others drowned
themselves trying to swim across the Hudson and reach the
Jersey shore. Only through a miracle did a good part of the
troops which had held lower New York escape. In a few
weeks the twenty thousand had been reduced to less than
fifteen thousand.

And during this time, the Philadelphia Associators made
themselves very small at Amboy. More than enough news of
what was happening in New York filtered into their lines,
and the only concrete result was desertion. It was a thing of
the past to call one's neighbor comrade, and as for citizen—

Paine had pleaded with General Roberdeau, with Colonel
Plaxton, "What are we doing here? Over there in New York,
the whole good hope of mankind is being smashed, and what
are we doing here?"

"Our duty, which is to garrison Amboy."

"Christ, no! We could march up through Jersey and cross
over at Fort Lee and join Washington. Better yet, we could
cross the Raritan and attack the British where they're weak-
est, in Staten Island. Or we could raid over into Bayonne—"

Roberdeau smiled condescendingly. "You're a writer, Paine, a dreamer, shall we say. The hard military facts—"

"God damn it, sir, what do you know about military facts?"

Plaxton blew up with rage, but Roberdeau only pouted and spread his arms helplessly. "First the others, now you, turning against me, talking treason."

"Treason! My God, sir, is everything treason? Isn't it treason to sit here on our behinds?"

"Orders—"

"From whom? Did the orders take into account that Washington's army would be shattered, that we should lose New York? Has any man in your command fired a gun yet or faced an enemy?"

Fat, his face jelly-like in its impotence, Roberdeau blubbered his appeal to Plaxton, the slim, dandified gentleman, one of the Penn family, sneering and bored at the two of them:

"Is my duty my duty? Tell me? Am I to blame that Washington's army is driven from New York? Am I to blame that instead of soldiers they give me shop clerks?"

Then there were the desertions; Philadelphia was not far enough away, and each night a few of the militia slipped out of camp. Almost no discipline was left, and for the most part the officers were drunk; if the general objected, they laughed in his face. Paine stormed, pleaded, exhorted; and strangely, the militia did not take offense at him; rather, they became like schoolboys being scolded. When he sat by a fire and read to them from *Common Sense*, they listened, fascinated, intrigued, and then for a moment he could fill them with passion:

"Do you understand, this is for us, for you and me, for

our children! We are the beginning, and we are making a
new world!"

But it didn't take; they were homesick, frightened, bewildered by the reports from New York. If the British had cut
to pieces Washington's great army, which had already been
under fire at Boston, what would happen with raw, untried
militia?

"Listen to me, comrades!"

Now they hated the word. What did words mean when
words led only to death. The revolution was a farce; and it
was doubtless true that the British hanged all rebels—or gave
them to the mercy of the Hessians.

As Jacob Morrison said, there should be at least twenty
who could be counted on; he had been sounding them out,
and he told Paine, "In this cursed Jersey, there must be at
least a few hundred others we could pick up, enough to
make a raiding party. I seen too many like Roberdeau, who
is no good, and in a little while he'll go home—mark my
word."   •

"I suppose he'll go home," Paine shrugged.

"Then what's to hold us back? The Continental Congress?" asked Morrison derisively. Paine sat down and put
his face in his hands; his head ached. He told Morrison:

"It's mutiny, you know."

Morrison asked him if he wanted to get drunk.

"All right."

There was no longer a pretense made of guarding the rum.
They had a quart each, and staggered around the camp,
roaring obscene songs at the top of their lungs. Like a helpless schoolmarm, Roberdeau called them names until Morrison ran at him with a bayonet. Paine stood on a supply cart,
swaying, exhorting the militia, who were not entirely sober

themselves, moving them and himself to maudlin tears, watching out of the corner of his eyes how Morrison staggered around, brandishing the bayonet, finally falling off the cart.

But when it came down to facts, the next day, they could not find twenty in the camp who would join them, not ten and not even one. Roberdeau, Plaxton, and a few other militia officers held a council of war, the outcome of which was a decision to march back to Philadelphia; and when the Associators heard the decision read, they cheered for a full fifteen minutes. Paine and Morrison sat on a fallen tree trunk, their firelocks on their knees, and watched the camp break up. It didn't take long, nor did Roberdeau speak to them; only when the Associators began to march did a few militiamen glance back and wave. Morrison began to hum softly, and Paine sighed and studied his rusty musket as if he had never seen it before.

"Not that I give a damn," Morrison said, "and I suppose they have something to go back for. The little man, Tom, is a timid rabbit—don't let it stick in your throat."

"No—"

"Do you want a drink?"

Paine nodded, and silently Morrison passed him a leathern flask of rum. They rocked it back and forth for a little while, and then when it was empty, they threw it away. "Ye that love mankind," Paine quoted, and Morrison said, "Shut up!"

"Ye that dare oppose not only the tyranny but the tyrant, stand forth!"

"God damn you, shut up!"

"All right," Paine nodded. "Only let's get out of here— let's get out of this damned place and not see it again."

They crossed the Raritan and set out to walk to Fort Lee on the west bank of the Hudson River, some thirty miles to

the north. There was a garrison and there was a place in
Washington's army for two men who held onto their guns.
They took the old pike to Elizabethtown, trudging along
through the cool September days, their guns over their shoulders, two left from all the Philadelphia militia, a tall backwoodsman and a slope-shouldered, broad-necked Englishman, profession: revolutionist, but just two of all the raggle-
taggle that drifted along the road—deserters, farmers, cow-
boys, milkmaids, and even a British patrol now and then to
send them diving into the underbrush. They had no money,
but the weather was good, and they could sleep in a field
and roast sweet corn over a fire.

For Tom Paine, there was a quality of relief in the dis-
banding of the Philadelphians; the weak went and a few of
the strong were left, and he had never had a comrade before
like this tall, slow-spoken Pennsylvanian. He read to him
from *Common Sense,* and respect became a bond between
them. Morrison told how his wife and child had died, leaving him alone in the dark forest, and trudging along they
shared their loneliness and knew each other's thoughts. In
those times, the flatlands of Jersey were not covered with
smoking factories and an endless maze of railroads, but between the pine barrens, the sulphur swampland stretched for
miles and miles, inhabited only by flocks of whirring birds,
by snakes and frogs, desolate by daytime, but shining with
an unearthly beauty at dawn and twilight.

Once they passed Elizabethtown, they walked for hours
through this silent, stretching plain, for Paine so reminiscent
of the British fens. He spoke to Morrison of the things he
had seen as a boy in the gin hell of London; hope which
had been so low in them rose higher, and the calm spaces
of the swamps gave them new courage. Now they laughed
at Roberdeau.

And then Morrison was shot through the head by a British sentry they stumbled over in the dark; the sentry, more frightened than Paine, ran away, and Paine, who had heard his first shot of war, took his friend's rifle and went on.

His way lost, his clothes soaked and dirty, he came into the light of a campfire where two deserters sat, boys of seventeen who snatched up their muskets and faced him like animals at bay:

"Who in hell are you?"

"Paine—Tom Paine."

"And what do you want, god damn you?"

"The way to Fort Lee, that's all," he said calmly, observing with speculative inward curiosity that he was not afraid of these two terrified children, not afraid but only deeply saddened and coming awake to the stuff his dreams were made of.

"That way," they said, grinning, easier once they had him covered and saw that he was alone.

"Do we still hold it?"

They shook with laughter that was partly hysterical. "We hold it," one of them said.

"Why did you run away?"

"You go to hell, you bastard, that's none of your business!"

"Why?"

And then the other lifted his shirt to show the fresh, raw marks of a lashing.

Like a low-crowned hat, Fort Lee sat on top of the Palisades, opposite Fort Washington on the Manhattan shore. The one was named after Charles Lee, the Englishman who had sold his services to the colonies for a substantial sum, who had been a professional soldier all his life, who lived on

his own lush visions of glory; the other was named for a
Virginia farmer who had blundered into the command of
all the continental armies, and had, since August, been
lashed by defeat after defeat. That farmer had already lost
all of Manhattan to the enemy except Fort Washington and
a few hundred acres of land surrounding it. He had been
driven out of Manhattan and almost extinguished as a military factor at White Plains. He was now trying to regroup
his shattered army and plan a campaign, and most of all
make up his mind whether or not to abandon Fort Washington.

General Nathanael Greene, the handsome young Quaker
in command of Fort Lee, believed that both points, facing
each other across the Hudson River, could be held as long
as was necessary. Rightly enough, he considered them a gate
to the Hudson, and the Hudson a gate to the colonies. Now,
at Fort Lee, he was informed that a man had arrived in
camp who called himself Tom Paine.

"Paine?" Greene asked. He had a book, a small Bible
called *Common Sense,* worn to pieces with two dozen read-
ings. "Well, bring him here. Paine, you say? Of course, bring
him here."

"I know you and I don't know you," Greene said to Paine,
when they stood face to face, the one tall, sunburned, handsome and dapper in his buff and blue which he had had
made in the style of his commander's Virginia militia uniform, the other broad and stocky, hook-nosed, hair in a knot
and cheeks with three days' beard, his old clothes stained
with dirt and blood. "You're Common Sense, aren't you?"

Paine nodded, and they shook hands. Greene, excited as
a boy, called over his aides, introduced them, ran into his
tent and brought out his own battered copy of Paine's book,

ruffled the pages, smiling and trying to believe his eyes that
Paine was here in front of him.

"You don't understand, of course—you don't know what
this has meant to us. Everything, do you believe me?"

"I want to."

"Good. You know we've been beaten, no use trying to
hide that. We were driven out of Brooklyn and we were
driven out of New York. All we hold in Manhattan is the
fort, yet we have hopes of getting it all back, not military
hopes entirely, but here, what you've given us, something
to chew on and bite into, something solid and substantial
that they can't take away from us. I've bought seventy-five
copies myself and forced men to read them who have never
opened a book in their lives—"

Paine shook his head dazedly.

"And now you're here. That's the wonder of it, your being
here. I swear, sir, I'd rather have you than a regiment, and
the general will say the same thing when he meets you."

For a day, Paine was left alone. He told Greene that was
what he wanted, to be left alone, to walk around the camp,
to clean himself up, to think. There were a good many
things he had to think about, he told Greene. Well, naturally, you'd expect that. "Do whatever you want to," Greene
said. "When you're ready, we'll talk."

Paine wandered through the fort leisurely, always coming
back to the high bluff where he could lean on the parapet
of tree trunks and look across the dancing little waves of
the Hudson to the green, wooded hills of Manhattan. Actually, Lee was more a bivouac than a fortification, poorly protected, but amazingly picturesque in its high setting over the
river. Paine found talking to the men easier than he had
expected; they were Yankees, many of them, from the little

villages of middle New England, but it had been noised
about the camp that he was the author of *Common Sense*,
and they were pleased to find him as simple as they were.
Working men themselves, they recognized in him all the
signs of a man who has used his hands unsparingly, the sloping shoulders, the heavy palms and short fingers, the thick,
muscular forearms. They talked to him about his book, and
he was amazed to find how keenly they could analyze material facts, the trade of the colonies, the potential for ship
building, for weaving, for manufacture. Ten minutes after
meeting him, they would be relating tales that Greene could
not have dragged out of them with torture; they told him
about their parents, their wives, children, farms. So many
of them were boys under twenty, red-cheeked children who
knew whole pages of his book by heart.

"You remember, sir?" they would say.

And he wouldn't remember. Here was none of the comrade, the citizen, the self-conscious dramatization of the Associators, but rather a subdued realization of what it meant
to face the best troops in the world and be defeated constantly.

"Yes, sir, you'll find it mighty pertinent," and they would
go on to quote him. "Now that matter of delegates to Congress, as you put it, I wouldn't take exception to it, Mr.
Paine, but I might offer a mite of a suggestion. You speculate that Congress could choose a president—"

They were argumentative and keen and alive, but their
education didn't include niceties. They were likely to pick
their noses in a ruminative fashion, to chew tobacco and
spit where it pleased them; they weren't clean. They were
an abomination to the Virginians and Marylanders, with
whom they bickered and fought constantly, and they couldn't
get along with the Dutch.

Paine gave away Morrison's rifle. For himself, his old musket was good enough, and he was very doubtful of his ability
to hit anything with it, even if he loaded with buckshot. He
gave the long rifle to a Virginian who could use it.

When Greene had heard from Paine the full story of the
Associators, he nodded and said, without passion, "Of course,
it isn't the first time. That's happened in half a dozen places.
It's happened with us, too, I suppose."

"They weren't cowards," Paine said.

"Men aren't cowards. It's a balance; either it's better to
stay and fight, or it's better to run away."

"They didn't have any direction," Paine said. "They were
molded by certain things for God knows how many hundreds of years, and how could you unmold them overnight?
And they didn't have any leadership. Back in Philadelphia,
Rush told me that revolution is a technique. What do we
know about that technique?"

"Nothing—"

"And yet I can't get used to the idea that the cause is
doomed. Do you think it's doomed?"

Greene said no, but not with assurance.

"No, of course, it's not doomed." Paine shook his head
and rubbed his heavy fingers into his brow. "Revolution is
something new, we don't know how new it is. I sometimes
think that April last year a new era for the world began."
He asked Greene how long it would be, how many years,
and Greene said he didn't know, it might be twenty or a
hundred years. They smiled at each other, Greene showing
his large strong teeth, his blue eyes wrinkled in appreciation
of the parts they both played in this curious comic opera.
Paine was relieved to find someone saying what he had been
thinking. Greene said he was glad that Paine was there.

"It means very little," Paine protested.

"No, I'm trying to learn how to make a campaign, but what's the good if they don't know why they're fighting?"

"Do you think I can tell them?"

"I think so," Greene nodded.

"All right."

"Do you want an officership?" Greene inquired. "It can be arranged, you know. A captaincy, easily; you could be a colonel or a major if you wish to—we have so many of them, God knows."

"No, I don't think so."

"In a way, it's a matter of respect," Greene said uncertainly.

"If I can't have their respect as Tom Paine, it's no good to me."

"Yes—"

"You see, all I can give them are reasons. I don't know anything about fighting."

He was in Hackensack when Fort Washington fell, dropping the ripe plum of three thousand men into the hands of the British. At Hackensack, five miles inland from Fort Lee, there was a larger encampment of the ragged continental troops, Jersey and Pennsylvania men, undisciplined, a swaggering, dirty, wretched camp that gave Paine a desolate reminder of the Philadelphia militia. The bivouac was overrun by camp-followers, women of all ages in all the stages of decay. The men kept chickens and pigs and spent their time earning the undying hatred of the local farmers. Greene had said to him, "Go there and see whether you can make those swine understand why they're fighting."

The "swine" grinned at him when he spoke of the revolutionary army. They pelted him with mud when he tried to tell them why a man should want to die for this little civilization on the fringe of the forest, and for the first time in many years he used his fists. He was deceptively powerful, and his big shoulders hid layers of leathery muscle. They respected him when he had laid a few of them on their backs.

Henry Knox, the fat colonel of artillery who was in command of the camp, grinned appreciatively. "They understand that," he said. He had been a bookseller once, had even done a little publishing on his own, and he considered Paine his own private gift from God, something to lessen the boredom. Talking about the fantastic success of *Common Sense*, he would keep Paine in his tent for hours, and having a good, solemn liking for the bottle, they were quietly and warmly drunk on many an evening. Knox was the last person in the world to be in command of this dirty, disorderly, mutinous camp, a fat, smiling young man of twenty-six, florid in complexion, talking constantly about his wife, and again and again pressing Paine for the story of the book's sale. Did it sell more than two hundred thousand? That was the story.

Paine didn't know; he wasn't sure and they had lost all track of printings. And then it had been printed everywhere without permission.

"But, man, man, there was a fortune in it," Knox said.

"I suppose so."

"And you didn't touch it. By God, that was magnificent!"

Paine shrugged, and then Knox began to speculate upon the number of readers there must have been. Possibly everyone in the colonies who was literate. Possibly a million readers, one of three persons—but that was hardly possible. Yet it was enough to stagger the imagination.

"And here?" Paine asked. "What do we do and where do we go?"

Knox said he didn't know; they were here and the British

were across the river, and it seemed like it might be that
way forever. It had been terrible at first, being beaten in
every engagement, but now they were learning how to fight.
Perhaps it didn't look that way, the camp being what it was,
but they were learning—

That was only a few weeks before Fort Washington fell.
The fort, standing on a bluff on the east bank of the Hudson,
was supposedly impregnable. Greene thought so, and so did
Knox; if Washington had his doubts, he kept them to himself, and it was only Charles Lee, commanding about five
thousand men in Westchester, who said out and out that the
fort could not be held. It couldn't; the hills around it were
taken, the defenders rolled back, flanked, cut off from retreat, the fort filled so full of fleeing continentals that it
could not even fire a shot in its defense. Some three thousand
men were taken, and Washington, watching the whole thing
from a boat in the Hudson, saw what little hope he had left
crumble and disappear.

Paine met him again only a few days before the fort was
taken, and the Virginian had said, almost desperately:

"It's good to have you with us here. They don't know in
Philadelphia—they think it's a very simple matter to make
a war and a revolution."

Paine thanked him.

"Talk to the men," Washington said. "Only talk to them
and make them understand this thing."

Then the fort was lost and the end was in sight. Paine sat
stolidly and watched young Knox weep out his rage and dis-
appointment, but when he turned to the Englishman for
sympathy, Paine, in one of his rare bitter moods, snapped:

"You poor damn fool, did you expect nothing to happen?
Did you expect them to give us America?"

"No, but the whole garrison—"

"And it will be more than three thousand men before we're finished. Don't be an idiot," Paine said brutally. "Stop crying—is that all you're good for, tears?"

At Hackensack, the camp was dissolving; daily, there were more and more desertions. Paine went from man to man, pleaded, threatened, used his big fists; and they listened to him, because he wasn't an officer, because he was as unkempt and as ragged as any of them, because he could say a few words that would set a man's heart on fire. It was hard, and it was going to be harder; he admitted that, but they hadn't looked for a picnic, or had they? They weren't paid, well, neither was he, and he turned his pockets inside out to show them. Their shoes had holes in them, well, so had his. Then why? "I know what I'm doing," he grinned. "I'm feathering my own nest." How? Well, for one thing, he told them, the United States of America would be a good place to live in, comfortable, good for a working man. He knew; he had been a staymaker, cobbler, weaver, exciseman, down the whole line; for another, the enemy wasn't going to forget what had been until now. "Give up, and you'll pay the rest of your lives," he told them. And once he wangled a keg of rum from the dwindling commissary and got drunk with them, the way they could understand, roaring, yelling drunk.

"All right, all right, citizens," he told them. "A little of this and a little of that. We're just beginning."

Then the enemy crossed the Hudson, flanked them, and Greene had to take his garrison out of Fort Lee, double-time, a panic-stricken crowd running down the road to Hackensack, Washington leading them, Greene and old Israel Putnam whipping them along, more panic at Hackensack when they tried to reorganize with the mob, and then the whole rabble plodding out of Hackensack on the road to Newark, less than three thousand of them now; and they, with the five thousand stationed in Westchester under Lee, were all that was left of the twenty thousand continentals who had held New York. It rained and they dragged through the mud, whipped and miserable; they were starting a retreat that had no end in sight, and this was all that remained of the glorious revolution and the glorious army. In Newark they were jeered at by the Jersey citizens who were so sure they were seeing the last act of a miserable drama. They ran, fell, crawled, panted through the town, and scarcely were they out of one end than the British patrols entered the other.

Rain changed to the winter's first snow on the road to New Brunswick, and marching through the slow-drifting flakes, they were a column of sorry and forlorn ghosts, muskets and rusty bayonets, here and there a cocked hat, a bandage, a cannon or two trundling clumsily, no sound and no song and no cheering, the officers walking their horses with faces bent against the cold. The road was bordered with stone walls, mantled in white now; the fields were dead and flat and the houses wore masks of shutters.

Paine walked beside a boy whose name was Clyde Matton, and who came from Maine. Carrying his own gun and the boy's, Paine had an arm around his thin shoulder. "The march is short," Paine said, "when one minds the road and not the steps."

"I reckon it's too long either way."

"There'll be a warm fire tonight."

"Little comfort in that. I'm thinking of going home."

"Home's a far way off. There're few men here, but good men."

He walked by the carts of the wounded and told them

stories. They found him a good story-teller; he could make
things sound funny, and he was a fine mimic of accents. Already, he had picked up the vernacular of the various colonies, and he had a deadpan method of delivery, his heavy
beaked nose inquiring for effect after each sentence. In spite
of what he had gone through, he had never been healthier
physically; his large, freckled face inspired confidence, and
whether it was a cart mired in the muck or a man fainted
from weariness, Paine's big shoulders and slab-like hands
were ready and willing. Before this, strength had meant
nothing, the power of mules and work-horses and slaves, but
now it was something that gave him a heady sort of happiness—as once, when remaining behind with Knox and Alexander Hamilton and a dozen others to hold a rear guard
crossing with a gun, he had alone driven off a flanking attack
of dragoons, wading among the horses and sabers and flailing
his big musket around his head like a light cane, taking
nothing in return but a slight cut over the eye and a powder
burn on the cheek. Telling about it admiringly, young Hamilton said:

"He's filthy and slovenly enough when you come to that,
but he's the bravest man I ever saw, and he has the strength
of a madman."

The bloodstains they left on the road where their bare
feet dragged made him refuse Greene's offer of boots; he
wasn't acting, but he was living the one life that was undeni-
ably his own, this thing called revolution, learning a technique among this defeated, fleeing army, learning the one
life he might live.

At night, they made their fires when they could not march
a step more, and it was Paine to do the cooking for a hundred men, Paine to calm a boy's fear, Paine to read a man
a letter from his wife and write one in return, Paine to sit

with his strong hands clasped about his bent knees and slowly, simply explain what they were suffering for, the politics of an empire and a world, the struggles of mankind from the Romans to now, the new day of small men, not only in America but the world over.

The officers left him alone. He had hardly anything to do with them now, and they, in turn, realized that a dirty, unshaven English staymaker was one of the few things that kept what was left of the American cause from dissolving into thin air.

Washington was not the man Paine had met in Philadelphia, not the long, carefully groomed Virginia aristocrat, not the richest man in America and lord of Mt. Vernon, but haggard and skinny, the face drawn, the light gray eyes bloodshot, the buff and blue uniform, for all its launderings, spotted with dirt-stains and bloodstains. Washington was a man who said to Paine:

"Whatever you can do—"

"It's little that I can do," Paine nodded. "If you mean write something, it's hard to tell a man who is suffering and giving that he must suffer more and give more."

"I don't know you," the Virginian said. "But there are so many things I don't know now I thought I knew once. I don't know how to put my faith in a staymaker, but I am doing it. I am glad to call you my friend, Paine, and I would be proud if you'd take my hand, not as the writer of *Common Sense*, but as one man to another."

They shook hands, Paine with tears in his eyes.

"If you can write something," Washington said, "not only for the army but for the whole country. We're so near to the end—"

Paine was thinking he would die gladly for this man, die or kneel on the ground he walked.

Well, writing was what a writing man should do. With the drum held between his knees, with the top tilted to catch the wavering light of the fire, he scratched and scratched away, all the night through. The men gathered around him, men who knew Paine and loved him, men who had felt the strength of his arms, men who had slogged side by side with him. They read as he wrote, sometimes aloud in their stiff, nasal back-country accents:

"These are the times that try men's souls. The summer soldier and the sunshine patriot will, in this crisis, shrink from the service of their country; but he that stands it now, deserves the love and thanks of man and woman. Tyranny, like hell, is not easily conquered. . . ."

They read:

"If there be trouble, let it be in my day, that my child may have peace . . ."

With bloodshot eyes, they read and spoke softly:

"I call not upon a few, but upon all: not on this state or that state, but on every state: up and help us; lay your shoulders to the wheel; better have too much force than too little, when so great an object is at stake. Let it be told to the future world, that in the depth of winter, when nothing but hope and virtue could survive, that the city and the country, alarmed at one common danger, came forth to meet and repulse it. . . ."

"I thank God that I fear not," they read, and others on the edge of the crowd begged him, "Read it, Tom."

"Not all the treasures of the world, so far as I believe, could have induced me to support an offensive war, for I think it murder; but if a thief breaks into my house, burns

and destroys my property, and kills or theatens to kill me, or
those that are in it, and to *bind me in all cases whatsoever*
to his absolute will, am I to suffer it? What signifies it to
me, whether he who does it is a king or a common man; my
countryman or not my countryman; whether it be done by
an individual villain or by an army of them? If we reason to
the root of things we shall find no difference; neither can
any just cause be assigned why we should punish in one case
and pardon in the other. Let them call me rebel, and welcome, I feel no concern from it; but I should suffer the misery of devils, were I to make a whore of my soul by swearing
allegiance to one whose character is that of a sottish, stupid,
stubborn, worthless, brutish man. . . ."

Hard, cruel, vulgar words they understood, and like a
harsh and angry roar, their voices came:

"Read it!"

9

THE LONG WAR

THE ARMY was across the
Delaware, safe for the moment on the south bank, when
Paine decided to go to Philadelphia with old Israel Putnam
and publish the paper he had written. Come out of the worst
crisis they had known yet, he called it that, *Crisis*, and both
Washington and Greene agreed that it might help. Putnam,
a tired, aging man was going to try to find volunteers, to
quiet the city and keep order, but he didn't put much faith
in his mission. Jogging into the city with Paine, the two of
them on moth-eaten nags, he muttered to the effect of its
being over.

"Well, it's not over, if that's what you mean," Paine said.

"Almost—" Putnam pointed out that he, Paine, was young;
he, Putnam, was an old man; he had rheumatism; and he
hated Philadelphia; he was a Yankee himself, and he hated
the midlanders.

"They're like other folk. You won't find much difference
anywhere, plain people are plain people."

"Are they, the damn, dirty bastards?"

Paine had had a letter from Roberdeau, a pleading, apologetic letter. Understanding took time, Roberdeau said. All
before the campaign had been like a storm coming up, and
no one believed it, and now the storm was here.

Paine spoke more forthrightly than he should have; lashing into old Putnam, he said:

"All of you officers are the same; nothing matters but a military victory, and as far as you are concerned the men you lead might as well be tin soldiers!"

"Less than that."

"You old fool, haven't we done enough in just being! Did you expect it to be over in a week?"

Putnam glowered and closed up, and after that they rode on in silence. The snow-covered pike was bare and cold and lonely; everywhere in the Jersey and Pennsylvania counties now, houses were shuttered. It was a suspicious, surly land, and both men felt it. They were relieved to see the church spires of Philadelphia in the distance.

This was a frightened city. He saw a house burning, and nobody moved to fight the flames, and as ominous as the devil a pall of smoke rolled eastward on the wind. Frightened and not the city of brotherly love—a shop window smashed, a printing press wrecked in the street, a cart of household goods overturned. People ran, slowed to a walk, and ran again, and on a street corner an itinerant Quaker preacher called out, "He who takes up the sword must perish by the sword!"

And there were deserters everywhere spreading the news of what had happened on the long, sad march from New York to Trenton, how it was that the army had dissolved into nothing, and Washington, the blundering foxhunter, had hanged himself, surely, and Charles Lee was a prisoner of the British, taken in a bawdy house, and the soldiers were eating the leather of their shoes, and Greene had turned traitor and murdered George Washington, and Howe had

Washington prisoner and the Virginian was going to lead a Tory army against his own people.

There were sad people going away with all they owned piled high on rickety wagons: *The enemy is here, don't you know?*

And hard people with set faces who walked to their work with muskets in their hands: *Let them come!*

And people who understood nothing of what was happening, when only yesterday it was peace.

It was not the city Tom Paine had left. The world goes on, and then suddenly something happens, and then never again is there peace and quiet. The thieves and cutthroats become bold, for they are the first to sense that an era has come to an end, and that never again will things be the same.

Bell would not print what Paine had written. "Mon, mon, do ye think me mad?" He was dismantling his presses. "When Congress goes, I go," he said.

"You're afraid."

"Aye, mon, and no' ashamed of it."

Paine was patient, a different man, Bell realized, a bulking, ragged man with a musket slung over his shoulder, but patient and explaining:

"You are wrong, Bell, the British will not take the city, and there are some things that have to be done, whether they take it or not. You see, this has to be printed; I call it *The Crisis*. We're in the first crisis, and we're going through it." Wheedling, "You and I can set it in one night."

"No!"

"God damn you, Bell, you made a fortune out of *Common Sense*. You're going to print this if I have to hold a bayonet at your throat!"

"No!"

For a moment they looked into each other's eyes, and then Paine whispered, "God damn you," and turned away.

Paine sold it to the *Pennsylvania Journal,* to an editor who told him, grimly smiling, that Congress had already left for Baltimore.

"Courage," the editor smiled, "is a nebulous conception. Of course, we must preserve the government."

Paine apologized for asking for money. He hadn't written this thing for money, just as he hadn't written *Common Sense* for money; but when a man's stomach is empty a few shillings become as necessary as breathing.

"Philadelphia is worse than the army," Paine explained. "The army is freezing and starving, but there's always a crust of bread. But you don't last long in the city without a shilling in your pocket."

The editor nodded, and wondered whether the army could use him. He was fed up with the city.

"Don't go away," Paine said somberly. "There are few enough left who dare to print what has to be printed."

They worked together, setting and printing, and then they began to smile as they pulled copy after copy of the black, sticky manifesto that Paine had written on a drumhead.

"It's fire," the editor said. "I've seen a lot of writing, but nothing that was hot as this."

"I hope so," Paine agreed. "By God, I hope so!"

He met Roberdeau in the street, and Roberdeau shook his hand and asked where was he staying.

"Nowhere."

"Then come home with me." It was strange how calm the general was in this panic-stricken city. "Come along."

"You have worries enough."

"No, come along." Roberdeau was older and leaner, a

shadow in back of his eyes that Paine had not noticed before.
When asked about the Associators, he shook his head. He
told Paine that then it had been a game.

"Of course, I didn't know. No one knew, I think. Is it all
through with Washington?"

Paine was able to smile now. "You don't know him."

"No—I don't." He told Paine that he had read *The Crisis.*
"Do you know what it made me feel? That I was rotten—all
through rotten."

Paine nodded; he had felt much the same, writing it.

"It must be printed, you know, as a pamphlet."

"Nobody has guts enough for that now. I asked Bell, and
Bell ran from the city with the Congress. The printers who
stay are going to climb a fence and stay there." Paine fingered his neck and said ruefully, "You know, I begin to
think of a rope myself. It doesn't matter so much with me,
I have nothing to lose and nobody would care a lot—but to
be hanged by the neck—"

"I know," Roberdeau shrugged. "Let's see about having it
printed."

"Let's have a drink."

A few drinks loosened them up. Paine told Roberdeau
what he had thought of him at Amboy, and Roberdeau,
smiling grimly, suggested that Paine have a bath. They shook
hands, Paine thinking of how a soft man past middle age can
change and stay in a city that was dead, and not worry too
much about being hanged by the neck. They went off to find
a press, bought a small one, and lugged it in a cart to Roberdeau's house. Paine was dead tired and wanted to sleep, dead
tired and dozing in the tub that Roberdeau and his son
filled with hot water, and then sleeping restlessly while the
general went off to find paper. When he woke, he had for-

gotten where he was, a feather bed that gave under his hands, quilts, and a bright room with good furniture.

When Roberdeau returned, Paine was sitting in the parlor, drinking black coffee and talking to a handsome girl of twenty-four, Roberdeau's niece. He had told her of the flight from New York, and she was leaning back, seeing it with her eyes half closed, her face and hands tense.

"But we begin again," Paine said. "It isn't over."

"I can see that," she nodded. "The way you tell about them, it wouldn't be over, ever. But how long—will it be years?"

Paine shook his head.

"But doesn't it matter to you?" she persisted.

"Not to me, no. You see, that's my life, nothing else. When it ends here, it starts somewhere else, and I go there."

"As if to say, where freedom is not, there is my place?"

Paine nodded.

"I pity you," she said.

"Why? I'm happy enough."

"Are you?" She felt like weeping; she rose and somehow left the room.

Roberdeau returned, successful in that he had been able to buy several hundred pounds of varying stocks and a few gallons of ink. He had also found a printer with guts enough to set on his own, a small man called Maggin who could print only a few hundred a day in his old-fashioned vise-type press. That night Paine set type, and all the following three days they printed, hardly sleeping, dirty with ink and working like madmen to turn out copies of the pamphlet before the city fell. Their courage was contagious, and other printers climbed off the fence. Within a week, *Crisis I* was circulating by the thousands, injecting new life into the Philadelphia bloodstream, bundles going to the army where they were read aloud, bundles smuggled into New York, which the British held, a sticky manifesto that screamed with rage, hope, and glory.

On Christmas Day, at night, Washington did the impossible. His army dissolving as quickly as wet sand, he found it beyond his power to do as once he had planned, retreat westward and further westward, beyond the mountains if necessary, but never risk an engagement with the British. After being battered and defeated time after time, he was coming to the realization that his course was not to fight a war of battles but a war of spaces, a war which might last for many, many years, but so long as his army was intact, one that he could not lose.

But his army was no longer intact. Unless some victory were achieved, some deed to spur the imagination of the people, it would cease to exist entirely. And at Christmas Day, at night, he recrossed the Delaware and attacked an encampment of drunken, sodden German mercenaries.

He took over a thousand prisoners; it was the first victory, sorely needed, and things that were almost at an end began again.

For the time, the city was saved; people who had fled came back to Philadelphia, even the Congress, and to half a dozen of them, in a coffee house, Paine said things that were not easily forgotten. He was a little drunk. To Roberdeau he made poor apologies, "Yes, I was drunk. How else can a man watch them?" They were planning campaigns on a table-cloth, and they had it figured up and down, forward and backward, how Washington could win the war in a month. "To hell with the lot of you!" Paine said.

They asked him what he meant, and he said he meant
that some had stayed in the city and some had run away.

"Without the Congress, the revolution ceases to exist,"
they parried.

"Without the Congress!" Paine roared. "God save us—but
tell me, what has the Congress done? A city like this with a
thousand men to hold the houses and barricade the streets
could last forever—forever, I tell you, and the whole British
Empire could not force its way through it. But the Congress
went, and the city lost its head, and I tell you, not you but
Washington, not you but a few hundred poor ragged devils
saved this cause! Not you!"

He was drunk, but they didn't quickly forget what he
said. And between themselves, they decided that Paine might
very well be dispensed with, that Paine was more a nuisance
than an asset. They pointed to the clothes he wore, clothes
not fit for a beggar, to his old, battered wig, to the fact that
he carried a musket in the streets.

The armies had settled into the torpor of a cold winter,
and Paine found a room where he could write. Another crisis
was over, and the devil sat on his pen; he no longer had to
seek for words; they came to him easily now, and every word
was a bitter memory. ". . . Never did men grow old in so
short a time," he wrote. "We have crowded the business of
an age into the compass of a few months—" He would sit
back and think of those months, and though he wrote easily
enough, what he sought for did not come to him; he sought
a rationalization, a scheme, and a progress for revolution; he
wanted the whole and this was only a part. When through
the murk a half-formed vision of a world remade appeared,
his own impotence and futility drove him half mad. Then
he would drink, and the righteous souls could point to him
and be sustained.

There were few pastors in Philadelphia that winter who did not preach a sermon on Tom Paine. One roared, "Look you upon the unrepentant! What cause is served or benefited by a foul mouth and a drunken brain? Is this liberty, this mocking specter that prowls the streets and defames all that is precious to mankind?"

To the few who stood by him, Paine said, "No, it's not war, not revolution; those who hate us sit on their asses and eat their three meals and sleep on feather beds, and who gives a damn that an army lies out there in the snow?"

Bell agreed to publish the second *Crisis,* providing Paine supplied the paper stock. Paine, who hadn't a coin in his pocket, stared at Bell speechlessly.

"Mon, mon, take a quiet look at it," Bell said, spreading his arms. "There's no stock coming in, and a mon does not make a penny, turning himself upsidedown to print a throwaway."

"And was *Common Sense* a throwaway? I didn't ask an accounting, but are you a rich man or a poor one for print-ing it? How many hundred thousand did you sell?"

"Ye're talking fables."

"Am I?"

"These are hard times."

"Do you know how hard they are?" Paine smiled. "You lined yourself well on my book. Be careful, Bell, more than one man has found himself a cist straddling a fence."

"Are ye threatening?"

"No, no—forget that. I want a good press, and I don't give a damn whether Satan himself drives it. Will you print if I find the stock?"

"That I will."

They shook hands on it, and then Paine went to find paper. Roberdeau was gone from town, as was Jefferson; Franklin was off in France, and his son-in-law was one of those who thoroughly despised Paine. Aitken hadn't enough stock to print ten copies. Paine, weary, without food for a day past, pressed his way through town trying to sell his credit, what it was worth, for a few thousand sheets of paper. John Camden and Lenard Frees, two merchants who had cornered sizable quantities of newsprint, had been warned to keep far from the author of *The Crisis*. They could not be reached; Paine stormed and threatened and pleaded; a skinny clerk said persistently:

"I am sorry, they have no paper for sale."

He could have bought a hundred thousand of foolscap, but the owner would sell only for cash, and British cash at that. To no avail, Paine insisted:

"I tell you, don't look at what I am! People have forgotten *Common Sense,* and I'm a damned beggar, dirty, a drunkard, I know, but ask them if ever I defaulted on a debt? Ask them that! Ask who in Philadelphia Tom Paine owes a penny to? Ask them!"

He sought out Aitken again.

"Go to see the Jew, Simon Gonzoles," Aitken told him.

Black and big, Gonzoles had a curly beard that swept down his chest to his waist. He wore a velvet gown and a skullcap, and looked curiously at a Gentile who smelled so strongly of liquor. Sniffing with his beaked nose, he nodded at the name of Paine, yes, he should cross the threshold. There was a girl in the big, twilit room, round and soft as a peach, and she stared at Paine, half in fright, half in wonder.

"I know little of paper," Gonzoles said. "In furs I dealt

once, and what have you done to the fur trade, with your revolution and fury?"

Paine shook his head, said nothing, but pleaded with his tired eyes.

"For disciples of the Book," Gonzoles said, "we Jews know surprisingly little of that on which the word is printed. If I desired to help you, where would I go?"

"I can buy—for English gold," Paine begged him. "For two hundred guineas a hundred thousand of foolscap—that's a fine paper, not like common print or book stock, a writing paper, you understand, for genteel purposes, but believe me, what I wrote needs to be said. That's all I can buy."

"I know what you write," the Jew said, not without a trace of bitterness, yet Paine never took his eyes from him as he went to an iron-bound strong box and counted out the money.

"I look like a beggar," Paine said. "I smell like a drunkard —but I pay my debts."

"This isn't a debt."

"I swear—"

"Don't swear!"

Paine stood a moment, stiff, trembling a little, then took the money and left, hardly able to keep from running, clutching the gold in both his hands, hiring a cart on the way to take the paper to Bell's.

All that night, he worked with Bell, all the next day, his hands wet with ink, the good, pungent smell filling the air about him.

Roberdeau came back and saw him on a street corner, looked as he would at a ghost, and then grasped one arm and cried sharply, "Paine!"

"Yes?"

He wasn't drunk, Roberdeau saw. "Come home with me," he said.

"Yes—"

He led Paine home, but he had to walk slowly, so that the stumbling figure could keep up with him. Roberdeau's niece was there as they came in, Paine edging shabbily forward clutching his hat.

"Irene, Mr. Paine is staying to dinner," Roberdeau told her.

Paine nodded and smiled and said nothing, nothing at dinner in the way of conversation; he ate slowly with control, but he ate and ate, smiling apologetically now and then. Bluntly, Roberdeau asked, "When did you eat last, Tom?"

"Two days, I think, or three."

The girl turned her head; Roberdeau, staring down at his plate, said brutally, "You can change the world, but you can't keep body and soul together. My God, Paine, are you mad?"

A shrug in reply, no words.

"What are you going to do now?"

"I don't know. I'm writing a crisis—we need one."

"You're writing a crisis—Paine, don't you realize that life goes on, even in wartime, that you're doing no one any good, not you, not Washington, not our cause by being a beggar and a drunkard on the streets of Philadelphia—"

"Shut up!"

"No, I'll talk, because you're worth something more than a damned filthy drunkard. I heard you at Amboy, and now you'll hear me!"

"I'm leaving," Paine said, rising.

"The devil you are. Irene, get out of here!" The girl left, but paused at the door a moment, giving Paine such a look of sympathy, of warm human kindness, that between that and the pressure of Roberdeau's heavy hand Paine sank back into his chair. Roberdeau sat facing him; he took some snuff, offered the box to Paine, and then filled two glasses with brandy. They drank and sat in silence for about five minutes.

"Say your piece," Paine nodded, and in that moment Roberdeau reflected upon a man who had sucked in the whole soul and being of America, even to the speech. In the unshaven, hook-nosed, wigless head, there was something both fierce and magnificent, a grinding savagery that might be sculpted as the whole meaning of revolution, unrest and cruelty combined with a deep-etched pattern of human suffering and understanding.

"Suppose you made this uprising," Roberdeau said carefully. "Let us say that without *Common Sense* there could have been no United States of America. Let us say that without the first *Crisis* we couldn't have pulled through the January of this year. What then: is it the beginning or the end? How many times have you said that we don't know yet what we've raised? At the rate you're going, you'll be dead in six months."

"I'm tougher than that."

"Are you? I don't think so. There are those who love you, Paine, but how many hate you?"

"Enough, I suppose."

"All right. You have to fight, and you're in no condition to fight. You have to live, and you haven't a penny to your name. Now listen to me, the Committee of Secret Correspondence is going to be reorganized as a permanent Office of Foreign Affairs. There's a post open for an official secretary, and I'm going to have Adams put you up for it."

"Through Congress?" Paine smiled.

"Through Congress."

"To hell with them," Paine muttered. "I'm a revolutionist, not a dirty, sneaking politician."

But Roberdeau said quietly, "Stay here with Irene. I'm
going to see Adams."

He was gone a long while. Paine sat in a deep wingchair
and listened to the girl play on the clavichord. He must have
dozed a bit, because when he opened his eyes, she had
stopped playing and was watching him.

"Tired?"

He said, no, he wasn't tired, and asked her what she had
been playing.

"Bach."

"Please play again," he asked her.

The little instrument rustled like a harp; Paine watched
the girl's back, the motion of her head, the strong muscles
that played her fingers.

She was less beautiful than strong and handsome; there
was a tawny color in her hair that spoke of a Norman strain
somewhere in the family, yet in every motion and gesture she
was French. Through playing, she turned to Paine and she
was startled by something in his eyes. For some reason Paine
thought she would go. He asked her to stay.

"Yes, of course." She sat down near him and said, "Tell
me about yourself."

He began to tell her, speaking in a soft voice, his eyes half
closed. In a little while Roberdeau would return, and there
might be a good chance that he had succeeded. Politics was a
career, and Paine was very tired.

"I think you're the strangest man I have ever known," she
said. "I think—"

"What?"

She walked over and kissed him, and then Paine was smil-

ing strangely. "Of course, it's no good," she admitted.
"You're damned, aren't you?"

Paine said nothing, and then they just sat and waited for
Roberdeau.

To his amazement, Paine got the office, in spite of a fervent objection by a small clique, headed by Witherspoon,
a Scotch pastor and one-time supporter of the bonnie Prince
Charlie. Witherspoon hated Paine, not only because he was
a fearless writer, but because he was both a Quaker and
English. The clique accused him of everything from murder-
ing children and being a secret agent for the British, to being
an apostate and a devil without horns. But Adams and Jefferson and others stood up for him, and at the time there
were reasons for the two parties to make a deal. Tom Paine
became secretary to the committee of the new Department of
Foreign Affairs, with a salary of seventy dollars a month.

It was a new feeling, respectability. Seventy dollars a
month was not a fortune; indeed in the recently issued continental currency, it threatened to become nothing at all
very soon; yet it was more than enough for Paine's simple
needs, enough to pay the few debts he had, to buy him a
decent suit of clothes, clean if not spacious quarters, pen and
paper to write with, and no danger of starving.

And the respectability, of course; Paine the revolutionary
was nothing; Paine the writer, whose book had been read
and reread by almost every literate person in the thirteen
colonies, and spoken aloud to most of those who were not
literate, whose book had caused the British ministry to curse
the day when the written word had been made available to
commoners, was a mere scribbler; Paine the pamphleteer,
who had done as much as any man in America to hold the
army together in its worst hour, was a rabble rouser and no

more: but Paine the secretary to the Committee of Foreign
Affairs was a person of some consequence, on the inside
among the circle of the gods that be, able to do a person a
favor and say the right word in the right place. Or so they
thought, and more hats were tipped to him, more hellos said,
more waists bent than ever before.

And Paine came to live in the world within, where the
ivory tower protected even the most sensitive. Soon enough
he discovered that where the quaint inner circle of colonial
politics began, reality stopped. That war was being fought
by a haggard, desperate little army led by a quiet and stubborn man called Washington, mattered so little to the Continental Congress of the United Thirteen Colonies that it
was only by deliberate resolution that they could recall the
nature of the situation.

On their side, it might be said that they were as impotent
as any governing body could conceivably be; able to make
treaties, they could not force observation of them; they had
the right to coin money, but no power to buy gold or silver,
and with the power to wage war, they could not raise a single
soldier. In the one worst moment of crisis, when Washington's shivering and defeated troops had finally crossed to the
southwest bank of the Delaware, they had abdicated volun-
tarily, fled in panic from Philadelphia to Baltimore, and
given to Washington the full power of a dictator.

Their knowledge of warfare was confined to the continental military tracts they read so feverishly; each had his
own personal military theory and fought for it, and the only
military fact they agreed in was that it would be ridiculous
to fight the war in the one style Americans knew, the silent,
terrible bushwacking tactics that had torn a British army
to ribbons between Concord and Lexington.

They were split into parties, the pro- and anti-confederation, the northern party, the southern, the pro-reconciliation and anti-reconciliation, the pro-Washington and anti-Washington. There were the isolationists who believed revolution was a property peculiar to Americans of pure British descent and of the eastern coast of North America and that all other persons and places should be excluded; and there were the internationalists, those who would rally the insular Dutch, Irish, Scotch, Swedes, Jews, Poles, French, and Germans, and add to them whatever liberal and anti-British feeling existed on the continent of Europe. Not the Sons of the American Revolution but the non-fighting ancestors were already working feverishly to make the roster exclusive.

And to add on the coals, they had discovered the good American device of lobbying.

They lobbied for everything: to have their local towns, counties, cities protected by troops; the Southerners to have tobacco adopted as a necessity for the troops; the down-easters to convince all that no one could fight without a liberal ration of rum; the wool-runners to sell woolen blankets at four times the price they had ever sold them; the midlanders to sell their grain; the New Englanders to have the troops fight on curds; the New Yorkers to have them fight on beef.

And they could agree on nothing, not on the style of the confederation, not on post-war aims, not on a constitution. The honest, sincere men among them fought and broke their hearts, and somehow things were done and somehow the war blundered along.

And into this Paine came, a revolutionist whom all regarded with suspicion. He did his work, he wrote another *Crisis;* he sat in a cubicle and pushed his pen as a clerk, and sometimes, when he closed his eyes, he would see men in rags with a rattlesnake banner. And he saw Irene Roberdeau and said, "Look at me. Do you like it?"

"I think you look better than you ever looked."

"Do I? And I tell you, something is dying inside of me." She noticed then what a flair he had for the dramatic.

"I can't stand much more of this," he decided.

"I hear you're greatly appreciated."

"You do? They're waiting for a chance to be rid of me, and the sooner it comes, the better. This is a people's war, and some day the people may awake to that."

"And can't you forget the war even for a while?"

"You told me I was damned," Paine smiled.

"But not beyond redemption," she said.

The carts came into Philadelphia with half a hundred badly wounded men, and Paine worked with others, feeding them, making them comfortable in the old Quaker meeting house to which they were taken. Some he knew; he was Common Sense to them. He found his *Crisis* papers among their belongings; a paper read a dozen times would end as dressing for wounds or wadding for a gun.

"A stout heart," he would say.

He sat all one night holding the hand of a boy who was dying, and the next day he washed the body and laid it out himself. It was before the time when women would go near a dying or a wounded man; the male nurses were tobacco-stained, filthy old devils. Paine told Irene Roberdeau soon after, "I'm going away, I must."

"Where?"

"To the army—I'm no good for this sort of thing."

She pleaded with him, asked him whether it was not enough to throw herself at his feet.

"I'm no good for you," he said. "I'm no good for anything except this stew I've brewed." Yet he lingered on in Philadelphia.

It was spring again, and the armies were moving in the field. Plowing over, farmers picked up their muskets, cleaned off the rust, and drifted down the country lanes toward Washington's encampment. Last summer was forgotten; the shop clerks forgot and left their shelves, and the mechanics laid away their tools. A lark and a campaign, and the war would be over. Spring does that, coming suddenly with the sky bluer than ever it was during the winter. The few thousand regulars, lean and hard, mocked the way Yankees mock at the summer soldiers, the militia who took their fighting as they would bird shooting, in between the planting and the harvest. "Where were you at Christmas Day?" became the taunt, harking back to the time they turned like wolves at bay and crossed the Delaware. This was the year for ending the war; they could prove that by the almanacs, by the stars, by gypsy fortune tellers. Ho and away; there were rations in plenty, and up from New Orleans by the bosom of broad mother Mississippi had come a thousand fat hogsheads of gunpowder, lead weight to cast a million of shot and three thousand shining Spanish bayonets. There was no treaty with Spain yet, but rustic farmers, suddenly turned astute politicians, winked and nodded their long heads as they ran a hard forefinger over the Toledo steel; one knew about those things.

It was in Washington's mind to make a campaign in the north against Burgoyne, but the middle country was screaming to be protected. Howe had packed his British and Hessians into their great ships and sailed away with them, and who knew where they would land? They were sighted off

Delaware, and then word came that they were sailing into Chesapeake Bay. The American army, swelled to a considerable size now by the influx of militia, began to march south.

Paine watched them strut through Philadelphia. It was summer and hot, and stripped to the waist, their muskets slung over their backs, barefooted most of them, they appeared fine and ready and trim.

Paine was neither seen nor minded; he stood in the packed crowd that cheered and hooted and waved at the sunburned marchers, bright and gay with sprigs of green tucked under their caps and behind their ears. Washington rode by in his buff and blue, looking healthier and younger than he had this midwinter past; alongside of him was the boy Paine had heard of but not seen before, young Lafayette in white twill and satin, beribboned all over with gold braid. Hamilton was there and fat Harry Knox, nursing along their lumbering guns, and Nathanael Greene to whom Paine waved—but a man is not to be seen in a crowd.

Paine went to Roberdeau's home, but Irene was not there. She left a note for him that she had gone to watch the parade.

And then they were defeated at Brandywine Creek, slashed to pieces, cut and routed, the old story of men who were willing to die but didn't know how: the old story of mistakes, a listing of blunders, each one worse than the last.

With a dead, white face, Paine heard the news, walked to the office of the Committee with dragging steps. "Of course, Congress must leave the city again," everyone said. No one had the truth of what had happened; they were running around like chickens freshly slaughtered; they were frightened.

The whole city was catching the virus of panic, the Tories

with fear that the rebels would take their revenge before they left, the rebels with fear that the Tories would not allow them to leave. Neither party quite knew the strength of the other. But the British would march on Philadelphia; that, at least, was obvious.

Paine found Irene, and she said to him what she hadn't dared to say before,

"Come with me—out of all this. Haven't you done enough and suffered enough? It's over now, and if they go on, how long will it be, ten years? or twenty? Paine, I've never loved anyone else—and if you leave me now—"

"And if I stay with you? What kind of happiness would you have with me! I have nothing, Irene, except an old shirt and a pen to write with. I'm a camp-follower of revolution, a scribbler, and a pamphleteer."

"I won't ask you again, Tom."

He nodded and went without kissing her, without saying anything else, and the next day he heard that she and her uncle had left the city. They were not alone in leaving. The Tories made a show of strength, brawls and gunshots and now and then a woman's scream—the city was dying and not gently. As during that last time when the city had been threatened, Paine tried to plead with the leaders of the Associators. Congress had gone, but there were one or two left, friends of his, with a little influence, and between them they managed to call a meeting in Carpenter's Hall. Less than two hundred persons appeared, and when Paine addressed them, they listened in silent apathy.

"A city," he cried, "is the best fortress in the world, the forest of the citizen soldier! Every street can become a fortress, every house a death trap! The army lost a battle, but this is a people's war, and the British army can break its back on the stout heart of Philadelphia—"

There was no stout heart in the city. Paine sat in his room and wrote a *Crisis* paper, and below him the streets were deserted. One by one, the pro-continental citizens went. At night, a pistol bullet whistled past his ear. There was a parade of Tories, with a great banner reading, "Death to every damned traitor!"

Paine carried his musket now; he saw them tar and feather a harmless old man, whose only sin was that he swept the hearths in Carpenter's Hall; he died after Paine and a few others had taken him from the stake to which he was bound. A round dozen had the nerve to remain—sullen, desperate men with guns in their hands, and they buried the old man openly. Paine said softly, "God help them when the day of reckoning comes."

Houses were burning; the volunteer fireman's association had gone to pieces completely; the houses burned and left their trail of smoke across the blue sky.

Paine reflected curiously upon what such a situation does to men, for among the few rebels who stayed was Aitken, a somber, aging man who nodded when Paine told him about the new *Crisis* paper.

"I'll print it," he said.

"And when the British come?"

Aitken shrugged; he didn't seem to care. Paine begged him to make some provision for leaving the city and getting his presses out, but he shook his head stolidly.

"A man does what a man can," he said. "I have no other place to go." And he stayed behind. When Paine came to say good-by, the Scotsman handed him five hundred freshly printed leaflets.

"Go on," he told Paine. "Get out before it's too late."

Paine found an old, swaybacked nag, bought a saddle for a few dollars, and rode out of one end of Philadelphia as the

Hessians marched into the other. And on the Baltimore
Pike, he drew up his horse and sat for a while, listening to
the beating of the British drums.

He asked himself, "What am I now, propagandist without
presses? Rabble rouser lingering at the scene of death after
the mob has fled? Revolutionist surveying the dead corpse?"
He rode slowly on the old nag, and often he looked over his
shoulder at the city that had nursed a thing called America.
He lay down to sleep in a copse, hobbling the nag first and
keeping his musket by his side, but his dreams were not
good. And the next day he stopped at a farm and called:
"Halloo!"

It was shuttered; a musket poked through a slit in the
wood told him to be off. "Where is the army?" he called.
"God damn you and the army," the slit said.

And wasn't it always that way when they suffered defeat,
the countryside growing black and sullen, the houses shuttered, the cattle locked away, the whole face of the land becoming black and fearful? It had been so in New York, in
Jersey, and now in Pennsylvania, and Paine began to wonder
who it was that made and fought the revolution, when the
fat, staid prosperity of the land was so awfully against it.
He rode on and in circles, and once when he faced a farm,
a bullet ripped the cloth of his jacket. In a cornfield, his
horse tethered beside him, he lay and watched the blood-
red sun setting; and never before had he been so lonely a
stranger in so lonely a land. He saw once, far off and down
a road, three men of the continentals, unmistakable, gaunt
and barefoot and ragged as they were, but as he whipped his
nag down on them they raced into the woods. And a milk-
maid, whom he would have asked for a drink, parched and
hungry as he was, fled into a barn when he made toward

her. A frightened land. Paine rode in broad, slow circles. He rode out of dawning and into sunset, a lonely Englishman, a renegade Quaker who pursued a will-o'-the-wisp called revolution; he lay alone and hungry, and remembered Irene Roberdeau's eyes and voice, her throat and her swelling breasts, and he cursed himself, his fate, all his destiny and all that was Tom Paine.

And then one evening, he was stopped by a fierce, half-naked sentry, who wore a bloodstained bandage over his matted hair, and demanded:

"Who goes there?—God damn you, answer up or I'll blow out your dirty guts!"

"Tom Paine."

"The hell you say!"

"Then look at me. What is this?"

"General Greene's encampment. Let's have a look—"

He sat having dinner with Greene, the flies of the patched tent thrown back, a fringe of autumn trees dropping their leaves against the orange light of campfires, and Greene saying:

"I tell you, Paine, you brought back my soul, I was so filthy tired and done in. Do you understand?"

Paine nodded; how was it that Greene looked on him as a savior, that Greene held his hand and tried to let Paine know how it had been at Brandywine? In appearance, they were closer now, Greene's handsome face worn and lined, incredibly aged for a man so young, Greene's buff and blue uniform faded and ragged, his boots worn through at the toes.

"So we lost Philadelphia," Greene said, after Paine had told him. "Not a shot fired, not a hand raised, but we gave

it up to them. It could have been a fortress, and was it you
who said this was a people's war?"

"I said it."

"Are you tired, Paine?"

"Tired, yes. There's nothing good about war, nothing
decent, nothing noble. You say, I will take up a gun and
kill my brother, because the ends justify the means, because
my freedom and my liberty are my soul's blood, and how
can I live without them? Make men free so that the land
will shine with God's holy light! And then they run away,
they leave their own houses, they close their shutters and
blow out your brains, if, God forbid, you should want a
drink of water, and they damn you for a bandit! If we were
like the Jagers, it would be different, but we're little men,
general, little, tired, hopeless men."

"Yes—"

"And now what?"

"God knows. We are beaten and beaten."

"And him?"

"Washington?" Greene shook his head. "We're going to
attack—he's bewildered, well, we all are. We had a count
and we still have eleven thousand men left—that's strange,
isn't it? And they're at Germantown with less than seven
thousand, so we're going to attack. But we are afraid; go
outside later and talk to them, Paine, and you'll see how
afraid we are. We had a talk about it, and no one knew what
to do. But Wayne, you know him?"

"I know him."

"He sat in a corner and pretended to read a book, didn't
say anything, just fire in him and sometimes he'd look at me
as if I hadn't the guts of a rat left, and finally Washington
asked him what would he do, what had he to say, and he
answered, 'I'd say nothing, I'd fight, sir, fight—do you hear

me, fight, not run away, but fight!' " Greene's voice slipped
away; Paine prodded him.

"And then?"

"And then we looked at each other, because we were all
afraid—and tomorrow we attack. For God's sake, Paine, go
out and talk to the men."

"Yes."

As he rose, Greene caught his arm. "What will you tell
them?"

"About Philadelphia—"

"Do you think—"

"They ought to know. It's time for them to begin to hate.
This isn't a revolution, it's civil war."

The nightmare of the Battle of Germantown Paine would
not forget until his dying day. And a nightmare it was, so
impossible a nightmare that not for months afterwards could
the actual action be pieced together. In four columns, the
American troops drove on the British and Hessians who were
very nearly trapped. But the columns could not co-ordinate;
it was dawn, and fog lay over the field like a pall of heavy
smoke. Paine rode with Greene and was separated from him;
lost, he ran into a whole regiment of continentals who were
also lost. They fired at him; screaming with fury, he got into
them and saw that half were drunk, the other half too weary
to do more than stand oafishly. Then a storm of firing broke
out ahead of him, and the men scattered. Riding toward the
firing, Paine came on a steady stream of wounded. Most of
them lay on the road, too weak to move. The fog made it
dark as evening, and only by voice did Paine recognize Doctor Mulavy, who had been with Greene at Fort Lee. In a
bloodstained apron, he yelled at Paine to find water, mistak-
ing him, mounted as he was, for an officer.

"Water, I say, water!"

"What's up there?"

"Paine?"

"Yes, what's up there?"

"God knows. Paine, where am I to find water?"

He rode on, blundering into a column of Jagers, green
clad, roaring in German as they rushed past him, taking no
notice of him. Then, above the sound of the battle, he heard
Harry Knox's booming voice. He followed it and through
the haze saw naked artillerymen swinging into position a
battery of twelve-pounders. Knox was bleeding and sweating and yelling, and when he saw Paine he ran to him and
pointed to a great stone house that loomed vaguely in the
drifting mist.

"Look at that! Look at that!"

Appearing like magic from the mist and smoke, half a
hundred figures raced over the lawn for the house; suddenly,
it exploded with fire, and the figures twisted, dropped like
punctured bags, some of them lying where they fell, others
crawling away. A perfect fury of musket fire broke out from
another direction, and Knox shrieked at his artillerymen.

"Load, you bastards! Load, you dirty bastards!"

A group of men appeared, running with all their strength,
and no one knew whether it was an advance or a retreat, and
an officer came by, spurring his horse out of the mist and
then back into it again. Paine's nag bolted, and it ran until
it was caught in a slow-moving band of cavalry. They were
speaking Polish, most of them, and they moved on slowly,
Paine with them, walking into a burst of grape that tore
them to pieces and sent their horses in every direction.

Coffee was served, and corn cakes and cheap molasses, all
put down on the claw-leg table, hot and steaming as they

came in, one by one, and stood around. It was nine o'clock in the morning, a day later, and they had been invited to the little Dale house to have breakfast. They stood around, and no one had an appetite, Paine and Greene and Sullivan and Wayne and Knox and Stirling and the Pole, Pulaski, and Stephan, as sorry and bloodstained and tattered and dirty a high command as had ever been seen. There was no talk, but rather a dazed, sullen expectancy as they waited for Washington. And then Hamilton came in, went to the table, and began to cram his mouth full, saying:

"Good, you know, have some."

"Where is he?"

"He'll be here. This is good breakfast, and you don't know when there'll be more."

"Angry?" Wayne asked.

"Just as always."

There weren't enough chairs. Some sat, others backed against the wall. Greene grasped Paine's arm and nodded. Then Washington came in, walking straight through and looking neither to left nor to right, pouring himself a cup of coffee and taking a piece of pone, and telling them, not harshly:

"Go ahead and eat, gentlemen."

Nevertheless, they were afraid of him. Paine had coffee; Greene stood with his legs planted wide, staring at the floor, as if there were some complicated problem there that defied his understanding. Pulaski pulled at his mustaches while tears welled into his very pale blue eyes, and Wayne bit his nails. And the big Virginian, eating slowly, said to them:

"There is no point in discussing yesterday, gentlemen. Tomorrow is more pertinent."

They looked at him, but no one answered.

"Make out your reports concerning the battle. We will go on, and perhaps our fortunes will fare differently—"

Then something broke the dam, and they all began to talk
at once—hoarse, strained voices trying to pierce through the
haze that almost destroyed them the morning before. And
Washington, taking Paine by the arm, said:

"Tell me, sir, you were at Philadelphia, and was it bad?"

"Very bad."

"And do you think it very bad with us?"

"No," Paine said definitely.

"Why?"

"Because you are not afraid," Paine said quietly.

"Just that?"

"Just that."

Then they shook hands.

Marching south to prevent reinforcements for the enemy
from sailing up the Delaware, and failing in that. Failing at
Fort Mifflin and Fort Mercer. Failing in a child's ambuscade
against a few hundred Hessians; failing in a simple ma-
neuver because the men tripped and fell from weariness.
Failure and failure and failure. Twelve miles through the
rain and muck, and a panicky scramble from a dozen British
dragoons. Two thousand men slop along from dawn to dusk,
and then one day the ground turns hard. The roads that
were swamps, cut or worn in between the two shoulders of
meadowland or forest, as most roads were at the time, become as nasty and sharp as corrugated iron. A cow's track in
the muck freezes and becomes a deadly weapon. A ripple of
mud drives its point through a paper-thin sole. A bloodspot
stains the road, and then another, and then still another.
Flakes of snow fall as if a down quilt were ripped open and
fluffed across the sky. As a mark on the road, as a sign is the
bright red blood in the cold white snow. Now march north
again, for word has come from the tall Virginian to join him.
There is a place called the Valley Forge.

"I tell you, comrade, that our cause is just!"

Paine is changing, and his flesh is gone. He was a strong man with broad shoulders and hands like flails, but the flesh is gone, the cheeks sunken, the eyes hollow. With his big musket a killing weight on his shoulder, he walks in the ranks, coughing, stumbling, falling as the others fall, leaving his own trail of blood. How else are comrades bound? "I tell you, our cause is just," he says, and Greene, who leads this pathetic army, thinks to himself, "They will kill him some day, because you can't whip dying flesh."

They don't kill him, they listen. And twenty who would have deserted hear a man say in a whisper:

"Men live by glory, so listen to me, comrades. All things come out of this, and the deed we dared is beyond my understanding and yours. But if you want to go home—"

"God damn you, Paine, we've heard that before!"

"Go home." And then silence until someone says, "Go ahead, Tom."

"Men are good," and he looks around at the circle of beggars.

"Why?"

"Even the simple fact that we want to go home. Bad men don't want to go home. We are good men, quiet men, little men. And we are taking the world for ourselves; they drove us like slaves for five thousand years, but now we are taking the world for ourselves, and when our marching feet sound, my God, friends, who will be able to stop their ears? But this is the beginning, the beginning—"

"I want you to stay with me," Greene told him one evening. "Tom, I need you. I want you to take a major's commission."

Paine shook his head.

"But why? I don't speak of rewards, that's a long time off, but where is the virtue in being nothing, in not drawing a shilling's pay, in knowing that if you're captured, you'll be hanged an hour later?"

"I'm not a soldier," Paine said.

"Are any of us?"

"This is your war to fight, Nathanael, and mine to understand. I am not even an American, and where is the end for me? You'll be free, but I'll have my chains—"

"I don't understand that."

"I don't want to talk about it," Paine said uneasily, and then smiled a bit as he reminded Greene that he was still the secretary for the Office of Foreign Affairs.

As they approached Valley Forge, Paine came down with an attack of dysentery. Colonel Joseph Kirkbride, whom Paine had first met at Fort Lee, was due for a leave, and asked whether the other wouldn't share it with him.

"You can stand a rest," he told him.

Paine, who could barely stagger along by now, agreed. Greene provided the horses, gripped Paine's hand, and begged him to come back again.

"I'll come back," Paine smiled. "A bad penny turns up, doesn't it?"

Kirkbride lived in Bordentown, in a comfortable frame house, hearths five feet wide, a feather bed at night, a steaming bath in the kitchen, and, best of all, books. He had Swift, Defoe, Shakespeare, Addison, Pope, Clairmont, the vulgar little novels of Dreed. Paine was sick and weak and tired, and he let go of reality, curled in front of the fire and wandered with Lemuel Gulliver, prodded the amorous filth of Gin Row with Muckey Dray, recaptured Defoe's England, dreamed, whispered parts from *Hamlet* and *Lear,* ate and slept. They had few visitors, and both men wanted to be left alone, to forget for a while. They drank a good deal, not to drunkenness, but to the warm, sleepy contentment of satisfied animals. They talked little; they looked out of the windows and watched the snow fall, the drifts pile up, always with the comfort that they could turn around and see the flame roar in the hearth.

In that way, two weeks passed before Paine rose one morning and announced, as if the thought had only just occurred to him:

"I'm going back."

Riding along a frozen road where his horse's hoofs drummed like musket shots each time they bit through the crust of ice, Paine saw a blur in the meadow beside him, and going over knelt beside a man frozen stiff and dead, musket beside him and face turned up to the sky—a deserter but a continental, a life gone and cold loneliness in a lonely land.

That was the way it was and had ever been, winter and the land against them, closed doors and closed shutters, no different in Pennsylvania than it had been in Jersey.

At night he crouched close to a small fire; a step could mean death and he kept his musket beside him; he warmed his hands; he lay in his blanket and looked up at the cold winter sky. It was not safe to ask one's way nor to declare one's party. He was looking for a place called the Valley Forge, and only one man whom he spoke to had anything to say about it, "A sad spot, mind me."

He stayed one blessed night in a Quaker household, a big, square man, soft-spoken, and a woman whose smile was innocent as a child's, and trying to thank them and tell them who he was, received from the man, "Nay, we know thee not, but as a stranger cold and hungry. And if thee are one of them, keep thee council."

"You don't like the continentals?"

"We love man, but hate bloodshed, murder, and suffering."

"And is it murder to fight for freedom?"

"Thee will find freedom a thousandfold more within thee."

Leaving, Paine said, "The road to the encampment?"

"The Valley Forge?"

"Yes."

"Thee will find it. God has chosen a place of perdition on earth. Look thee in the sky, and where the devil stands, they be."

This was the Valley Forge. When he came, it was night, and a sentry, muffled in a blanket, barred his path. There was a bridge across the Schuylkill and a pink sky over the snowy hills. There were dugouts, lines of them back and forth like dirty lace, half dirt holes, half log. On a frozen parade ground, a flag waved. Fires burned, and dark figures moved in front of the flames. The hills jutted like bare muscles, and the leafless trees swayed in the wind.

"I am Paine," he told the sentry, and the man coughed, laughed, showed his yellow teeth at the feeble pun.

"So we all are, citizen."

"Tom Paine."

The man sought in his memory, found a reminder, and shook his head. "Common Sense?"

"Yes. Where's the general?"

"Yonder—" The man had lost interest, huddled back in his blanket.

"Yonder" brought him past dugouts, an artillery emplacement, a log hospital where the wounded groaned, sang and screamed, and other sentries to whom he gave the same answer:

"Paine."

"Go on."

He had walked a mile through the encampment, along the river with the hills over him and to his left, when he saw in the dusk the fieldstone house that was Washington's headquarters. There was a drift of smoke from the chimney, a light in the windows, a sentry in front and a sentry in back. They let him in. Hamilton, a thin, hollow-eyed boy, years older than when Paine had last seen him, stood in the vestibule, recognized the onetime staymaker of Thetford, and smiled and nodded.

"Welcome."

Paine blew on his hands and tried to smile.

"You like our little place?" Hamilton asked.

There was something in his tone that made Paine ask, uncertainly, "Is it worse than what I've seen?"

"That depends on how much you have seen."

"I walked through from the bridge."

"Then the best is yet to unfold," Hamilton said bitterly. "You must go to the dugouts, Paine—you must go and talk to them, and probably they will cut your throat. Do you think you have seen them at their worst—but we are breeding a new brand of beast here. Why don't you ask why?"

"I know why," Paine nodded.

"Do you—but you worked for that swinish Congress of ours. Do they know that we're starving, naked, dying of hunger and disease and cold, rotting—rotting, I tell you, Paine!"

Going up to him, Paine took him by his jacket and said quietly, "Get hold of yourself. I don't even know where Congress is. Get hold of yourself."

Hamilton giggled and swallowed. "Sorry." He giggled again. "Go in there—he's in there."

"Don't be a fool."

"Sorry," Hamilton said.

Washington rose as Paine entered the room, peering for a moment to identify the stranger, and then smiling and holding out his hand. He looked older, Paine noticed; war was making old men of this young and desperate group; thinner, too, and strangely innocent as he was now, wigless, in a dressing gown with an ancient cap on his head, his gray eyes larger than Paine had ever imagined them to be. He was genuinely glad to see Paine, begged him to sit down and take off his coat, and then, in a very few words, described the tense and terrible situation at the encampment, the lack of food and clothing, the alarming increase in venereal disease, due to the abundance of women who lived with the men, some of them camp-followers, some of them wives, the daily desertions, the shortage of ammunition, the increasing anger even among the most loyal at the fact that they had not been paid for months.

"All that," Washington said softly. "I tell you it is worse than last year, and you remember that. Unless the country helps, we will break, I can tell you that, Paine. I can tell no one else, but, Paine, we are close to the finish—you must know. Not through the enemy, but ourselves, and then the revolution will go like a bad dream."

"What do you want me to do?"

"Go to Congress and plead. Go to the country and wake them up. Make them understand—tell them!"

"I want to stay here."

"Don't stay here, Paine. Here it is hell, and I don't think even you can help us. Go to Congress, and somehow we will last out this winter—I can't think of the next. Somehow, we will endure."

10

REVOLUTIONIST AT LARGE

He found the Congress at York, and curiously enough he was welcomed. A dinner was given for him, and there were Rush, Abington, the Adams cousins, Lee, Hemingway, and others. The guest of honor was Tom Paine, shaven and with a new jacket and shoes. "What he has seen and suffered," Hemingway said, "should be an inspiration for all of us." Well-fed, honest men they were; claret was the drink of the evening, bottles sparkling up and down the table like a whole line of British redcoats. James Cranshaw, at whose beautifully furnished home the dinner was given, played host as in old times, carrying in the whole roast suckling pig himself. Two beef and kidney puddings flanked the roast, and two platters of fried chicken flanked the puddings. Hot bread, both corn and wheat, gave off their good smell, and there were cornucopias full of dried fruit. "For the land is plentiful, let it be known far and wide." Sitting next to Paine, Cranshaw pointed out the beauties of his Philadelphia Chippendale:

"You will note, sir, the simple lines and the undecorated backs of the chairs. For the highboy, I confess nothing equals the mahogany product of Newport, in particular the brothers Granny. For chairs, Philadelphia holds the crown and nothing in England is as good, I say nothing, sir. In New England they desecrate the product with ladder backs and peasant seats of rush; here our sidechairs are quiet songs of beauty, the ball and claw arrived at its final function, the fretted back become Grecian in its gentle curves. Shall one doubt the future of America?"

"I wonder," Paine thought.

They plied him with food and drink, and they talked of everything under the sun but the war. Not until the meal was done, the flip served, and the ladies had retired to the drawing room, did they come to the point. Then, over snuff and cigars, they pumped Paine about what he had seen at Germantown and Valley Forge.

"But you will admit that the leadership was mediocre?" they prodded him.

"The leadership, gentlemen, is sacrificing and courageous."

"But stupid."

"I deny that! Soldiers are not made overnight. We are not Prussians, but citizens of a republic."

"Yet you cannot deny that Washington has failed constantly. What you told us you saw at Valley Forge is only final proof of his unfitness!"

"Unfitness!" Paine said quietly. "My good gentlemen, God help you!"

"Aren't you dramatizing, Paine?"

"What is the case in point?" Paine asked. "Do you want to be rid of Washington?"

"Let us say, rather, co-operate with him," Lee said smoothly. "What Gates has done at Saratoga, his capture of Burgoyne's entire army, proves—"

"Proves nothing!" Paine snapped. "Have you forgotten that Gates deliberately abandoned Washington at the Delaware last year? I'm not afraid of words, gentlemen, and I'd as soon say traitor as anything else. At a price, Gates will sell, and I am not sure others haven't a price—' staring from face to face.

"Paine, you're drunk!"

"Am I? Then I'll say what I would never dare to sober—I'll say, gentlemen, that you disgust me, that you are breaking down all that is decent in our Congress, that you are ready to sell, yes, damn it, ready to sell, and that when you lose Washington, you lose the war—"

The next night, someone tried to kill him, a pistol snapping and missing fire, and a week later a note that said politely that some things are spoken of, some not. But Rush sought him out in a tavern and said:

"Don't misjudge us, Paine. We aren't traitors, believe me."

"But you would rather see me dead?"

"What do you mean?"

Paine told him, and Rush's face clouded and darkened. He assured Paine that he knew nothing about the attempt. "We are not assassins," he said grimly.

In the streets of York, one day, he meet Irene Roberdeau. She greeted him warmly and seemed genuinely pleased to see him. She and her uncle were stopping at the Double Coach, and he walked there with her, telling her briefly what he had done since he had last seen her.

"You will never rest," she said. "You will never have peace, Tom."

"I suppose not."

She told him that she was engaged to be married—when they reoccupied Philadelphia. He nodded, and she wondered from his face whether it mattered at all to him.

"We will take Philadelphia again?" she asked.

"I am sure we will."

"Tom—"

He looked at her.

"It could have been different," she said.

"I don't think it could."

Work piled up as secretary to the committee. Again he was a clerk who sat up nights doing *Crisis* papers, yet somehow he managed to let his weight be felt, putting pressure on those he knew, speaking constantly of Washington's need, threatening, using himself as a wedge in the countless little plots, breaking them open, writing false orders to commandeer shoes and clothing, talking to the food brokers, promising everything under the sun, actually maneuvering a shipment of grain toward Valley Forge, drinking again, more than he should, writing words that cut like knives—

A change was coming over things. At the end of that winter of 1777-1778, the crucial point of the war arrived, and the Americans won, not through battles, but simply by existing as an army, as a military force. The tall, unhappy Virginian, who had failed so as a commander, proved his worth as a rallying point, and throughout that dreadful cold winter, he held a nucleus of his men around him. Perhaps if Howe, the British commander, had attacked Valley Forge, the American army—what was left of it—might have been utterly destroyed. But Philadelphia was comfortable, and Howe did not attack, and with spring there was not only a French alliance, the product of old Ben Franklin's careful work, but a reoccurrence of that incredible phenomenon, the American militia.

Once again the summer soldiers, through with their plowing, poured into the encampment—householders, farm hands, men and boys. The four thousand left after the winter at

Valley Forge became seven thousand, then ten, then twelve thousand. And as a nucleus there was the bitter, hard kernel that had kept alive in the hellish encampment.

Howe became frightened. Once he could have been the attacker; now he was in a position to be attacked. He marched out of Philadelphia, north through Jersey; and at Monmouth, Washington barred his path. Not for nothing had three years of war, three desperate, losing years, put iron into the ragged, lean continentals. For the first time they fought and held their ground, stood through the shot and shell and fire of a day's burning battle, and then lay on their weapons and watched a broken British army retreat from the field.

The war was not over; it was not much more than begun; but now there was an American Army.

Paine was beginning to understand his new profession, the skill called revolution which he was the first to practice as a sole reason for being. He had seen the people take power, and the means by which they took power; he had seen their appointed leaders, citizens whose livelihood was not war, rally them against the enemy. He had seen the counter-revolution rear its head again and again, in New York, in Philadelphia, in Jersey, and in Pennsylvania. He had seen the army split up into opposing groups, and he had seen staunch patriots eager to sell out to the highest bidder. And now he was watching one of the final phases, a cleavage between the people's party and the party of finance, of trade and power and aristocracy. And strangely enough these latter forces were united against one who was reputedly the wealthiest man in America: the Virginia farmer, Washington. First, it was a plot to deprive Washington of the command and give it to Gates; then, to dirty his reputation and split the high command from him; and now, lastly, a direct sell-out to Great Britain. England sent across the ocean a party of gentlemen with very broad powers; they knew whom to contact. Paine sent a messenger to Washington and wrote with fury in his pen.

A *Crisis* appeared in which Paine, raging mad, wrote: "What sort of men or Christians must you suppose the Americans to be, who, after seeing their most humble petitions insultingly rejected; the most grievous laws passed to distress them in every quarter; an undeclared war let loose upon them, and Indians and Negroes invited to the slaughter; who, after seeing their kinsmen murdered, their fellow citizens starved to death in prisons, and their houses and property destroyed and burned; who, after the most serious appeals to heaven, the most solemn adjuration by oath of all government connected with you, and the most heart-felt pledges and protestations of faith to each other; and who, after soliciting the friendship, and entering into alliance with other nations, should at last break through all these obligations, civil and divine, by complying with your horrid and infernal proposal. . . ."

Working underground himself, he fell deeper and deeper into the snarl. He hadn't the restraint to refrain from direct accusations, yet he could not unearth a scrap of written evidence to back up his suspicions of the plots against the revolution.

Not trusting Samuel Adams—sincerely believing that Adams and a good many others of the Boston crowd could be bought if the proposals were properly put, the price high enough, and the settlement such as to give them the positions they longed for—he could, nevertheless, find no solid grounds upon which to accuse them. And Richard Henry Lee, stopping him on the street, told him bitterly:

"You seem to enjoy making enemies, Paine."

"I have so many that a few more don't matter."

"A friend might help. A quiet tongue might, too."

"My only friend is the revolution. And my tongue wags like the tongue of any damned peasant."

"Just a word of warning—"

"I don't have to be warned, my friend," Paine smiled.

And then, hard on that, came the affair of Silas Deane.

As secretary to the Committee for Foreign Affairs, Paine had come, time and again, upon some very curious matters. There was a European firm called Roderique Hortalez and Company. He himself had had some dealings with them when things were most desperate the winter before. It was a matter of military boots for an army that bound their bleeding feet in rags and sackcloth, and a Mr. Steffins of Charleston said he might obtain a thousand pair of good boots—for a price. The price was a livre a pair; that was high, but in wartime one expects things to come high. Paine negotiated the deal, and when the boots arrived they proved to be of Spanish leather—and the bill was presented by Roderique Hortalez and Company. The company was already widely known among the continentals, but who had hired Mr. Steffins and who had paid him? Going into the matter, Paine discovered that almost all outside help to America—shiploads of wheat from France, flatboat fleets of powder, shot and cannon that came upriver from New Orleans, cargoes of rum from the Indies, clothing from Spain, dried cheese from Holland, even one consignment of Scotch plaid that had somehow been smuggled from the British Isles—all bore bills of sale from Roderique Hortalez and Company.

Too many people seemed to know all about Roderique

Hortalez and Company; too many who were unwilling to talk. For Paine to get details was like pulling teeth. Henry Laurens, the president of the Congress, an honest man trying to fight his way through a wilderness of lies, deceits, and selfishness, one whom Paine respected and liked, told him:

"What does it matter, so long as it helps the cause?"

"But the prices," Paine pointed out.

Laurens had smiled; that was some time ago.

From Arthur Lee in Paris came word that it was a probability, no more than that, that both France and Spain had made secret gifts to America, possibly as much as a million livres apiece. Deane was getting a five per cent commission on all sales through the company, and bills were being presented. Then, in a letter from Franklin, Paine found what he considered almost conclusive proof that all supplies were purchased with a gift of gold from the two governments, a gift handled by a mysterious and incredible person called Caron de Beaumarchais, incredible because he appeared to be the power behind Roderique Hortalez and Company, mysterious because the French government preferred him so, being not yet at war with England when the funds were advanced to him. A neutral power could not show preferences among belligerents, but an international concern could deal with whom it pleased.

To all this, Henry Laurens had said, "What does it matter?" smiling. Nations could very well act like children about international affairs; face had to be preserved. The world knew that the Continental Congress was perhaps the most impoverished governing power on earth, that it had hardly enough money to buy pen, paper, and ink for the sessions.

Thus, when bills began to be presented to the Committee for Foreign Affairs, they were politely ignored, recorded, filed, but ignored. One understood those matters.

"But did one?" Paine wondered.

He asked Roberdeau to arrange a small dinner at which Laurens would be present, and then he carefully led the talk to the subject of the bills.

"Why do you harp on that, Paine?" Laurens asked, somewhat impatiently. "Those bills will never be presented for payment. France is at war with England now and the goods advanced to us by Hortalez, or shall I say by the French ministry through Hortalez, are only a mere fraction of the military advantage France has gained through the years we have been at war. Franklin made that plain."

"Yet if Hortalez and Company demand payment, it would be rather embarrassing for France to insist that we had received the goods as gifts. Do you know what the bills amount to?"

"I have some idea," Laurens said testily.

"They amount to four and a half million livres," said Paine. "Beaumarchais can become a millionaire—we've paid double for everything, you see—if they present claims. Even Deane's five per cent would make him a rich man."

Roberdeau whistled and Laurens shook his head. "I had no idea it was that much."

"The greatest swindle of our time," Paine prodded.

"What do you propose to do?"

"Attack Deane before payment is demanded and what miserable credit we have is broken."

"You have no proof that Deane expects to receive a commission. First the bills must be presented for payment."

"Proof—my God, isn't it proof enough that Deane handled all the negotiations. If the goods are a gift, Deane gets nothing; if we are forced to pay, Deane is a rich man."

Hard on that dinner, the scandal broke. Beaumarchais, through the mysterious firm of Hortalez, flung his hand into the pot of fortune and demanded payment, and Deane came back to America to collect. The split that had been brewing for so long in America, between the party of the people and the party of trade and power, snapped wide open. Congress, writhing under the impact of four and a half million livres that could never be repaid, demanded of the French ambassador:

"Was or was not the money a gift?"

"It was," they were assured, but it could not be acknowledged publicly. The honor of France was at stake.

Hortalez again demanded payment; Deane appeared before Congress and smilingly asked for his five per cent. He was not afraid; he knew too much about Congress, too much about what went on in France with Arthur Lee and Franklin. When Congress refused to hear him, he took his case to the papers, attacking the whole Lee family, declaring himself the savior of his country and asking for justice. That was more than Paine could stand, and he wrote a furious, biting reply.

Deane claimed credit for the supplies sent to America. Paine opened the books of the Committee for Foreign Affairs and proved that the French and Spanish gifts had been made before Silas Deane ever went to France. Philadelphia began to boil.

And then the French ambassador, Gerard, saw Paine privately and told him, "This must not go on."

"Why?" Paine asked bluntly.

"For reasons I cannot explain. Certain personages are involved. You must drop your attack on Deane."

"And if I refuse?"

Gerard shrugged and spread his hands. "Do you refuse?"

"I am sorry," Paine nodded. "This thing we are doing; it isn't a little intrigue for the crowned heads of Europe—it's revolution, do you understand."

"I understand," Gerard said, and the next day told Congress:

"All the supplies furnished by Monsieur de Beaumarchais to the States, whether merchandise or cannon or military goods, were furnished in the way of commerce, and the articles which came from the King's magazine and arsenals were sold to Monsieur de Beaumarchais by the department of artillery, and he has furnished his obligations for the price of these articles."

Paine writhed and pleaded to Roberdeau, "Proof—if only I had proof." He wrote bitterly of Deane:

"It fell not to his lot to turn out to a winter's campaign, and sleep without tent or blanket. He returned to America when the danger was over, and has since that time suffered no personal hardship. What then are Mr. Deane's *sufferings* and what the sacrifices he complains of? Has he lost money in the public service? I believe not. Has he got any? That I cannot tell. . . ."

Gerard did not warn Paine again; he sought out the faction in Congress that hated Paine so bitterly. Congress acted, summoned Paine, and demanded whether he wrote *Common Sense to the Public on Mr. Deane's Affair.*

"I wrote it," Paine acknowledged.

In secret session, Congress attacked Paine mercilessly; he heard rumors of what was going on, but was denied all his pleas to answer the charges. He heard that the wealthy Gouverneur Morris of New York had said, during session:

"What would be the idea of a gentleman in Europe of this Mr. Paine? Would he not suppose him to be a man of the most affluent fortune, born in this country of a respectable family, with wide and great connections, and endued with the nicest sense of honor? Certainly he would suppose that all these pledges of fidelity were necessary to a people in our critical circumstances. But, alas, what would he think, should he accidentally be informed, that this, our Secretary of Foreign Affairs, was a mere adventurer from England, without fortune, without family or connections, ignorant even of grammar?"

Laurens told Paine, "Resign before they have a chance to dismiss you. God knows what is coming, Paine—I don't." And Laurens added, "I am doing the same, you see. They will have to find a new president for their Congress."

Paine resigned.

And in Philadelphia hell was brewing.

Only outwardly was Philadelphia tranquil, and even that tranquillity was fast disappearing. The Quaker city was a revolutionary capital, occupied by the British, reoccupied by the Americans. It was not only geographically the center of the states, but ideologically as well, for Boston soon cooled and the Massachusetts farmers, who had once ripped a British army to shreds at Concord and Lexington, had for the most part gone back to their spades and plows. Their cold, bitter Yankee sense of personal freedom was bound inextricably with their own rocky land, and their fierce individuality made them poor material for any other warfare than the kind they fell into instinctively, guerrilla tactics. That guerrilla warfare might have ended the struggle much sooner was beside the point; it was not being fought that way, and the Yankees drifted off.

The bulk of the struggle was left to the midlanders, Pennsylvania men for the most part, Jersey men and New York men, Connecticut, Rhode Island, Delaware, and Maryland regiments; and in the South, Virginia and Carolina men. But the core of the regulars, the men who starved and froze and thirsted, the few thousand who clung by the spare figure of

Washington in the worst of times, were almost all Pennsylvania and Jersey men. For them, Philadelphia was the altar
of revolution, and for them, the blackest day came when
Congress fled without even an attempt to defend the city.

The British, who considered the city worthless, since they
already held New York and could not afford troops to garrison both towns, had evacuated it with as little attempt at
defense as the Americans before them. Marching to reoccupy
the place on the heels of the redcoats, the continentals were
not happy or gentle. They wanted revenge, and some they
took. The city was dirty, littered, houses in ruins, houses
looted, the beautiful Philadelphia Chippendale, the pride
of the colonies, hacked and ripped and broken. The Americans walked back into the city with their bayonets bared.
Wayne, a hard knife-blade of a man, led the Pennsylvanians.
"A Tory," he said to a committee of important citizens, "is
a son of a bitch with —— inside of him." They were used to
strong language, but not that strong. They proclaimed their
loyalty.

"As I understand loyalty," Wayne said, "so I would make
you understand it—"

But to untangle the Tory from the rebel was impossible.
Of the thousands of citizens who had remained behind when
the British came, who was to say which was loyal and which
was not? Of informers, there were plenty, but even those
most bitter shied away from the bloody terror that wholesale
accusation would bring. The midlanders were hard men, but
not that hard.

And Pennsylvania was a democracy. Of all the countries
that made up the union, Pennsylvania was the nearest to a
government of workers and farmers—militant workers and
farmers who had framed their own liberal constitution, their
own single-house form of government in the days when the

war started. The backbone of this group were the leather-
clad frontiersmen who had sworn that they would have a
thing or two to say with their long rifles before the aristocrats took their land.

Into this brew was flung the Silas Deane affair—to split it
wide open.

Roberdeau showed Paine a letter, addressed to Robert
Morris, who had lately cornered the flour market of the midlands. The letter had come to Roberdeau through means he
was not anxious to disclose; there were ways. The line he
pointed out read, "It would be a good thing for the welfare
of the gentle folk of the country if Mister Thomas Paine
were dead. . . ."

"If they wish to, they can kill me," Paine shrugged.
"They've tried before—"

"Don't be a fool. The time is over when you can fight this
thing alone."

"What do you suggest?"

Roberdeau suggested that they show their hand. He offered his house for a meeting place. He knew a few who
could be trusted, and Paine knew a few. Tomorrow night,
he said.

"Tomorrow night," Paine agreed. He was very tired; a
man could take up a gun, preach revolution, write papers
pleading with his fellow citizens to support the war, unearth
plots, oppose factions, lose his reputation and his livelihood,
be hated and despised, scream aloud that men fought and
died, that Philadelphia did not exist for the sole purpose of
raising the price of food, clothes, munitions, livestock—but a
man reached his limits. It was not easy to know that people
wanted to kill you; it made him afraid the way he had never
been afraid on the battlefield; it made him afraid of dark

streets, afraid to drink too much, afraid to sleep in his miserable two-shilling room without locking the door.

The last time he had looked in the mirror, it was with
the sudden realization that he was growing old. A network
of little lines picked out his eyes and cheeks. That was Paine,
the staymaker. Irene Roberdeau was married and carrying
a child. The world went on, but facing him in his mirror
was Paine, the mendicant of revolution.

It was a good group that gathered at Roberdeau's house,
Paine told himself. A solid group, each person picked, each
to be depended on.

There was David Rittenhouse, the scientist and mechanic,
a person of substance, but nevertheless one who had worked
with his hands; there was Jackson Garland, who, before his
forge had been destroyed by the British, had cast forty-nine
cannon for Harry Knox. Garland was Scotch, thin and sour
in appearance, but a man with a mind, one who had often
explained to Paine his theory of the coming trade unions.
There was Charles Wilson Peale, captain in the Continental
Army, a painter of amazing skill, and completely devoted to
Washington. There was Colonel Matlack, a Quaker who had
decided that some things were worth fighting for, who had
said publicly that he would die fighting his own brothers
before he saw the Morris clique destroy the Pennsylvania
constitution. And there were young Thomas Shany and
Franklin Pearce, both captains and veterans of Wayne's
Pennsylvania Line. In addition they could count on the ac-
tive support of both Laurens and Jefferson, neither of whom
was present.

Roberdeau had wine and cake served, and then called the
meeting to order. The group was quiet, grave, and somewhat
bewildered; vaguely they sensed the possibilities and results

of an open split in the Continental Party, and for that reason they felt they were treading on gunpowder. Organized revolt was still a very new thing in the world; organized radicalism, splitting from the rightists within the body of the revolution, was entirely new.

Roberdeau, his fleshy face red and excited, suggested that Paine take the floor and explain the purpose of the meeting. To which Paine pointed out anxiously:

"I don't want to intrude myself. It might be said that I am the least of the company here. I feel—"

"Damn it, no! This is no time for hedging nor politeness," Matlack said. "You know what this is, and go ahead and speak, Paine."

Paine looked around at the others; heads nodded. Paine said, speaking quietly but swiftly, "I don't need much of a preamble. A time was when revolution was new to all of us, but we've lived with it a good many years now—perhaps not long enough to understand it completely, to know the whole devil in this broth we're brewing, but long enough to have some comprehension of its structure. Revolution is a method of force by a party not in power, as we understand it by the party of the people, which has never been in power in the history of this earth. When the thirteen states of our confederation aroused themselves to seize the power, the confederation as a whole was in revolt against the British Empire. That we recognize, and the confederation as a whole is now engaged in war with the sovereign state of Great Britain.

"That is one thing. But the same method of revolution was singularly applied in each of the states of the confederation, and in each of the states the party of the people fought for the power. In some states, the people won; in others they lost, but in no case was the issue clear-cut. The act of revolution goes on in thirteen lands on this continent; there is civil war everywhere; in New York a man takes his life in his hands if he dares travel alone through Westchester County. In Massachusetts, the Tories are so powerful that they openly paint their chimneys with bands of black to identify themselves. In the lake country the Tories and the Indians have allied themselves, in such power as to engage our armies in force. In the Carolinas brother fights brother, and whole families have been wiped out by this civil strife. No one who traveled through the Jerseys in the retreat of seventy-six will ever forget how the whole countryside rose against us, shot at us from behind their shuttered windows, let us starve, just as they let us starve in Valley Forge a year later.

"In only one place did the revolution triumph, instantly, decisively, and without doubt, and that is here in Pennsylvania, the wealthiest land on this continent, perhaps the most loyal, certainly the most powerful. If the midlands fall, then the revolution falls; and if the midlands go up in smoke, who will say that the Pennsylvania line will not desert Washington and march back to defend their homes?

"Though I don't have to remind you, let me briefly reconsider the revolutionary enactments of Pennsylvania. You remember how, even before Concord and Lexington, the working men of Philadelphia formed themselves into an armed citizenry. Alone, unskilled as they were in any sort of warfare, they might not have triumphed, but fortunately they were joined by several thousand hunters and homesteaders from the back country. It was by the long rifle and the buckskin as well as by the musket that we overthrew the anticonstitutionalists. The aristocrats gave way when we threatened them with civil war and when they saw our guns. We won a constitution and we won a democratic state legislature, and then, loyal to the confederation, we sent our men by the thousands to fight with General Washington. I saw that myself. I was at Newark when the Pennsylvanians held the rear, at Valley Forge when they lay in the snow and starved, but held; at Monmouth our buckskin men broke the British backs. And, gentlemen, I was at the Delaware in seventy-six, when Washington fled across to the poor safety of the west bank, when he ordered a count and there were eight hundred men—eight hundred to defend the future of men of good will and make a nation out of this suffering of ours—and then I saw something that I will not forget if I live a hundred years, I saw the working men of Philadelphia, twelve hundred strong, march up from the city and hold the Delaware line until Sullivan joined with Washington. Six months before, the Associators ran away, and that was to the shame of no one; it takes six months of hell to put iron into a man's soul, and when they marched up out of Philadelphia again, the clerks and masons and smiths and millers, weavers, mercers—they were different. Pennsylvania gave freely, and now we have our deserts.

"Congress fled and gave our city to the British and Tories. We have it back so that it can become the speculator's dream, so that Deane can fleece us, so that Morris can corner flour, so that Graves can run up the price of tobacco twenty-two dollars a barrel, so that Jamison can pile up his wool on the river front while the army freezes, so that Mr. Jamie Wilson, whom you know as well as I, can corner a million dollars' worth of back-country land—easy enough with the woodsmen away fighting—and not content with that, attack everything the people of this state have fought for through his rotten and seditious paper, the *Packet*. And he has as his good ally, the equally vicious *Evening Post*. All this, gentlemen, is not a matter of chance, but a concerted attack against the revolution in Pennsylvania. The so-called Republican

Society of Mr. Robert Morris is about as much republican as George the Third; its sole purpose, as far as I can see, is to destroy the constitution in which lies the power of the people.

"I think I have talked too much, gentlemen. There is the situation which I was trying to fight alone, and which General Roberdeau thinks we can fight better together. I leave the rest to you—"

No applause; he sat down in silence, all of them watching him. He was very tired, and his head ached. Matlack said thoughtfully, thinking aloud more than anything else:

"Whatever we do, we will need the means of force. Washington—"

"I think he'll be with us," Rittenhouse nodded.

"Will he, though?"

Paine said yes. Peale said direct action: if men were profiteering, they would be brought before a tribunal, judged, punished. The constitution would be defended by force—

"Then that's civil war."

"So be it. They've asked for it."

"Support?"

"Bring this out in the open and people will declare themselves. Then we'll know."

Roberdeau sighed; he was growing old; peace was a dream now. Worried, Rittenhouse said they must move cautiously, cautiously.

"To hell with that!"

"Bloodshed—"

"They've asked for it," Garland said harshly. Most of them took that stand; they had been with the army; when campaigning started, they would be with the army again. But, Paine pointed out, this thing must come of the people. Peale suggested a mass meeting, and Roberdeau said he would organize it. A vote was taken, and the others agreed to the method.

They shook hands and each went home. No one smiled. It was something a long time coming, and now that it was here, they were not happy.

The meeting was held at the State House, in the courtyard. Several hundred people attended, and both Paine and Roberdeau spoke. Matlack moved for the establishment of a Committee of Inspection, and an open vote was taken. Paine was the first elected, then Colonel Smith, a solid supporter of the Constitution, a militiaman and therefore from the people. Rittenhouse, Matlack, and Peale finished the roster. The crowd was grim and earnest. The Republican Society had tried heckling, but the crowd was too somber for that, and it was only by the efforts of Rittenhouse and Roberdeau that violence was avoided.

The next day Peale and Paine dined with Captain Hardy, in command of a company of Pennsylvania regulars, temporarily bivouacked in the city. Peale explained what was coming. "I'm afraid of the mob," he said. "If your men support us—"

At first, Hardy refused. It was not in his province. If Wayne agreed—

"But there's no time for that!"

They argued for an hour, and then Hardy agreed to put it up to the men. Both Paine and Peale spoke, and the troops, after some consultation among themselves, agreed to support them.

In a way, war had been declared in Philadelphia.

The city knew. It was like an armed camp. Men kept their muskets at hand; mobs roamed the streets; there was work

for Peale's company of troops. The Committee of Inspection
set up its tribunal, and merchant after merchant was hauled
before it, ordered to explain their business, ordered to produce books and vouchers. A Mr. Donny was found to have
thirty-six hundred pairs of shoes in his warehouse, purchase
price averaging eleven dollars, asking price, sixty dollars.
Paine prepared the evidence carefully. A Mr. Solikoff, a mysterious gentleman of Baltimore, was found to be Morris's
partner in cornering the flour market. Indictments were
drawn up.

The *Philadelphia Post* had a rush of courage and attacked
Paine more scathingly and filthily than ever before. Paine
would have let the matter pass. "It's not the first time," he
explained.

But they were out in the open now. Matlack had the *Post*
building surrounded by soldiers, and Towne, the publisher,
was asked whether he would like to hang by the neck for a
while. The warning was enough.

"I don't like that," Rittenhouse said. "Freedom of the
press—"

But the committee assured him that once the revolution
had triumphed, there would be time enough for freedom of
the press.

The committee had no power to punish, but it had a tremendous power for intimidation, and it was solidly sup-
ported by the rank and file of Philadelphia. It stored up its
evidence for the coming election, and at a great public mass
meeting, it presented its case against Morris. The following
day, thoroughly frightened, Morris let his corner on flour
fall to pieces.

From a meeting of the committee one night Paine walked
home, suddenly as weak as a child, barely able to mount the

rickety wooden stairs to his room. He lay on his bed, alternately hot and cold, trembling, delirious, plucking at his memory, whimpering sometimes, but too weak to light a fire in the hearth. All the next day he lay in bed in the same semi-conscious state, half the following day. Too many things were happening; for the moment Paine was forgotten. The tribunal sat over Philadelphia, and the city was frightened, angry, divided in itself. Mobs surged though the street by torchlight, and Peale's soldiers, spread too thin by far, tried vainly to keep order.

Roberdeau remembered the absent writer, and by that time Paine was almost dead, a haggard dirty figure in a foul and dirty chamber. When Paine regained consciousness, the first person he saw was Irene Roberdeau, and it was a dream, and this an angel. He said, "I'm dying—" but it didn't matter. He was too weak to feel anything but a lonely sort of happiness, only strong enough to resist Roberdeau's efforts to take him out of the place he called his home.

For nine days she stayed with him, an impersonal, competent nurse, and then Paine, who could stand it no longer, begged her to go. She went, and it was lonelier and bleaker than ever. When he got out of bed and looked into the bit of glass he called his mirror, it was not Paine who faced him, but a yellow mask stretched on jutting bones, hollow eyes, a monstrous nose, and long, scraggly, thinning hair.

While Paine lay sick, civil war raged in Philadelphia. He heard the gunshots of the pitched battle between Wilson's group and the constitutionalists. He heard, all through one night, the ragged sound of musketry, and wept like a baby because he was confined here, feeble, unable to move. And he was still sick when the state election swept the constitutionalists into a power beyond dispute.

Peale told him about it, and Paine nodded and tried to smile. "So long as we won," he said.

Another dark winter dragged through; it was seventeen-eighty; part of the Pennsylvania Line mutinied, for lack of food, of pay, of clothing. Five long years they had been fighting, and they wanted to see their homes, their wives and their children. Charleston fell. The mutiny was put down. Washington poured his heart into begging letters, and Paine read them. He was clerk of the Assembly now. Washington wrote, "My dear Paine, is there nothing that can be done, nothing?"

The election had been very decisive. With the constitutionalists in power, Morris, Rush and other leaders of the Republican party threw in their hands. The counter-revolution had been blocked and broken, and it would not rise again for many years. Paine had to live somehow; *Crisis* papers could be written and printed, but the people who read them had not a penny to give the author. It was then that Roberdeau and Peale had offered Paine the position of clerk to the State Assembly, and Paine had taken it. "I hoped to go back to the army," he apologized. He didn't have the strength; strangely, quietly, age crept up on him. His hair was graying, and the curious twisted eyes had a shadow of fear in them.

As clerk of the Assembly, he read an appeal from Washington: ". . . every idea you can form of our distresses will fall short of reality. . . ." To Pennsylvania, this was, when all else had failed; to the men who had taken power and organized the first revolutionary tribunal. "Such a combination of circumstances to exhaust the patience of the soldiery. . . . We see in every line of the army the most serious features of mutiny and sedition. . . ." To Paine, it was more than that, the tall Virginian pleading, "You, Paine, who did this thing with your pen—you who could talk to the men." He was sick, and his hand trembled. The Assembly sat with dead features; afterwards, he would get drunk. The discussion was hopeless; a delegate saying, "What can we do?"; another putting it into different words.

He had a thousand dollars in continental money. He took half of it and made the first step of reconciliation with the party of finance. Sending the five hundred dollars to Blair McClenaghan, dealer in tobacco and linens, a Scot who had a grudging admiration for Paine, he suggested some sort of moving fund for the relief of Washington. The Scot mentioned the idea to Salomon, a small and rather mysterious Jew who made his headquarters in a coffee house on Front Street. It was rumored that Salomon had broken the wheat combine, that he had knocked the bottom out of the price for woolen blankets. At any rate, he was involved with the constitutionalists, whose chief financial backing came from Jews.

"Do it," Salomon told the Scot. "It's the only thing—but I am not your man. I can spare a few thousand, five perhaps, but you'll need capital, a great deal of money. Go to Morris and Reed and Rush. I think they'll go in."

"After the way Paine fought them? It's his idea."

"After the way he fought them. They want it their revolution, but they don't want to lose the war."

McClenaghan went to Morris. Morris said bitterly, "I hate that man—but he's right. We're going under. If I can convince Wilson—"

"If you can—" the Scot smiled.

"Nevertheless, one day Mr. Paine will pay," Morris said grimly. "We won't forget."

The sum of hatred Paine had aroused was left for further

collection, and that night, on the basis of his five hundred dollars continental, the Bank of Pennsylvania was organized to supply the army with food, clothes, and munitions.

Paine wrote *Crisis* papers in the same white heat, but he had to drink more and more to put the flame in his pen. Twice he went off to the army; old Common Sense was thinner, more haggard than ever, but the men welcomed him and still flung the cry at him, "My God, Tom, this don't make no sense whatever." He explained patiently, again and again; they were his children, dirty, haggard, worn as he. Washington said to him, "Don't let me ever estimate, Paine, what you are worth."

In the *Crisis Extraordinary* he was at his calmly furious best, appealing to the merchants for a common front, begging them to believe that only in a democracy could a man of business have full play for his abilities. In the *Crisis on Public Good,* he begged the confederation to fight together, not to fall out among themselves, not to let regional differences turn them from the common enemy. He began to think of a national government now; what had happened in Pennsylvania was a warning.

There was a week of sheer drunkenness when his brain bogged down, when he felt he was over and through and could go on no longer, and then he came out of it, thinner than before, yet more resolute—with a scheme for carrying the revolution to England personally. He would go there himself. A *Common Sense* to the British citizen, the British working man and farmer.

Nathanael Greene talked him out of that. The Benedict Arnold affair had just run its course, and the British were burning with the execution of André.

"If they could hang Paine," Greene said, "that would even things. I am afraid we still need you."

Suddenly, not in a day nor a week, but suddenly enough after all the years, the war was being won, not over yet, no treaty of peace signed, but nevertheless won, the heartache and hopelessness finished, a British army trapped at Yorktown, the British cause in America torn to shreds, a French grant of several millions solving the financial problem, the Tories shattered. Then it was Paine alone and frightened, looking at all this, and wondering, "Where am I? Who am I?"

The props had been knocked from under him; always on the outside, always the man behind the scenes, always the propagandist, he found a time now when there was no need for propaganda, no need for men behind the scenes. In a victorious army, the pleading, exhorting figure of Paine would stir only laughter. His trade was revolution, and now he was without a trade.

"Go back to staymaking then," he told himself morosely. His friends, his companions were turning their hand to statecraft, construction; others were grabbing, because victory meant spoils. And he, who was so definitely not a statesman, had no desire for spoils.

There was a trip to France. His old friend and the one-time president of the Congress, Henry Laurens, had been taken prisoner by the British while sailing to Holland. Paine, who knew Laurens' son, tried to lift the boy out of his misery.

"It won't be forever," he told John Laurens. "There'll be an exchange of prisoners soon. The war will be over—"

Paine had a way with men, and the boy came to worship him. Then, when young Laurens went to Paris to help push

the French loan, he begged Paine to accompany him, and
Paine, who saw his work on this side of the ocean coming to
an end, agreed. In a way, it was a holiday, the first he had
ever known in all his life, he an honored visitor in France,
men of distinction begging him to autograph their copies of
Common Sense, making him understand, as he had never
understood before, that he, Paine, really mattered.

It was over all too soon. The mission was successful; everything, it seemed, was successful now, and Paine, coming
home on a ship loaded down with two and a half millions
of livres in silver, could not help reflecting on the curious
change in the little union of colonies which called itself
America. As for instance when he wrote his last *Crisis* paper,
just before the trip to France. No trouble about publishers
then; a dozen printers clamored for the privilege of printing
it. *Crisis* papers were safe investments now that the crisis had
passed.

They asked Paine to dinner soon after he had returned to
America, Mrs. Jackson, who had been Irene Roberdeau, and
her husband. Frank Jackson had no jealousy of Paine; he
said to Irene, quietly, "Why, he's almost an old man!"

Irene was still young and lovely. As she sat with her child
at her knee, she confirmed Paine's aging lassitude. He was
old; he was finished; it was only in a dream that he had
dared to love this woman.

"What are you going to do now, Thomas?" she asked him.

And he tried to smile his way out of it, implying that
there would be much to do. He was a busy man, he said, so
much writing, so many dinners—

"The revolution is done," Frank Jackson said, and there
was nothing for Paine but to agree.

"They won't forget you."

A sop to him. "Why should it matter?" he muttered.

"You look so tired," Irene said.

He was tired; damned tired and wanting to get out of this place and get good and drunk. Who were these people, and how did he come to be sitting there in their house? Who was he but a wandering staymaker who had been something else for a while?

"You'll need a rest," Irene said.

"I imagine I will," he agreed. After that, he could not get away quickly enough.

He was not even the clerk of the Assembly now—nothing, Tom Paine, former revolutionist, a little more ragged than usual, a little more empty under his belt. The expected thing after Yorktown was a spree, and he had been drunk for four days; but that didn't go on. You had to eat and drink; you found that shoe leather wore out; you needed a room, no matter how small and dirty and disreputable.

The loneliness was not to be abated. Roberdeau had gone to Boston. Greene was campaigning in Carolina, and when he wrote that it would be like old days if only Paine were with him, Paine thought ruefully, "Not like old days. I was needed then. I'm no part of victory."

Wayne was knifing through Georgia with the now famous Pennsylvania Line; the best soldiers in the world they were called. The years made a difference; Paine could remember five hundred of them by name.

Washington came to Philadelphia for a triumph, but it was a hollow triumph; his stepson had just died. The tall Virginian looked wasted and empty, and when he called for Paine, they were like two men left over. Paine was ashamed of his dirty clothes, his appearance, his mottled face.

"My old friend," Washington said.

Paine began to brag; he was thinking of doing a history of the revolution. Did Washington know how many copies of *Common Sense* had been printed?

"I know my own value," Paine boasted.

Thinking of how perspectives changed, of what a wretched creature this scribbler was, away from the campfires and disillusioned, mutinous men, Washington smiled and said, "My dear Paine, no one of us will ever forget your value." Why did revolution leave such a backwash? Everyone was looking for rewards, but how did this fit into a world of peace and order?

"Even Morris recognizes what you have done," Washington said quickly. "On two fronts, the home front and the fighting front, it was Paine who kept the cause together—I tell you that with the deepest conviction, my good friend—"

They parted soon after, and Washington was not there to see Paine weep.

A delegation of rank and file soldiers called upon him. Months and months of back pay was owed to them; would Paine be their spokesman? Would Paine organize their demand and present it to the government? No one knew better than Paine what they had suffered through the years of war; no one had been closer to them than Paine. His pen had flashed fire for the revolution, and now had it a little fire left for those who had fought the revolution?

"Our aims are being accomplished," Paine told them wearily. "Now you must wait. Any sort of demands backed by force would be close to sedition—"

The soldiers stared at him dumbfounded.

He took the case to Robert Morris, the minister of finance. "Of course, their claims are just." he pointed out to Morris.

No one could say otherwise. But was this the time? Could Morris do something?

"Something, naturally," Morris said. It seemed so long ago that they were fighting each other. "These men are deserving, they will be paid," Morris assured Paine. "You were right not to encourage sedition. If the war may be considered won, then certain legal practices must be observed—"

Thoughtfully, Morris said, "You could turn your very considerable writing ability to our use, Paine. The government could be made to realize—"

"I didn't come for that."

"No, merely a thought, let us leave it in a place where we can take it up again." After a moment, Morris said, "There is no reason why we should be enemies."

Paine nodded and left; of course, no reason. Revolution and counter-revolution were done now. Men turned their hands to reasonable things.

Some writing, drawing pay from a government that no longer needed him, a new suit of clothes, a piece explaining the revolution to Europe, an emasculated piece, another *Crisis* with a touch of the old fire—why isn't peace formalized?

A few weeks with Kirkbride. Old soldiers dropped in; they talked of a thousand years ago, when they marched from Hackensack to the Delaware; but there was another trend of talk. The future bulked bright and large in America.

But how for him?

Desperately, he tried to interest himself in the future of America, the spoils and the glory, the boasting and memories, the speculations, the coming boom, the pride of being a free citizen in a great republic.

"Where freedom is not, there is my country," he had said once.

The peace came; America strutted like a peacock, free and independent. Fireworks and flag-waving and speeches and banquets and glory without end.

A tired Englishman who was once a staymaker, among other things, wrote:

"The times that tried men's souls are over—and the greatest and completest revolution the world ever knew, gloriously and happily accomplished. . . ."

He might have signed it: Tom Paine, revolutionist at large.

PART TWO
EUROPE

11

GIVE ME SEVEN YEARS

Blake, the painter and the
poet, said to him, to Tom Paine, "They are going to hang
someone, and it might as well be you. They intend it to be
you. They've longed to put a rope around your neck since
1776. You can't bait the lion in his den interminably, and
England isn't America—"

"England isn't America," Paine agreed. He knew that by
now.

"Then get out of London. Get out of England. Dead,
you're no good to anyone."

"Run away," Paine murmured, and Blake laughed grimly.

"I can't laugh," Paine said. It had come down like a castle
of cards; it was the year seventeen ninety-two, and he was
Thomas Paine, esquire, revolutionist at large, packing an
old valise hurriedly, preparing to flee from London and not
be hanged—not yet. He was only fifty-five. He had said,
"Give me seven years, and I will write a *Common Sense* for
every nation in Europe." And now it was done in England.
He had written a book called *The Rights of Man,* but somehow there were not the same bitter, stubborn farmers who
had taken up their guns at Concord and Lexington. And
he was fifty-five and tired and running away.

It was still dark, an hour or so before dawn, when Frost and Audibert pounded on his door and demanded to know what on God's earth was keeping him.

Anything into the valise now; a copy of *The Rights of Man*, an undershirt, and a half-finished manuscript.

"I'm coming—"

"The Dover stage won't wait—and the hangman won't!"

"I said I'm coming!"

Then it was done now, and England had slipped back to what England had been before. The bright, quick flame of glory was over; the little plots hatched in cellars and taverns were over. The forty-two muskets in Thaddeus Hatter's basement would stay there until they fell apart with rust. The barrel of gunpowder had been rolled into the Thames, and the shipworkers and miners and weavers and shopkeepers would stare at each other with the guilty, ashamed look of men who had for a moment dreamed the impossible and dared to believe it.

"I'm coming," Paine said.

In the stage, lurching over the pitted road that led to Dover, Frost nudged him and whispered, "In front, Leonard Jane." Jane was an agent of the crown, one of the many sharp-faced men who made their way here and there and saw things; it was before the day of the secret service.

"And I thought you said no one would know," Paine complained petulantly.

"Well, they know—"

In the pale tint of the early dawn, and then flushed by the bright red sun of morning, he had to sit and realize what it would mean to die, to be stretched, hanged by the neck, to have that bit of doggerel shrieked by every ragged urchin as they rode him to the gallows:

"Paine, Paine, damned be his name,
Damned be his fame and lasting his shame,
God damn Paine! God damn Paine!"

In his rush of thought, he whispered to Audibert, "If they take me, go to America, and go to Washington who remembers me, tell him how it was here, tell him there's no difference, England or America, only the want of a man like him—"

They didn't take him, but only because they weren t sure of themselves. "Even here," Audibert said, "you can't arrest a man without a warrant." And something had gone wrong; when they reached the customs at Dover, the warrant hadn't come through yet.

The customs men searched every bit of their luggage, found Paine's book, and tore it in half and threw it on the floor, "That for the rights of man and god damn you!"

Paine forgot what it meant to be hanged and said, "Shut your dirty mouth," a ringing tone in his voice that harked back ten years. Paine had been a soldier, and his eyes flashing he said, "Shut your dirty mouth!" Then he picked up the two halves of his book.

They were locked in a room, the three of them, and down from the barracks marched a detachment of six redcoats to stand guard outside the door.

"If the packet leaves without us," Frost said—and then drew a line on his throat with one finger.

A crowd began to gather around the customs house, and soon they were screaming, "Paine, Paine, damned be his name!"

"Your people," Frost said caustically, "who would rise to the banner of freedom and righteousness."

"Poor devils."

"Don't waste sympathy on them. If we're not out of here soon, we'll require all your sympathy."

"What are they holding us for?"

"A warrant, what else?"

Then the captain of customs opened the door and said, "Only by the grace of God, Paine, do you leave here. Don't come back to England."

Then Paine's party pushed through the hooting, screeching crowd onto the packet. The anchor came up, and two barges began to warp out the little Channel ferry. Paine stood on deck.

"Will you come back?" Audibert asked him, as the white chalk cliffs receded.

"I'll come back. It will be France, England and America—and then the whole world. I'll come back."

Safe on board the Channel boat, leaving England, leaving the hangman and the mob, Paine reflected how easily, how insidiously all this turmoil had begun. Back in America, when the struggle was over, he had put the revolution behind him; he had wanted to be Thomas Paine, esquire, dreaming of something for himself akin to what Washington had at Mt. Vernon. He was not an old man when the revolution ended; he was only forty-six, and a man's life isn't over then. Look at Franklin.

There comes a time when a man wants to sit back and say, "I've done enough; I want to eat and drink and sleep and talk and think." There was one magnificent, never-to-be-forgotten afternoon, when he sat for hours in the warm sunlight with Franklin talking of things scientific and things philosophical. "Play with science," Franklin told him. "That's the new age, the dawning."

"I would like to play," Paine said, his eyes curious.

Well, he was deserving of it, wasn't he? Not that he had made the war alone; but neither had Washington, nor Jefferson, nor Adams either. His part was not so slight that he was greedy in asking for some small reward, in petitioning Congress to give him some sort of livelihood, since he had nothing but revolution, since he was a specialist in change, and change was over.

They voted him a little money and a place in Bordentown and another in New Rochelle. It was enough. He lived simply, some drink, plain food, a workshop—correspondence with the scientific minds all over the world who were pricking at the future.

"Thomas Paine, esquire," he signed himself.

It was to be expected that a man would change; the times that tried men's souls were over. He dabbled in politics, but in a gentlemanly way, the way Morris or Rush would dabble. And when he saw a beggar now, a poor drunken sot, an aging veteran, racked with dysentery and syphilis, a one-armed garrulous soldier, an artilleryman whose eyes had been blasted away by flaming powder, he did not say, "There, but by the grace of God, goes Thomas Paine."

But that was to be expected too.

And sometimes he was a little ashamed of these louts who came to his house and cried, "Hey, Tom, hey there, old Common Sense, hey there, old comrade."

Talking of old times, look what they had made of themselves! The old times were over.

Better than that to dine with Washington, the tall fox-hunter whose name was spoken so reverently now, but who had nevertheless not forgotten the cold march down through the Jerseys.

"Madeira, Thomas?"

"I incline to claret."

"But Madeira, Thomas, with all tne sunshine of the blue sky of Portugal."

Better to dine with Morris, Reed, Rush, now that old feuds had been patched up, old differences set aside; these were quality and these were the men who counted. They sipped their brandy and they talked of high financial matters, and they were the powers behind this new United States of America; and Paine was permitted to sit in and see what delicate maneuvering made the world go round.

A man changes; or perhaps that is wrong and a man never changes. Here, in this year of seventeen ninety-two, leaning on the rail of the Channel boat that was taking him over to France, away from an England that would have hanged him, watching the white chalk cliffs of Dover, he cast back in his memory and let the events run by, one by one, as they had happened.

There was the iron bridge, a scientific experiment—and hadn't Ben Franklin said that he had an eye and a mind for science? The bridge was something new in the world, of course, but a dreamer could see that iron was the coming master of man's fate. And why not a bridge to begin, so useful a thing, so common a thing? So he played with the idea, sketched, and made, in model, a bridge of iron. People came forty miles to see it. Anyone could see that the bridge was just "Common Sense," they said, making a poor pun of what had once been glory. The copies of the book *Common Sense* were turning yellow, stuffed away in attics and chests, but folks said, "Mighty smart feller, Paine. Thinks like a Yankee."

He took the model to Philadelphia and set it up in Ben Franklin's garden in Market Street. What a time that was! So many citizens called him Doctor Paine that he began to believe it—almost. He was toasted at dinners, luncheons, parties; four white wigs he owned, and his shirts were starched and faultlessly clean.

And once Rush mentioned, "How does it seem now to read *Common Sense,* Paine?"

"*Common Sense?*" as if it were some small matter that he could not easily call to mind.

"It was good for the times," he said judiciously.

"And what times they were, those old days," Rush laughed.

"At each other's throats."

"But now there's enough for all."

"For all, of course," Paine agreed.

Then he took his bridge model to France. Five years ago that was, 1787, Thomas Paine, esquire, crossing the broad ocean to France, not a bumpkin sick in a dirty, festering hold, but a gentleman of parts, philosopher, scientist, politician, financier you might say; first-class stateroom, walks on the deck while passengers pointed him out to each other.

His leaving America was in itself a reminder of the past; he still had enemies, enough to keep the State of Pennsylvania from erecting his iron bridge; and though he had hoped to go to France anyway, it was mostly bridge matter that sent him there. He had corresponded with the French scientists, spoken to Franklin about them, and he was quite certain they were the cleverest in the world, not to mention the wittiest. France would take up his bridge, then the world, then acclaim, then fortune. On shipboard, he felt youthful enough to have a mild flirtation with a Mrs. Granger of Baltimore, a flirtation which Paine pressed to the bedside with a grace and tact of which he would once not have thought himself capable. But why not? He was only in the summer of his life, healthier than he had ever been before, famous;

forgotten as staymaker, cobbler, excise man, but Paine the philosopher and scientist.

France welcomed him; old, imperial France. King Louis sat at royal court at Versailles. If there were mutterings somewhere, what had Paine to do with them? This was France, not America. Taking a hint from Franklin, he played the part of the simple but wise American, plain brown breeches, no wig, no scent, white shirt, black coat, black shoes, cotton stockings, a cordial, winning smile that made up for his ignorance of the tongue. He met them all, the politicians, philosophers, the wits and the fops, the scientists, the high lords and the humble scholars. To a man of talent, there were no barriers—and the French food! He would say:

"Ah, we in America eat, but we do not cook. . . ."

And why not England? Why not go home again—it was so close, and so many years had gone by? The bridge hung fire in France; they liked it, but not enough. And in England, too, old hates were forgotten; you might fight a people once, but you did business with them indefinitely. And wasn't it said that in England George Washington was a greater hero than he was at home in America?

Paine crossed to London.

Dinner with Sir Joseph Banks, president of the Royal Society, Marcus Hawley, the astronomer, Sir John Tittleton of the East India Company—each one shaking hands with Paine, bowing to him, expressing their earnest belief that it was an honor, "Upon my word, sir, an honor—"

And of *Common Sense,* "Vigorous, sir, vigorous and thoroughly British, reaffirmation of the ancient dignity of the Magna Charta. America rebuffed us, but there was good English stubbornness in the rebuff, and who will say that the

two countries are not wiser and more inclined to be one
when the opportunity presents?"

"One?"

"The war was a mistake. We are intelligent men, we grant
that."

How could he do otherwise than agree? Did they once
bring up the fact that he was a staymaker, that he had rolled
in the filth of Gin Row, that he had kept a tobacco shop?
They were too well bred for that. Their superiority was lived
rather than expressed, but so apparent that Paine, dazzled,
could only smile, drink more than was good for him, smile
and agree. You spent an evening with such men as these, and
you saw why they ruled—brilliance, wit, charm, elegance;
and perhaps you thought of the Massachusetts farmers, leaning on their big, rusty firelocks, spitting, or perhaps you did
not think of that at all.

And when he brought out his bridge model, there was a
chorus of praise.

"Trust the colonies to be a hundred years ahead of us in
inventiveness."

A part of Paine's mind thought, "They still call us the
colonies."

Then Thetford, and it shocked him that the old place had
not changed, not at all, not a stone moved, the furrows
plowed in the tracks of a thousand years of furrows, a crow
perched on top a fence where he thought he remembered
it perching so long ago. After America, this was entirely out
of the world, for America lived by change, tear down the
house and build a better one, tear down the barn and build
a better one, pave the streets, sewers? Why not? The Romans did it. A higher church and a higher steeple, a bigger
town hall.

But Thetford was the same, the tenant farmers brown clods of earth, not the tall, gangling, stubborn rustics of America, the new squire as fat and ruddy and overstuffed as his father, already gouty in one leg.

They didn't remember Paine; no one remembered him. The peasants pulled at their forelocks and said, "Eee, sir, thee be looking fur the Paine place?"

His mother was alive, a withered little thing, ninety years old, partly blind, partly deaf; she didn't remember him.

"Ah," she said, when he told her who he was. "Thee be my son?"

"Thomas, Mother, Thomas," feeling an awful sense of repulsion, of separateness, of having gone such a long distance that it was blasphemous to come back.

"Thomas—he be dead."

"Me, look at me, Mother!"

"Thee be Thomas?" so incredulously, rubbing her withered face, yet in a way, not surprised, not even troubled.

He supped with the squire, the boy who had once hanged him up by his feet, roast beef, heavy boiled pudding, big mugs of beer. This was the landed gentry that had once glowed with a halo not so different from that on Christ's forehead; you grouped them together when you stood rooted in the soil, looking up. Now the squire was so busy stuffing himself that it was all he could do to fling a word in edgewise now and then.

"Back with us, Paine—"

Carving a slice of beef and lifting the whole of it into his mouth, picking up a lump of pudding with his fingers and depositing it on the beef, then half a mug of beer drained down so quickly that part ran from the corners of his mouth, splashing over the napkin he had tucked into his neckpiece.

"Beef?"

Another slice jammed into his mouth, the long carving knife bearing the function of fork, spoon, and plate.

"Find the place different? Out in the world, scooping fame and fortune. What d'y think of the colonies, Paine? Whig myself, but can't stomach Americans, crude, Paine, too bloody damn crude."

And then another gob of pudding swimming into a mouthful of beer.

Soon after, Paine left. He had provided that nine shillings a week be paid to his mother for as long as she should live.

This was life as it should be lived; a man of wit, of parts, of philosophy did not remain in one place. Once he had said, "The world is my village, where freedom is not, there is my country"; and again the world was his village, and wherever witty men chatted over brandy and coffee, there was his country. He crossed the Channel back to France, and the bright life of Paris opened its arms to him. Paine actually became gay; scratch and scratch and scratch at the surface, and still you would not find the staymaker, the cobbler, the rabble rouser who crouched over a drumhead one freezing night and wrote:

"These are the times that try men's souls . . ."

In Paris, after these many years, he again met Tom Jefferson, not so young now—but neither were any of them, the old group that had stood together in Carpenter's Hall—but not so different, the long, sensitive face more deeply lined, the voice a little deeper, a little more puzzled when it spoke out at the world. He was genuinely glad to see Paine, and as they shook hands, Jefferson said:

"Tom, Tom, it does my heart good, it's a little of the old days, isn't it, when two friends come together? A man grows

lonely so far from home, the more so when he mulls over
his memories and begins to doubt them."

Paine spoke of his bridge, of his previous visit to France,
his trip to his old home.

"And how do you find it here?" Jefferson asked.

Paine shrugged. "Louis will make reforms—the world
moves that way."

"Does it?" Jefferson wondered. "Did it move for us or did
we move it? There were some cold winters then, Tom."

Then let be what may! He could recall how he was again
in England, looking in his mirror, telling himself, "I've done
enough, enough!" In August, September, October of 1788,
the social world of London opened its arms to him. Then,
at the close of the eighteenth century, London was England
as far as fashion went, and with the rumbling and muttering
in France, it seemed that London might very well be the
whole fashionable world. Four hundred years of sedulous
effort on the part of the British ruling class had made of
themselves the tightest clique of privileged titles anywhere
in the world. Society was fixed, glazed, and varnished, and
the only time the bars were ever let down was when a man
of talent became as much a piece of fashion as skin-tight
breeches or the Beau Brummell cravat.

And Paine was that. Burke adopted him; Burke, who had
once made the great speech on conciliation with America,
had a reputation to uphold as a liberal of a sort. Actually,
liberalism with Burke was a memory of his youthful past;
he saw in Paine the beginnings of a change in a thinking
man, a change that he himself had already passed through;
it was as ominous and as certain as hardening of the arteries,
and therefore he concluded that Paine was a safe diversion.
He had him to his country place; he gave him dinners, took

him to various iron works that might be interested in doing
his bridge. He introduced him to such great persons as Pitt,
Fox, the Duke of Portland—rivers of port, five hundred candles burning in one small room, great and beautiful ladies.
Paine was introduced into the exclusive Whig club of
Brooks's, the same Brooks's that he had stood outside of so
many years ago, his heart full of bitterness. His heart was
not full of bitterness now as Fox offhandedly begged him to
step to the tables and have a look at what passed.

Fortunes slipped across the table at Brooks's. Ten thousand pounds on the turn of a card, a whole estate on the
deal of one hand. Somewhere in London, poor wretches still
starved by the thousands, ripped out their guts with hot gin,
lived twelve in a room, worked for threepence a day; but at
Brooks's ten and twenty and thirty thousand pounds hung
on the turn of a card.

He recalled the slip of a thing at some ball—was it Lady
Mary Leeds or Lady Jane Carson?—who had said to him:

"Mr. Paine, do you know to what I attribute the success
of you colonials in the American war?"

"Indeed I do not know, madam."

"To your beautiful, beautiful, beautiful, beautiful blue
and white uniforms. I loathe red—and I told that to General
Arnold, to His Excellency's face, I loathe red!"

Then a disturbing element broke in upon the life of Tom
Paine, gentleman—calm, dispassionate letters began to come
from Jefferson in Paris, telling Paine how the French revolution had arrived. They became a canker that ate at his
soul, turning him bitter and sour until finally he gave in to
it and went to France once more—to see, only to see, only
curiosity.

Like smoke to a fire-fighter, that morning in Paris, when

he, Tom Paine, who had come from fashionable London to revolutionary France, merely out of curiosity, as befitting a world traveler and philosopher, walked slowly through the workers' quarters, saw the black looks thrown at him because he was so obviously an Englishman, saw the muskets in the shops, handy to the storekeeper's grasp, saw the Bastille which had been so recently taken by the mob.

It was like Philadelphia, in the old days, citizens grimly mindful of their responsibility, citizens suddenly aware that they were human beings and not dirt under foot. Smoke and fire to Paine, and he breathed it in.

And then the welcome they gave him, the people when they learned who he was, his old comrade, Lafayette, who was commander of the National Guard, saying, "Militia, Thomas, but you and I know what they can do," Condorcet, then still a person of weight.

Condorcet had said to him in his very bad English, "I tell you, citizen Paine, that the written word does not die. I sat the other night with *Common Sense,* and I lusted, I lusted, friend Paine. We are a good people, we French, we are a strong people, and uncomplaining. Civilization will not have to be ashamed of us."

"Civilization is proud of you," Paine whispered.

Lafayette gave Paine the great, rusty key of the Bastille, and the onetime staymaker held it in his hands and fought to keep the tears back. That was how it happened, so insidiously.

"Weep, weep, my friend," Lafayette said impulsively. "We wept at other times; we moved worlds and awakened the sleeping ages. What have we to be ashamed of?"

"What?" Paine wondered.

"The key goes to America," Lafayette smiled. "Give it to

our general." It still meant Washington and no other when they spoke of their general.

Paine turned the key over and over in his hands.

He told himself, "I am old and tired, and what have I to do with all this?" He lay awake one night with the old sleeplessness, his brain teeming with fifty years of not too pleasant memories, fighting himself, trying to find relief in a bottle of brandy, dozing a moment to dream of a Pennsylvania farm where love had come so briefly, asking himself again, "What have I to do with all this?"

And then, getting out of bed, he felt for the key; how had they stormed the Bastille? Little people did such things; he knew; he remembered how the people of Philadelphia, clutching big muskets in uneasy hands, had marched up to the Delaware because he, Paine, wrote something about the times that tried men's souls.

He sat in the dark and turned over and over in his hands the key that had unlocked the Bastille. Lafayette had given it to him to give to Washington; Washington stood in the clouds, and Lafayette was a leader of France, and he, Paine, in between, was nothing. But in between was the moving impulse of revolution, a force summed up in himself, a passionate preaching that gained neither glory nor distinction, but by the power of the written word moved worlds.

Asking himself, "Who are you, Paine, and what are you?"

Still, there lingered like a dream the fashionable world of London. Burke and Pitt and Fox were great minds, brilliant men; why did Paine have to make a decision between the poverty and filth of his former days and the genteel world he had tasted? Does a man go back and reach out for dirt? If he could see in this slow and orderly unfolding of revolution in France, the bright dawn of a new world, a brotherhood of man, then wouldn't the great minds of England see it as well? Civilization was reasonable, and France, England, and America together could form the unshakable basis of a new order. In England, they admired him, and they would listen. They would see that the revolution had to come, and they would give in without causing blood to be shed.

Thus reasoned Paine, a man past fifty who had tasted so briefly of quiet and comfort, writing to men in England, to Burke and Pitt bright, glowing letters of what had happened in France—

"It embraces a new hope for all of us. . . ."

"The result in its fullness, in its exaltation of the human spirit, will be shared by you as well as by the meanest chimney sweep. . . ."

"Be of stout heart. . . ."

And then he heard that Burke stood up in Commons and delivered so fierce, so heartless a blast against the revolution in France that it spoke more of madness than anger.

"And you will answer him?" Condorcet said to Paine.

Paine nodded.

So it was Tom Paine, staring at the pen he held in his hand, sharpening one point after another, breaking a quill, cursing with the ripe, rich Anglo-Saxon oaths that he had learned in the London underworld, pleading with words; unshaven again, a bottle of brandy next to him, Paine again would be recognizable to the barefooted men who had marched with him down through Jersey. He had taken a room at the Angel, an inn at Islington outside of London, and he had a book beside him, a book called *Reflections on the Revolution in France*, written by Edmund Burke. It was a book that attacked, not only the French revolution, but all revolution, all progress, all hope, all man's poor bruised faith in his ability to climb to where the gods sat.

Burke had said that man, as man, had no rights. Paine set himself to write of the rights of man, to tell what he had seen of the French revolution, and to explain it—justification, it did not need. He wrote furiously, hotly, angrily, as he always wrote before the battle, before the guns sounded.

And he was young again.

"Loose, 'e is," they said in the taproom down below. "Loose an' black."

" 'oo is 'e?"

"Bloody damn colonial."

"What's 'is grouch?"

"The 'ole bloody world's 'is grouch."

But when he came down, to stare at the bar, lean on it, stare at his big splay hands, order rum, more rum, more rum, they left him alone.

Thomas Clewes, heading a deputation of miners, came to see him, short, wide-set men, the grime in their hair, in their eyes, in their skin, talking a broad Welsh brogue, Clewes saying:

"Be you Paine?"

"I'm Paine."

"And it's said you're preparing an answer for that damned jackal Burke?"

"I am."

"We be miners," Clewes said. "We're looking for a way, a leader, and a means. Things are bad, and I'll not have to tell you how bad they be. What are ye writing?"

"A handbook for revolution," Paine smiled.

"And what's in it to set a man to thinking?"

Paine read:

"The foreign troops began to advance towards the city—" Paris, he explained. "—The Prince de Lambesc, who commanded a body of German cavalry, approached by the Palace of Louis XV, which connects itself with some of the streets. In his march, he insulted and struck an old man with his sword. The French are remarkable for their respect for old age—"

The miners, watching him narrowly, nodded slightly.

"—and the insolence with which it appeared to be done, uniting with the general fermentation they were in, produced a powerful effect, and a cry of 'To arms! To arms!' spread itself in a moment over the city.

"Arms they had none, nor scarcely any who knew the use of them; but desperate resolution, whenever hope is at stake, supplies, for a while, the want of arms. Near where the Prince de Lambesc was drawn up, were large piles of stones collected for building the new bridge, and with these the people attacked the cavalry. A party of the French guards, upon hearing the firing, rushed from their quarters and joined the people; and night coming on, the cavalry retreated.

"The streets of Paris, being narrow, are favorable for defense, and the loftiness of the houses, consisting of many stories, from which great annoyance might be given, secured them against nocturnal enterprises; and the night was spent with providing themselves with every sort of weapon they could make or procure; guns, swords, blacksmiths' hammers, carpenters' axes, iron crows, pikes, halberts, pitchforks, spits, clubs, etc., etc. The incredible numbers in which they assembled the next morning, and the still more incredible resolution they exhibited, embarrassed and astonished their enemies. Little did the new ministry expect such a salute. Accustomed to slavery themselves, they had no idea that Liberty was capable of such inspiration, or that a body of unarmed citizens would dare to face the military force of thirty thousand men. Every moment of this day was employed in collecting arms, concerting plans, and arranging themselves into the best order which such an instantaneous movement could afford. Broglio continued lying round the city, but made no further advances this day, and the succeed-ing night passed with as much tranquillity as such a scene could possibly admit.

"But defense was not the object of the citizens. They had a cause at stake on which depended their freedom or their slavery. They every moment expected an attack, or to hear of one made on the National Assembly; and in such a situa-tion the most prompt measures are sometimes the best. The object that now presented itself was the Bastille; and the *éclat* of carrying such a fortress in the face of such an army could not fail to strike terror into the new ministry, who had scarcely yet had time to meet. By some intercepted cor-respondence, it was discovered that the Mayor of Paris, M. Defflesselles, who appeared to be in the interest of the citi-zens, was betraying them; from this discovery, there re-mained no doubt that Broglio would reinforce the Bastille the ensuing evening. It was therefore necessary to attack it that day; but before this could be done, it was first neces-sary to procure a better supply of arms than they were then possessed of.

"There was, adjoining to the city, a large magazine of arms deposited at the Hospital of the Invalids, which the citizens summoned to surrender; and as the place was not defensible, nor attempted much defense, they soon suc-ceeded. Thus supplied, they marched to attack the Bastille; a vast mixed multitude of all ages, and of all degrees, armed with all sorts of weapons. Imagination would fail in describ-ing to itself the appearance of such a procession, and of the anxiety for the events which a few hours or a few minutes might produce. What plans the ministry was forming were as unknown to the people within the city as what the citizens were doing was unknown to the ministry; and what movements Broglio might make for the support or relief of the place, were to the citizens equally as unknown. All was mystery and hazard—"

Paine looked up at the broad, dark faces of the Welsh miners, and saw in their eyes a light, an almost warlike gleam that he knew of old. He went on—

"That the Bastille was attacked with an enthusiasm of heroism, such as only the highest animation of Liberty could inspire, and carried in the space of a few hours, is an event which the world is fully possessed of. I am not undertaking a detail of the attack, but bringing into view the conspiracy against the nation which provoked it, and which fell with the Bastille. The prison to which the new ministry were dooming the National Assembly, in addition to its being the high altar and castle of despotism, became the proper object to begin with. This enterprise broke up the new ministry, who now began to fly from the ruin they had prepared for others. The troops of Broglio dispersed, and himself fled also. . . ."

Paine finished reading, and the miners stood there silent, impassive except for their eyes—fire in their eyes—regarding him as they turned over in their minds what he had just read, stories current in the newspapers only a few months past; but how vastly different in Paine's account from the mocking, supercilious sneers of the British reporters! Paine saw, and he thought that they could see the turmoil in the Paris streets as the mob became something else than a mob, as they died and organized and found their own strength.

Clewes said slowly, "So that would be yer writing, Mr. Paine."

"That and more. Does it set a man thinking?"

"It sets him thinking of this and it sets him thinking of that," Clewes smiled. "But what is a man to do?"

"For the time being, wait. Have you any arms?"

"We be working men, not soldiers and not gentlemen hunters, so where would we be hiding muskets, Mr. Paine?"

"There's none among you can work with iron?"

"Aye, we have a smith or two."

"Can he turn his hand to a musket barrel instead of a horse's hoof?"

"That he might. But we be peaceful family men, Mr. Paine. We nurse a grievance, and it might be a small one or a big one, according to them what judge. What the Frenchies did is a matter of their own, and I don't judge a cousin of mine who took up arms with yer General Washington. Some say it's wrong for a man to go down into the pits for tuppence a day; some say it's right. Some say it's wrong for the man that raises the beef to starve while the squire that eats it is fat and red as a jack o' lantern. Some say it's not a nice thing to watch yer wife die in childbirth for want of a little hot broth, to see yer children's bellies blow up, and others say it's something that has always been and always will be. To my mind, there were some free men on these islands once, and there might be again."

"There might be," Paine said evenly.

"Then we'll be waiting, and who knows but that the smiths might not turn their hands to this and that."

So he was in it again, neck deep, and again when he walked the streets—of London this time—it was with the knowledge that many men might sleep better if Tom Paine were dead. The book was finished and published, dedicated to George Washington, titled *The Rights of Man*. Actually, the publication came about without too much difficulty, with

less than had attended *Common Sense*, considering that this
was London and not Philadelphia. The first printing, under-
taken by a Mr. Johnson of St. Paul's Churchyard, was suddenly indignantly thrust back at Paine, Johnson exclaiming:

"My God, sir, this is treason, treason pure and simple!"

"And you've just discovered that," Paine smiled. "Here
the book is set and gone to press, a thousand sheets folded
and dry, and you've suddenly discovered that it's treason. Is
that your publishing policy, not to read nor to understand
a manuscript until it's set and printed—or have you been
entertaining a little correspondence with Mr. Burke and Mr.
Walpole about my scribbling? I think you're a dirty little
man!"

"I'll not be insulted in my shop, sir."

"You can't be insulted," Paine said.

Romney, the painter, recommended that Paine go to see
Jordan, on Fleet Street, and Paine did, with the preamble
to Jordan:

"It's probably treason, sir, so don't print first and discover
that later."

"So you're Paine," Jordan laughed. "And neither horns
nor whiskers—I'm glad to meet you." Grimy with ink, thin
and hatchet-faced, he made Paine think, "In love with his
trade and ready to die for the right word. He'll print the
devil's manifesto, if he believes in it."

"Let's look at the treason," Jordan said.

They put heads together, and for a whole afternoon they
read. When they came to the sort of thing such as the following, Paine read aloud and Jordan pulled on his lower lip
and became very judicious:

"Titles are but nicknames, and every nickname is a title.
The thing is perfectly harmless in itself, but it marks a sort
of foppery in the human character, which degrades it. It re-

duces man into the diminutive of man in things which are great, and the counterfeit of women in things which are little. . . ."

"Treason?" Jordan grinned.

"Depending how you look at it." Paine felt more alive, more vital than at any time in the past eight years. He did not reflect that he had become in thought as well as in practice, a professional revolutionist, and that there was no other real happiness for himself than the plying of his trade; he only knew that he was in the rat trap of London, that soon he would be a hunted man, and that he minded the prospect not at all.

"I like this," Jordan chuckled, and read: "Toleration is not the *opposite* of Intolerance, but is the *counterfeit* of it. Both are despotisms. The one assumes to itself the right of withholding Liberty of Conscience, and the other of granting it. The one is the Pope armed with fire and faggot, and the other is the Pope selling or granting indulgences. The former is Church and State, and the latter is Church and traffic.

"But Toleration may be viewed in a much stronger light. Man worships not himself, but his Maker; and the liberty of conscience which he claims is not for the service of himself, but of his God. In this case, therefore, we must necessarily have the associated idea of two beings; the *mortal* who renders the worship, and the IMMORTAL BEING who is worshiped. Toleration, therefore, places itself, not between man and man, nor between Church and Church, nor between one denomination of religion and another, but between God and man; between the being who worships, and the BEING who is worshiped and by the same act of assumed authority by which it tolerates man to pay his worship, it presumptuously and blasphemously sets itself up to tolerate the Almighty to receive it.

"Were a Bill brought into any Parliament, entitled, '*An Act to tolerate or grant liberty to the Almighty to receive the worship of a Jew or a Turk*,' or '*to prohibit the Almighty from receiving it*,' all men would startle and call it blasphemy. There would be an uproar. The presumption of toleration in religious matters would then present itself unmasked; but the presumption is not the less because the name of 'Man' only appears to those laws, for the associated idea of the *worshiped* and the *worshiper* cannot be separated. Who then art thou, vain dust and ashes! by whatever name thou art called, whether a King, a Bishop, a Church, or a State, a Parliament, or anything else, that obtrudest thine insignificance between the soul of man and its maker?"

"Treason, very possibly," Jordan said. "Do you want me to publish your book, Mr. Paine?"

"I do."

"Then I say the hell with treason and God damn it! I like your stuff." They shook hands on that, and then Jordan, thoughtfully, suggested, "If you won't take offense, Mr. Paine, let me suggest an edition to sell for three shillings, the price of Burke's book. Wait a minute—"

Paine was staring at him, demanding, "Who can buy it for three shillings?"

"I said as a minor precaution, so that the wolves won't come howling before the presses are cool. You know how they reason—they'll see a good format and they'll say, well, the people it reaches don't matter, and at least that will give us time. Then, if you want me to, I'll put out fifty thousand for sixpence and see myself hanged—"

"If I could believe you," Paine said.

"God damn it, man, I don't intend to live forever! Maybe

only you can say what you put down here, but others have
thought such things, and if you don't believe me, you can
get to the devil out of here!"

Paine smiled, offered his hand again, and said, "I don't
think, Mr. Jordan, that any of us will live forever."

The book was published, and Paine was drunk for two
days; the body drunk, the smallness, meanness, wretchedness of himself apparent only too well as he lay over a table
in a tavern and saw exactly what was Paine, hated it, but
triumphed mightily and exulted over what he had done,
Common Sense, the *Crisis Papers,* and now *The Rights of
Man:* that was himself, that was the brief, immortal spark;
that turned empires upside down and gave man hope and
brought him face to face with God. Drunk and howling foul
songs, he was found by Blake, the poet, Romney, the painter,
the former demanding of him:

"Paine, my God, what has gotten into you?"

"Glory! Glory!"

"Paine, get out of this stinkhole!"

"Glory! Glory! Glory!"

Blake took him home, gave him a bath, preached to him
and confided, "Paine, you and I are much the same—that
way is no good, I tell you, no good." He had met Blake some
months ago, spent an evening talking to him and telling
tales of the revolution in America. Blake liked him, and
after that they were together a good deal, Blake, Romney,
Sharp the engraver, Hull, Barlow, Frost, and Audibert,
friends of Blake, friends of Romney, curious misfit liberals
in the fashionable world of eighteenth-century London. Now
Blake read him poetry in his soft, deep voice, while Paine
sighed, "Glory, glory, glory—"

He came to Jordan the next day and said, "Let me smell the ink—let me get a hand on the presses."

The new books were stacked already, one hundred in a pile. All over the world, in England, in France, in America, the good smell of printer's ink was the same. Jordan described the selling, slow at first, mostly across the stands of his own shop; but it was picking up—three hundred copies to Wales, that at three shillings. "Have three hundred people in Wales three shillings to spend on a book?" Jordan asked.

There were a thousand of the cheap edition that crawled into Scotland; a sheriff, out from Carlisle, got two hundred, and that was before they were judged treasonable. But the sheriff had a nose for that sort of thing, and what else were you to say of something entitled *Rights of Man?* But a thousand got through and then two thousand more, and then it was set in Edinburgh by Thatcher McDowell, pirated, you might say, thirty thousand run off on cheap paper—was it any wonder that the mayor of Glasgow screamed that every Gillie in the hills, every weaver, every hand at a mill, and every smith's apprentice was reading a piece of treasonable filth called *Rights of Man?*

They took out three thousand words and printed it on scrap and waste in Cardiff—a thousand copies to go into the mines in a man's breeches.

London began to eat the three-shilling edition; every fop had it—for grins and wit and the sauce that could be flung at this man, Paine. " 'Od's blood," they would say. "Listen to the beast go at the pater!" Walpole had it, Pitt had it, Burke and Fox—and they didn't joke. At White's, the Duke of Devonshire, who lived more of his ducal life at the gambling tables than anywhere else, kept an open copy of Paine's book beside him, tearing leaves from it whenever he needed to light his pipe. Lord Grenville, the Foreign Secretary, read the book, tore it to shreds, and made a mental note to hang the writer. But the Tory government, after they had collectively flushed through their first passion of rage, held a meeting at which Pitt arose and said firmly, thinking perhaps of his father, who had not desired to lose America, or thinking perhaps only of the Tory government:

"For the time being, gentlemen, we will do nothing at all. A book, even a scurrilous rag, which costs three shillings can do no harm unless we publicize it enough to make three shillings a price that must be paid. . . ."

In that they were wrong. Jordan told Paine, "Nothing can account for the way the expensive edition is going. I've published books long enough to know the size of the fashionable reading public here—even taking into account the politicians who read it as a chore. There's a new audience here, an audience that never read a book before, an audience that's reaching into its pockets and somehow finding three shillings. . . ."

A weaver, Angus Grey, sought Paine out and said, "And what would you think of weavers, Mr. Paine?"

"I've not thought of them. Who are you?"

"Nobody that matters," the man said—ill-dressed, gaunt, dark-eyed, licking his lips slowly and purposefully. "But we have been reading your book and we have a mind to set things right. If we had a weapon or two, a musket or a little pistol, would there—" He let the question hang in the air.

"There might be," Paine said.

"And when, Mr. Paine?"

"When the time comes," Paine said. What more could he say? What more could he say to any of them who approached him, to any of the pinched, starved faces that hungered for

a utopia they found in a book, a utopia of which America
was the living proof.

And then ten, twenty, fifty thousand of the cheap edition
disappeared into the gaping maw of London, Manchester,
Sheffield, Liverpool . . . a fire was burning under England
and the muffled reverberations began to be felt.

It came down like a pack of cards, and in the gray of dawn
he ran away. It came tumbling down upon his head because
he had not understood that no one thing, no one man, no
one cause can move the world. When he wrote *Common
Sense,* he told a people already stirred to war, already fiercely
indignant, with arms in their hands, why they had roused
themselves in their wrath, why they should go on fighting,
and what they were fighting for. They had behind them a
hundred years of armed independence, factual if not political; they had fought the Indians and they had fought the
French, and they lived by their arms—and, for the most part,
they were religious dissenters, Methodists, Puritans, Congregationalists, even the Catholics and Jews among them had
fled to America for freedom.

With *The Rights of Man,* it was different; he flung that at
the heads of a people totally unprepared, a people who in
many cases imagined themselves in possession of a mythical
freedom that was in no way actual, but existed in song and
story and legend as the possession of every Englishman.

They were not armed, they were not prepared, they were
not religious dissenters; they looked at his book, yearned for
freedom, and then went back to their work, their slums, and
their gin-mills—and those few who had a germ of organization, the broad-faced miners of Wales, the weavers in the
northern counties, the ironworkers——those few pondered
their copies of Paine's book, counted their bullets, and then,

frightened, buried their muskets and did nothing—and when they heard that Paine had fled from England, even their dreams stopped.

His initial mistake—afterwards he realized that—was his first return to France. Then the idea, the vague shape, the conception so huge that he had hardly dared to think of it until now, fixed itself in his mind as a reality; a united states of Europe allied with a united states of America, a brotherhood of man that at the most would take seven years to accomplish, and eventually, possibly before the end of the eighteenth century, would spread over the entire world. It would be a people's government for the people, a government to see that no man starved and no man wanted, to see that hate and misery and crime disappeared through education and enlightenment, to see the iron grip of organized religion loosened, replaced by a gentle, deistic creed wherein the brotherhood of man turned its face to the singleness and goodness of God, a creed without hate or rancor or superstition. There would be an end of war, an end of kings and despots. Christ would come to earth in the simple goodness of all men—a goodness he believed in so fervently—and all men, turning their faces to God, would never lose sight of the vision.

That was Paine's dream, his conception—and one so awful and terrible and wonderful in its implications that he hardly dared speak it fully, even to himself. It depended on too much, the course of revolution in France, his power to sway men with the written word, the course of the post-revolutionary world in America—and finally the revolution in England.

He recalled that he had crossed to France again, further arousing the suspicion of the Tories, who were beginning to believe that he was in league with the French. With Lafa-

yette he had discussed the organization of a republican society that would eventually have world-wide ramifications.
Madame Roland and Condorcet had joined in the nucleus,
and Paine wrote a flaming proclamation of republicanism
that raged against the king's flight from Paris and called for
his abdication. The British Tories still held back, and Paine
began to believe that he could bring all his plans to a head
without ever rousing the Tory government from its apathy.
This was the first step—to the American republic would
be added the republic of France. He did not know that even
at that moment British agents were filing carefully written
reports of his activities. He returned to England then and
found that Paine, once deliberately ignored, had become an
apostle of the devil.

The forces of the government closed in slowly. England
was rumbling, but they had heard her rumble before, and
they judged the temper of the people well. If you crushed
a revolt, you admitted a revolt, and then the demon could
never be forced back into the bottle. On the other hand, if
you implied, intimidated, threatened softly, arrested secretly,
you could destroy a revolt before it ever realized its own
strength. America had taught them a lesson.

Paine's friends and supporters had planned a meeting at
an inn called the Crown and Anchor—where they would
drink to the second anniversary of the downfall of the feudal
system in France. A government agent saw the landlord, and
suddenly the inn was not available. Clewes disappeared; a
man called Luneden, who had approached Paine with an
idea for an unofficial militia group modeled after the Associators of Philadelphia, was found dead in a ditch near
Dover. Masterson, the ironworker, was arrested on a
trumped-up charge. On the other hand, young Lord Edward
Fitzgerald of Ireland, told Paine:

"Think on the green isle when you want for fighting men, Mr. Paine, and it might be that you'd find more than enough."

"Whatever happens," he told himself, "I must write, explain, make this thing clear." He did a second part to *The Rights of Man*. His bridge was forgotten, his dreams of scientific and social glory so much in the past that he wondered how he could ever have entertained them. It was the old Paine now, not too well dressed, his twisted eyes gleaming, darting rapidly as he talked, his broad, powerful shoulders bent again, as if the burden they carried was heavy, terribly heavy.

He wrote quickly, now that most of his doubts were gone. The first part had been a handbook for revolution, and this would be a plan—elementary and crude—but a sort of plan nevertheless for the new world he dreamed of. While writing, he knew that he was being watched, and he expected some interference from the government; when there was none, he was more wary than surprised. Then Chapman, the wealthy publisher, came and asked whether Paine would agree to his issuing the second *Rights of Man*.

"Clumsy," Paine thought, "oh, my lord, how clumsy." And he said, "I publish with Jordan."

"Jordan is nobody," Chapman replied smugly. "Jordan is a little mouse gnawing at the edges of the publishing cloth. A work with the strength and importance of yours, Mr. Paine, deserves nothing but the best imprint, the finest paper, and a binding a writer can be proud of. You and I are men of the world, and we know that the buying public, fools that they are, judge a book by its cover; the best Morocco, the most exquisite tooling—"

"I publish with Jordan," Paine smiled. "There are some

who have said, and not too quietly, Mr. Chapman, that my work touches on treason. A publisher of your standing—"

"Risks are a part of publishing. We champion the printed word, the freedom of the press."

"And the arrangements?"

"A hundred guineas for all rights."

"All rights?" Paine smiled. "No royalties?—Really, is my work worth so little?"

"I mentioned the risks. You will admit—"

"I publish with Jordan," Paine said.

"Two hundred guineas."

"Then my work increases in value. Would you also purchase the right to hand my manuscript over to Mr. Walpole once the price is paid?"

Mr. Chapman kept his temper admirably. "Five hundred guineas, Mr. Paine," he said.

"A writer's life is never dull," Paine laughed. "Go to hell, Mr. Chapman."

"Don't be a fool, Paine. I'll give you a thousand guineas, not a penny more."

"Go to hell!"

"I warn you, Paine, take the thousand. A man hanged by the neck has no use for money."

"Get out before I throw you out," Paine said.

That settled Chapman, but not other things. When Paine brought the manuscript to Jordan, the printer said, "I don't frighten easily, but things are tightening. Do you remember Carstairs, who took a thousand of the cheap edition for Scotland? He was found at the bottom of a cliff with his neck broken—mountain climbing— When has he climbed mountains?"

"Don't you think I see them tightening?" Paine growled.

"I'm not afraid, mind you."

Paine gave him a written statement, in which the author declared himself to be the publisher—and said that he and no other would answer for what *The Rights of Man* contained.

"You don't have to do this," Jordan protested.

"I want to."

"And don't walk the streets at night."

Paine smiled, recalling other times when that same warning had been flung at him.

Then, with startling suddenness, it came to an end. All the carefully organized revolutionary cells, miners in Wales, cutlers in Sheffield, the dock workers at Liverpool and Tyne, the potters and the wheelwrights—all these who had looked for Paine's leadership were cracked wide open by the government, before he had had a chance to call a congress, to order a rising of militia, before the thin threads of revolution were even in shape to be drawn together. Then as an anticlimax, there came a message from Jordan.

Paine went as quickly as he could. He had just heard of the arrest of the leaders of four of the cells; he was ready for anything, but he could not smile when the tall printer showed him an order commanding him, Jordan, to appear at the Court of King's Bench. The charge was treason to the Crown, as of the publication of a criminal book called *Rights of Man*.

"I'll answer it," Paine said.

"You will not," Jordan told him firmly. "If they hang you, that's the end of everything; if they hang me, it's much ado about nothing—you see, Paine, you've been here and there and everywhere, knocking about, and as you say, the world is your village. But I'm an Englishman, that's all, pure and simple, and I have a crazy liking for this little

island and the people on it. I see them going like horses
chained to carts, and I want to cut the traces. That's why I
published your book—and that's why I am going to die for
it, plain and simple, if I have to. You're the revolution, I'm
a printer; that's all, Paine."

Paine pleaded, but he had met a man more stubborn than
himself. He went to his Whig liberal friends to plead, but
the few doors not locked to him opened to reveal bland,
ironical faces that told him:

"But really, Paine, you never imagined we'd countenance
revolution. Really, we are British, you know—" And advice,
"Get out of England before you're hanged."

Romney sent him a message, "They're going to hang you,
Paine, sure as God."

Blake wrote him, "Paine, for god's sake, flee."

He issued a manifesto to the cells that remained, and only
a dead silence greeted him. "This is the time to act," he
wrote, and there was only a dead silence.

The next move of the government was a royal proclamation which forbade all unauthorized meetings and all seditious writings. Anyone knowing of such and not reporting
them would be open to prosecution.

But the book was selling, madly, wildly, by the thousands.
In the small time left, Jordan kept the presses going day and
night; the written word, once launched, could not be re-
claimed, not by all the power of the crown. And Paine wrote
constantly, letters, proclamations, appeals—if the cells had
failed him, he would go to the people. And the people read
his appeals, whispered among themselves, and did nothing.
They were not the armed farmers of Massachusetts, but
poor, frightened peasants and shopkeepers.

Thus it was over. Blake, in an hour of pleading, convinced him that final orders had gone through; Frost came

with news that a warrant had been issued. And a messenger from France pleaded:

"See this, Paine. France needs you. In England everything is done, and when you are dead, the hopes of the English people will be dead, too dead to ever be raised, I tell you, Paine. In France, it is beginning, and when the name of the Republic of France sounds through Europe, the people of England will find their strength. But don't stay here to be hanged."

"Running away," he told himself. "When I could stay and die. But I'm an old man. In seventy-six, I was young, and there were other young men with guns in their hands—and I could talk to them. And where are they now?"

And he told himself, "I'll come back!" He swore to himself, "I'll come back—only seven years at the most, and there'll be brotherhood among men who have never known anything but hate and fear. The dead never come back, but I'll return. . . ."

All that he turned over and over in his mind, standing on the Channel boat and watching the white cliffs of Dover fade, on a fall morning in September, 1792.

12

THE REPUBLIC OF FRANCE

It was always the beginning.
The cold, fresh wind blowing across the Channel was a
tonic, the blue sky, the gulls, the sway of deck under his
feet, and the breathless exhilaration that comes to someone
who has narrowly escaped death. His mood changed and the
black despair lifted, and his failure in England took its place
in the natural order of things; for thousands of years of recorded history, it had been the other way, and a brotherhood
of man does not come in hours nor in days. He would return to England with a United States of Europe at his back,
and then the people would rise triumphantly at his call. How
long? Five years, ten years; he was only fifty-five. Always
until now, it had been training, training, and more training;
he was Paine, the champion of man.

He said to Frost, "Do I look old?"

"You never looked better," Frost answered, somewhat surprised, now that he had thought of it.

"Tired?"

"Hardly—"

"What are you afraid of, Frost?"

"A man doesn't miss being hanged by the neck by inches,
and smile at it."

"Don't be a fool! Your life is nothing, just a little makeshift that you play with for a while, a machine that you put to use. And if something cracks it, then it's cracked, that's all."

"I'm sorry I can't see things that way," Frost said bitterly. "That was my home," nodding over his shoulder at England. "Now it's gone, now I don't come back."

Taking the young man by the shoulder, Paine waved an arm at Europe and said, "That's bigger—that's all the world. I have nothing, not a shilling from my book"—what there was, he had left with Jordan—"not a penny in my pockets, just a rag in my valise and the clothes on my back. And I'm fifty-five and I'm not afraid."

As they made the coast of France, one of those quick, dark Channel storms blew up, and it was raining when they docked. But notwithstanding the weather, almost the whole of Calais turned out to welcome Paine, a file of soldiers, fife and drum squealing first the *Marseillaise* and then *Yankee Doodle,* apparently under the impression that it was the revolutionary anthem of America. The citizens cheered and whistled and waved their arms at the astounded Paine, who had expected nothing like this.

"Vive Paine!"

The soldiers marched back and forth and back and forth, and Captain Dumont, half Paine's size, embraced him time after time. Then there was the mayor to give his embrace, and then four councilmen, then two lieutenants of the national guard. They informed Paine, first in French and then in very bad English, that he was deputy to the National Assembly—and from Calais, the honor, to them, of course, the overwhelming honor.

"I am most honored," Paine murmured in English. French, which he could hardly understand, flew about his ears. He could not speak now, and his eyes were wet; they wept with him, wept and cheered and wept again.

"If you accept," they said. "Naturally, only if you accept. The pay, eighteen francs a day, it is nothing, for you less than nothing. But to have Calais represented by Paine—"

He nodded, and they bore him away to a banquet they had prepared.

There was dead quiet at first as Paine walked in to the Assembly to take his seat. All eyes turned on him as news of who he was sped about, there was a soft murmur, hats were removed and heads bent in a completely French gesture of honor, even of worship, and then soaring acclaim as the voices rose. This was Paine and this was Paris and this was the revolution—and he had come home.

He sat down and wept, and all over the hall they wept with him. He arose, and they drowned his voice in another blast of sound—and then all order vanished as they rushed to embrace him.

That was one thing; he was Paine, the stepchild of revolution; not of the parlor variety, but a man who had given his propaganda to revolutionary soldiers at first hand, marched with them, fought with them, engineered a workers' revolt in Philadelphia, and guarded like a madman those liberties America fought for. That was one thing; Paine, who would make the world over, was another.

Paine who would make a world over could not speak French—yes, a few words, ask for a cup of coffee, ask for a piece of bread, a night's lodging, but no French at all to handle swift political talk, the rushing, frenzied French of Paris; and is the language of freedom universal?

In the days that followed he was to be reminded again and again of what Lafayette had said to him, not so long ago:

"Friend Paine, I think that you and I both were born too soon—and that we will have to pay for it."

But a man is not born too soon, Paine had smiled. The world waits for men and dreamers, so how can a man be born too soon?

Yet he thought often of what Lafayette had said. Paine's handbook of revolution was made in America, among long, drawling farmers who were slow to speech, slow to action, but not turned once they were on their way. You declared a liberty and you fought for it. Men died and men suffered, but the world became a better world—or so you hoped. Your comrades were Washington and Jefferson, and Peale and Anthony Wayne and Nathanael Greene and Timothy Matlack, and even the workers rising in a city were not a mob. And then you conceived an idea, a dream of a whole world a republic, and you tried to make a revolution in England —and you fled for your life but were welcomed in France, where a revolution was being made. It was still the beginning.

But was it? The Legislative Assembly dissolved, he sat in the National Convention. His friends were called the Girondins, liberals headed by Condorcet and Madame Roland; he was with them, naturally, they were his old friends, they had listened to his ideas, his orderly presentation of the revolution in America. Yet their stock was falling lower and lower as the Jacobins, called the party of the Mountain, gained a firmer hold on the poor of Paris, crying for their dictatorship of the city over the provinces. For Paine, it was confusion where there should have been order—ominous confusion. There had to be a representative Congress, regardless of the impotence or corruption of that Congress. He

didn't understand the endless ramifications; freedom was
freedom, and once you had gained power, it was a simple
thing to arrive at. And here was France being invaded by
foreign armies, being threatened by traitors within and traitors without, being threatened by starvation, fighting herself,
party of the Plain, the Mountain, Girondins, the left and
the right and the center. And why? why? he kept asking.
They all had only one enemy—power, privilege, aristocracy.
That must be crushed, and there must be only a party of
freedom.

Danton said to him, "The majority of the people are with
us, with the Jacobins—I tell you that, Paine; the left has the
majority."

"I have no quarrel with the majority," Paine answered
him. "I live for the majority of the world—and when France
is free, that will be another nation for the brotherhood."

As he sat in the Convention, he told himself, "I must
remember that Freedom is on trial." It was good, at first, to
see the galleries filled with the people of Paris; he hungered
to talk, dreamed of soon speaking French well enough to
speak directly to them, to the people.

Yet when the first decision came, he shied away from the
majority. They were with Danton, who proposed complete
reform of France's medieval, torturous judicial system, and
Paine could see in that only unending complications. "Con-
stitutional reform, not judicial reform," he kept harping. "A
free legislature can make just laws—"

Danton smiled and agreed, but nevertheless the motion
was pushed through under the cheering of the galleries.
Paine could not see that it mattered too much—complications, of course, but the thing was done—and the next day
he was horrified when Buzot, a Girondin deputy, trembling

with passion and fear, demanded an armed guard against the citizens of Paris—"The mob," as he called it. Thus Paine was inaugurated into the strange, complicated, terribly ominous situation of revolutionary France, so bright and hopeful in ways, so deadly and nightmarish in others. He argued with his friends:

"But the people, they're the basis of everything. Law and order, reason, of course, I want that—who wants it more than I do? But you must depend on the people, they're everything, they're the ones who take the guns in their hands and fight, they're the ones who work and produce. If you don't trust the people—"

"Well enough for you," they cut him short. "You know the American farmer, but this scum of Paris!"

"Scum of Paris," he thought. "That's all it is to them."

For a moment, he considered being on his own; after all, he was Paine—he was the voice of revolution and he called no man his leader, and what did language matter? A truth was a truth, and he knew—or forced himself to know—in his own soul that this Parisian "scum" were no different than the small, frightened people he had worked with and fought for elsewhere in the world. If he appealed to them, they would listen. Wasn't he coming to know the true heart and core of revolution?—the strength was in the people, the fury in them; but for the direction of it, there must be a plan, an order, and a final goal. That was what all the impatient rebellions of small people had lacked until now, and to formulate such a goal was his purpose.

Thus he wrote and published an *Address to the People of France*. France, he said, was not fighting for France alone, but for the coming Republic of the World, for mankind. France must be unified; France must be bold, yet calm and courageous. The world waits for France. . . .

Did the people hear him? When he sat in the Convention
again, he realized that even if they did, the deputies were
completely immersed in their own personal struggles. Who
was Paine? He could not even talk French. He sat helpless
while the shrill arguments raged about his ears, the Girondins calling for a government in which all France partici-
pated, the Mountain reaffirming the strength and stability
of the Parisian proletariat, the hot-headed deputies coming
to blows again and again, the galleries screaming, hissing,
booing, spitting, drowning out the voices of those they disliked, the whole impression being one of disorder, for all
the vigor and strength. When someone was good enough to
sit by him and translate, and when Paine saw a place where
he might say something that mattered, throw a little oil on
the waters and point them back to the fact that the freedom
of France was at stake, and when he rose, he was usually
ignored—or, if noticed, found the language a hopeless bar-
rier. If he prepared something and had it rendered into
French, the argument and debate had passed so far on that
what he said was meaningless.

Again and again, his instincts told him where he belonged,
with the Jacobins, for all their violence and extremism; but
he could not bear the way Danton and St. Just and Robespierre smiled at his ordered theories of revolution, his sys-
temized description of step-by-step procedure, always heark-
ing back to the struggle in America. They implied that
Paine was a figurehead, an ideal, but not a person to listen
to, to trust. Perhaps he was getting old.

He asked himself, "Am I afraid?"

He dreamed of having his old American comrades around
him once more, and then he returned to Madame Roland's
salon, where at least they respected him; even if they, in

their bright talk of a middle-class government of all France, foreshadowed their own doom.

Hope came again when the Convention named him to the committee of nine who were to frame a new constitution for the Republic of France. Along with him, there were Condorcet, Danton, Sieyès, Barère, Vergniaud, Petion, Brissot, and Gensonné. But except for Sieyès and Danton, they were rightists, Girondins. Danton could accept a place on the committee and remain with the left; but when Paine accepted, he cast his lot once and for all with the Girondins. For the first time, he said to himself, "I don't know."

But there were times when his doubts left him. Paris was not a place in which to doubt constantly; for Paine, it was a city of vigor, strength, and beauty; he did not see only the dirt of the people, the patched clothes, the way they hissed and booed in the galleries, their lack of manners and breeding; he knew that you did not put away a thousand years overnight. He saw their strength, their lust after a life just revealed to them, and when the republican armies swept the invaders back to the frontiers, he let himself be carried away by the general wave of rejoicing. The British expatriates, the rebels, radicals, poets and philosophers who had been driven into France by the Tory government, planned a great party at White's Hotel, their headquarters. Paine was one of the guests of honor, and it was a good feeling to go there and mingle with old friends who spoke his own tongue, Frost, Edward Fitzgerald, Carry Clewellen, the Welshman, Allison—

"By God, it's Common Sense!" they roared as he entered.

He had let himself go shabby, but out of his eighteen francs a day, he had saved enough for a new coat; no wigs in France now, his own hair drawn back and tied, and the old sparkle in his twisted eyes as Fitzgerald asked him,

"Thomas, will we be crossing the Channel the other way soon?"

"Who can tell?"

Fitzgerald had had something to drink, and his brogue was broader than ever, his light blue eyes dancing as he enumerated, "America, England, France—by God and little Jesus, Thomas, tell me you will be in Ireland next! Her green hills run with blood—I tell you, Thomas, land there and when you step off the ship a hundred thousand good men will be waiting to march with you!"

The military band blared and they stood to the *Marseillaise* bareheaded, and when they picked up *Yankee Doodle*, as tribute to Paine, he threw back his big head and roared:

"Father and I went down to camp, along with Captain Goodin,
  And there we saw the men and boys as thick as hasty puddin'!"

The punch was good, the rum better, the French brandy hot as fire in his throat. Paine got drunk, Fitzgerald got drunk, Frost too, and when Petion came to join them, they fell on his neck and kissed both his cheeks until he drew himself up to his five feet four inches and exclaimed:

"Gentlemen, for the dignity of the Republic!"

They drank a toast to the Republic, of France, of America —of the whole world, Paine perched on a chair and crying:

"Listen to me, my friends, my good comrades, I am drunk —drunk but inspired. I said once, not so long ago, give me seven years and we will usher in the brotherhood of man! My friends, I say five years and the glorious armies of France together with the glorious armies of the United States of America will carry the flag of freedom to every nation and every people on the face of this earth! Already we have seen the Prussian dogs flee like the swine they are; we see fat, half-witted George of England cowering on his throne, your own Louis abdicating to the people! Comrades, who shall say what miracles cannot be? Join me, I drink a toast to my good friend, my old comrade, that best of men and truest of friends, George Washington of Virginia!"

They joined him, but Paine was already so drunk that half the brandy ran down his chin. As the band again picked up *Yankee Doodle,* he strutted across the room, swaying from side to side—yet strangely enough not ridiculous, not provoking laughter even from those drunk, but rather pitiful admiration for a man at once so exalted and so forlorn.

He was afraid of himself, and he said to himself, "Tom Paine who never feared man or beast on God's green earth is afraid."

He was afraid because his body was becoming old and unwilling and tired, because his own dream of world brotherhood was becoming more precious and more real than actuality. Forcing himself to walk through the narrow, cobbled Paris streets, to go into the shops and into the workrooms, he could nevertheless not establish a kinship with the citizenry. He would say to them, "Thomas Paine," and they would smile delightedly, pour wine, cut sausage, and set out bread for him. A great gesture, because they were so close to starvation, and he had to eat a little, while they rattled their Parisian French at him, so quickly that he caught no more than a word out of ten.

They were good people, simple people, swelled with their own power because the power of little people was a new thing in the world, but a good, strong, sound people—and seeing that, recognizing it without reservation, he still could not put his trust in them—as once he had put his whole trust, life, and dreams into the hands of the ragged continental militiamen. The difference, the change was in himself; he feared the anarchy of the people, and preferred the order of the middle class; he knew that, and he could do nothing about it. He wanted order; he had the sense of oldness that hurries time; he wanted a quick, orderly fabric of republicanism to which one country after another might be added.

He had never been a man troubled by God or greatly given to prayer; his approach to religion was emotional, a fervent belief in an undefined deity, so composed of love for man and for all things living that he had never troubled himself with the nature of that deity. His business was with this world, and moving in a circle of atheists and agnostics, here as well as in America, he could afford to smile when hot words were spilled on the subject of religion; his belief was not subject to ritual, nor was it subject to argument.

But now he prayed, excusing himself with the knowledge that he was growing old. Death loomed up, and he didn't want to die. He had only begun, and it was harder, a thousand times harder than he had ever thought it could be.

Canais, the young disciple of Marat, came to Paine's lodgings and said, in very good English:

"Would it be presumptuous for me to talk about things that are none of my business, Mr. Paine?"

Paine liked the boy; he poured some brandy and nodded for him to go ahead.

"I've read every line you've written," Canais said.

"Yes—"

"And I would die tomorrow, content, if I could have written or done even a little part of what you did."

Paine fumbled his thanks; the boy's eyes were fixed full and clearly on him.

"So you see that I respect you, even as I love America—would you say that we are ushering in the citizen's century, Mr. Paine? I think so; I think that France can never repay her debt to America, and I hope that there will be a debt the other way. And I also say, Mr. Paine, that the world will never be able to repay its debt to Thomas Paine."

"And that is all?" Paine smiled.

"Not all. What happens to a man—?" The boy hesitated, disturbed by the thoughts that were crowding his mind. "What has happened to Tom Paine—if I anger you, stop me, throw me out and tell me that this is no business of mine."

"Go ahead," Paine said, miserably conscious of youth, vibrant, hot youth gone from himself forever, a boy telling Tom Paine what Tom Paine knew so well, yet feared to admit to himself.

"What has happened to you? In Philadelphia, you were with the people, in America—and who but the people made up your militia, who but the people starved and died at Valley Forge, ripped a dream of empire to pieces at Bunker Hill and taught little men how to fight on the green fields between Concord and Lexington? Have you forgotten? Were there bankers behind the stone walls at Concord? Did the rich merchants die at Monmouth Courthouse? Did your fine manufacturers and ship owners march up from Philadelphia to save Washington after he crossed the Delaware, or were they plain people, peasants and workers and clerks and small shopkeepers?"

"I remember," Paine said harshly. "Get on with what you have to say."

"Then are we so different? Is it that we're French? Is it because your militia drove back the German swine half-naked, and ours drove them back wearing blue smocks and wooden sabots, that they are different? Is your Boston massacre to be admired and our storming of the Bastille to be despised? For the sake of everything, Mr. Paine—come with us, come to the people and they will welcome you with open arms, make the world or else there will be no world to make for another hundred years!"

His fists clenched, his broad, powerful body stooped over, Paine stared at the boy moodily.

"It's no use, is it?" the boy said after a moment. "You are committed to your friends, the Girondins, to the bankers and merchants and all the apostles of the half-way, the liberalism that fears the people."

"I am past an age where I can enjoy anarchy," Paine told him. "We are fighting an organized enemy—and the people are not an organization; they're a mob. And a mob does not make democracy; a mob looks for someone to lead it, and if someone is clever enough, it can be led into the devil's mouth."

"And that's all?"

"That's all," Paine nodded.

Well, it was done, and he knew where he stood. He was getting old; he would go on fighting; somehow, things did not matter any more—and he almost regretted that he had not remained in England, as Jordan had. Jordan had been martyred, tried, punished, jailed while the man whose work he published ran away.

Paine was a sadder, older man when he stood in the Convention again. The question up before the house was whether the king should go to the guillotine, or be imprisoned until the end of the war—and then banished from France forever.

For Paine, the situation was complex and many-sided; and he could not agree with the simple reasoning of the Paris masses—that the king was a traitor, and therefore the king must die. Even if he could grant that the king was a traitor —and kings in specific and aristocracy in general had no greater or more bitter enemy these past eighteen years than Tom Paine—even if he could grant the accusation, he did not see that death must be the penalty. He knew that something inside of him had hardened and slowed, that the old fire was gone; he who would have seen every Tory hanged by the neck now grasped for the straw of reason. The king had not betrayed what he lived by. Once he had said, "We, Louis, are France," and that statement he hadn't betrayed.

Marat said, "He must be cut out like a foul growth!"

And Paine asked for justice, imprisonment now, a trial afterwards. He pointed out that George Washington, who was reverenced so deeply in America, would not forget the debt the colonies owed to France's king.

"And without America," Paine said wearily, "how far can we go? If men look for a brotherhood, will they be satisfied with blood?"

Thirty-six hours the question was debated in the hall of the Convention. Not in all the history of France had there been such high, tense, terrible drama as this, for not merely the king's life hinged on the final vote, but all the future course of the revolution. From the first it was apparent that the Girondins could not retreat, that they would have to fight, upon this issue, for control of the revolution. Christiani, a somewhat obscure member of the party, a mild man, gentle as a woman, said ruefully to Paine:

"It is hard to die for something one hardly believes in—but it is harder to throw away the last scruple. A wretch like Louis, who is better off dead, holds the destiny of man about his fat neck; and it makes one want to laugh at this life."

"You are not on trial," Paine protested.

"Ah, but we are—all of us."

And a letter to Paine, delivered in the Convention hall, unsigned, said:

"Citizen, for all that you once held dear, go with the people of France."

Like a lonely, lost man, he listened to the rocking currents of the debate. One does not understand; one sits, elbows on knees, hands cradling chin; one is alone and all that one has are memories. To Irene Roberdeau one says, Where freedom is not, there is my country. Arm in arm, one walks with Peale and Matlack—good comrades; then there was youth and fire and hope, and never the intrusion of doubt. One remembers and dreams, and then, waking out of the dream one comes back to the hall of the Convention in revolutionary Paris.

And hearing his name in all the melodious, frantically quick chattering of a foreign tongue, he seized old Bancal who was sitting beside him and asked:

"What are they saying?"

Duval had just spoken. Bancal translated, "That Thomas Paine is a man beyond suspicion will not be doubted. By the example of this man, one of the people, a long and a deadly enemy of kings and aristocracy, a defender of republican liberty—by his example, I vote for imprisonment during the war and exile after the peace."

In the roar that followed Duval's statement, Paine could hardly hear Bancal's voice, but saw the tears in his eyes and saw how proudly and calmly Duval stood among the tumult.

When the vote came, it was for the death of Louis.

The friends of Lafayette, men with connections in America, men who had a claim on him, came to Paine and told him:

"You can do this—because you are Paine."

"Because when we fall there will be only confusion."

"Because when Louis dies, it means war with England."

"Because Louis came to America's aid in the hour of her need."

Their plan—Condorcet's, Roland's, Brissot's—was for Paine to arise on the Convention floor and make a plea for the king's life. Tom Paine might carry the day; no one else could.

For all their arguments, Paine saw that the king's life meant nothing. The French revolution had split between the Girondins and the Jacobins, the right and the left, and in the middle was an aging staymaker whose name was glory.

"I can't speak French," Paine said miserably.

"Bancal will translate. The people will listen to Bancal— and they will listen to Paine."

"And to make it reasonable to myself—" Paine said bitterly.

"Only remember what Louis did for America." And knowing that they lied in their teeth as to their purposes, yet knowing there was truth in what they said—that in the hour of their need France's king had come to the aid of America— Paine agreed.

When Paine stood on the platform the next day, there was quiet in the house. Every eye was fixed on this man, whose name was synonymous with freedom and brotherhood; he, at least, was theirs, without subterfuge; he was the symbol of all they fought for; he was Paine.

And then he spoke through Bancal, standing silent, but with a forlorn dignity that rose over Marat's furious interruptions. Even when what he was saying became plain enough, the gallery did not hiss him; he was Tom Paine. He finished:

"Ah, Citizens, give not the tyrant of England the triumph of seeing the man perish on the scaffold who has aided my much loved America to break her chains!"

It made no difference; the vote was for death and on January 21, 1793, Louis of France went to the guillotine.

Then the world was changed and the revolution fled past him. In a matter of days after the death of the king, almost every nation in Europe, including England, was at war with France. And while the enemy armies made preparations beyond the frontiers, within the city of Paris the Girondins and the Jacobins fought their own deadly struggle.

Paine proposed that he go off to the frontiers with the troops. The military leaders smiled at him.

"You are too old to be a soldier, monsieur," they assured him, deliberately misunderstanding.

And when he said valiantly, "An army fights with more than guns," they raised their brows and smiled.

Then, with others, he was appointed to formulate a message to the people of England.

"Just a message?" he said. "And that will do what all my planning and work failed to do?"

"It is what you are fitted for."

"Just that—"

But he wrote as vibrantly as he had ever written, turning out the message that would never be seen by ninety-nine per cent of the British people. It helped him—his writing; it occupied him; but it answered none of the doubts that were plaguing him.

"Leave France?" he asked himself. But then what? Then what reason to live? He had forgotten his trade of staymaking. He was a revolutionist; it was all he knew, all he was fitted for.

No, he could not leave France, not yet, not while there was still hope for the revolution, not while the Girondins and the Jacobins might forget their hatred for each other long enough to permit France and the Republic to survive. But as time went on, the break increased rather than healed. A new situation had arisen, the hatred of the people for the middle class, fear of the people by the middle class.

More and more muskets were distributed to the people of Paris. And keeping pace with Paine's growing hatred of Marat and his party, there grew in him a mounting disgust for the Girondins who would destroy the revolution before they would give an inch.

Those were dark days, and Tom Paine walked alone.

Alone, he wrote to Marat and Danton, pleading. Danton ignored his letter; a pall of fear was beginning to hang over Paris, and Danton, who had looked askance now and then at the dictatorship of the mob, was beginning to feel gingerly at his own neck. Marat stormed to St. Just:

"No man knows when to die! I am sick of Paine, sick to death of him. Does he think that a revolution is distilled from roses, like perfume?"

"I have doubted that Paine thinks," St. Just smiled.

"Well, I am sick of him."

Alone, Paine prayed to God. A man does not pray easily when he is like Paine, when he is strong and his hands are broad, when he has a brain and a heart and contempt and hatred for those who made God's name the disgrace of the centuries. A man leaves God alone and turns to men and tries to do what is right. But Paine was old and tired, and he prayed, self-consciously, "Give them understanding."

Alone he said to the Girondins, "Show your honesty, your

love for France and mankind, and I will lead the people to you."

And the Girondins showed their honesty by as fine a piece of fraud as they had ever indulged in.

There was a young, blue-eyed, dream-saturated Englishman, Johnson by name, who had followed Paine everywhere for weeks now, dreaming of becoming his Boswell. Johnson was not very stable; he saw himself as a knight-crusader; he saw himself also as a revolutionist, and the two did not go well together. He wrote bad poetry, and he fell in love with a French girl.

His love-making was as bad as his poetry, and Paine had to listen patiently to both. The girl wasn't so patient, and sometimes she laughed at Johnson, usually when he told her how he would die for her, or kill anyone who came between them.

"You will not die for me, my little fool," she said calmly. "And if there is anyone else, that's my affair."

There was someone else, a Jacobin, and out of that Johnson built an entirely abnormal fear and hatred of the party of the left. When she told him, as kindly as she could, that she was through with him, he came to Paine and cursed Marat and his whole party as the source of every ill.

Paine dismissed the matter from his mind, thinking nothing more would come of it, but Johnson, after playing with the thought of suicide for several days, finally made the attempt. He used a knife, not knowing the fortitude needed to end one's life in so primitive a fashion, and as a result succeeded only in gashing himself.

But before he took the plunge, he wrote a letter to Paine, blaming Marat.

Alarmed until he learned how Johnson had fumbled the attempt, Paine showed the letter to Brissot, remarking,

"Marat has done a good deal, but I'd hardly blame him for Johnson's sticking himself."

"Yet if he dies—" Brissot mused.

With that flimsy excuse, the Girondins dragged Marat before the revolutionary tribunal. It was their last brief flash of power—and exactly the opening Marat had been seeking. Before the tribunal, Marat tore the charges to pieces, stood in such dignity as he had never shown before, and calmly portrayed himself as the just anger of a just people.

The Girondins had overstepped themselves—and so the end began. And Paine could only sigh tiredly, "The fools— oh, the poor, witless fools."

The end of the Girondins came with awful suddenness. One day Paine was telling Brissot, "In the end, it will not be the Jacobins who destroy Republican France, but you. For the sake of everything we've lived for, make your peace with them. Do you hate Marat more than I do? I tell you, the Republic is dying." And the next day it was over.

The Girondins were flailing about; their blows fell everywhere and accomplished nothing. They arrested Jacobins; they banned assemblies; they flung out accusations. And then the people of Paris picked up their muskets and began to assemble. On a much vaster scale, it was Philadelphia all over again, but this time Paine was in limbo. This time, the people neither remembered Paine nor turned to him; their wrath was against the Girondins, and if someone suggested that Paine was a mainspring of that party, they simply shrugged their shoulders. Thirty-two thousand of the volunteers stood over their muskets throughout the city, and all day long delegations stormed the Convention hall to scream for the arrest of the Girondins, who had betrayed the revolution. At last, the weary and frightened Convention adjourned for the day, and one by one, with shoulders bent over in despair, the Girondin deputies left the hall, the yelling mob hardly parting to make way for them. But when Paine left, there was a moment of silence. . . .

There was no sleeping that night. They went to Bancal's house, Duval, Condorcet, Brissot and Guadet, and they sat there until dawn turning over and over what had happened, what would happen to them, some even suggesting suicide.

"And either way," Paine said somberly, "the Republic is dead. Tomorrow the dictatorship of the mob, and after that anarchy—and after that, God only knows what."

The dawn of that day bore out their fears. The number of Parisians armed and assembled had increased almost to one hundred thousand; they made a dark, angry cordon around the hall of the Convention, and within, the deputies, not knowing precisely where the ax would fall, decreed as the people wished. The Girondin leaders were expelled from the Convention and placed under arrest. The French Republic was dead; the middle class had been overthrown by the hungry, angry poor of Paris, and the course of the revolution was turned into a strange and dangerous channel that had never been explored before.

Yet they left Paine alone; Paine, who had been a Girondin —or at least a friend and associate of Girondins—was still Tom Paine who had bent into the mire where mankind lay through the centuries, and had proclaimed freedom. Even the Parisians, the small men of the shops and the factories and the looms and the benches, even they who hated the Girondins so, would not lift a finger against Paine.

Silent and lonely he stalked the streets. They all knew him; his fierce hooked nose, his twisted eyes, his broad, sloping shoulders and his meaty, peasant hands were instantly recognizable; this was the godfather of revolution; this was the person who, across three thousand miles of water, somewhere in the American wilderness, had awakened sleeping mankind—and because they knew that, they were not cruel to him, they did not abuse him as they abused the Girondins, and now and then a kind word was spoken to him, as, "Good day, Citizen," and, "It looks different, Citizen, wouldn't you say?" or, "You're with us, Citizen. We've disposed of the traitors, and now you are with us—"

When was he not one of them? he asked himself. Their poor little bit of power had ripped out into anarchy, and the Republic was dead. His dreams were dead.

He fought sleeplessness with a brandy bottle and he fought wakefulness. He made up his mind that when they came to arrest him, he would stand erect and say, "I am Citizen Paine," and just look at them. But they didn't come to arrest him. He heard how in England men had copper coins with Paine's likeness on them fixed into the soles of their shoes, so they could vicariously stamp him into the mud. That, too, dissolved in a bottle. He drank himself into insensibility; for ten days, he had only enough control of himself to crawl down to the tavern for more brandy—after the waiter at White's had told him:

"Drink I'll sell you, but I'll not have the death of Paine on my conscience."

For a day, he was sober and haunted; he woke in the night, screaming, and when one of the Englishmen at the hotel, Jackson, told him, "For Christ's sake, Paine, you are killing yourself," he answered, "It's time, isn't it? Damn it, it's time!"

And then he was drunk again, day after day after day, vomiting, sick, seeing things that were not and things that were,

unshaven, dirty, dragging himself about his room and mouthing:

"Where is that damned bottle, that damned bottle?"

That way, for almost thirty days—until anger came, anger
so fierce and terrible that it sobered him while he vomited
and trembled. There were two bottles of brandy left, and he
smashed them against the floor. He strode back and forth
across the room, pounding a clenched fist into his palm, and
telling himself repeatedly in a calm, cold voice:

"You fool, you damned, accursed fool, it's only the beginning. You said seven years and even in seventy, it would
still be only the beginning. You dirty, damned, drunken,
besotted fool!"

13

REASON IN GOD AND MAN

The revolution goes on; a man does not make the revolution, not a thousand men, not an army and not a party; the revolution comes from the people as they reach toward God, and a little of God is in each person and each will not forget it. Thus it is the revolution when slaves shake their chains and the revolution when a strong man bends toward a weaker and says, "Here, comrade, is my arm." The revolution goes on and nothing stops it; but because the people are seeking what is good, not what is wicked or powerful or cruel or rich or venal, but simply what is good—because of that the people flounder and feel along one dark road after another. The people are no more all-seeing than their rulers once were; it is in intention that they differ.

Some of this, or all of it, Paine came to know, and he came to know that he was not the revolution, but only a man. There are no gods on earth, only men, and it had taken a long time for him to learn this.

His face was drawn, his figure leaner, his broad shoulders sloped more than ever as he entered the hall of the Convention once again. They had made no move to arrest him. "Let him run away," Marat said. "Let him be off to the devil!" But Paine did not run away, and now he was back, his lips tight as he strode through a thousand fixed eyes to his seat.

There was a rustle and a murmur and the sound of many persons rising as Paine came back. Galleries and floor wanted to see him, the fool who walked back into the lion's mouth. Paine found his place, stood a moment, looking from person to person, and then sat down.

"Citizen Paine," the speaker acknowledged.

There was a ripple of applause, in spite of themselves. Paine wiped his eyes and stared at the floor.

St. Just attacked him, St. Just at his best, shouting, "I accuse you!"

Citizen Paine rose and came forward and asked, "Of what, sir—of what do you accuse me?"

"Of treason to France!"

"I committed no treason to France," Paine said calmly.

St. Just went on to accuse Paine of being in illegitimate correspondence with part of the royal family outside of the country's borders, at which Paine shook his head and said, "You are speaking to Tom Paine, sir."

Even the galleries roared with applause at that. "Accuse me of many things," Paine said. "Accuse me of being a republican, of being loyal to my friends, of loving an Englishman or a Frenchman as well as an American—but not of treason, sir, not of consorting with kings. I am not a young man; I have enough to look back upon, and I will not defend myself."

St. Just said no more.

So Paine sat in the Convention, but said practically nothing. History was rushing on too fast, and he was left behind. He attended because he was a delegate and because he was practicing the only trade he knew, but there was nothing for him. And he was terribly alone, his friends in prison, others who might have been his friends avoiding him because he was suspect. A whole era was crowded into a week or a month. Marat died under Charlotte Corday's dagger, and Robespierre took his place, a disarming man, so delicate and so French, but strong as iron and unbending as rock. A humanitarian, he called himself, telling Paine:

"I am of the people because I feel all their wants, their hurts, their pains, their sufferings. You were of the people once, were you not, Citizen Paine?" That was his way, to sink a barb deepest where it hurt most.

"I was a staymaker," Paine said, "and a cobbler and I swept a weaver's shop and I grubbed in the dirt for tuppence a week. I don't speak of being of the people—"

And that was something that Robespierre would never forget.

Still, the new ruler of France was a man of iron; he had to be. All around the nation enemy armies were closing in; provinces were in full revolt, and here and there the counter-revolution had gained full control of a local district.

Reorganized, the Revolutionary Tribunal set to work, and there began that period known as The Terror. There was neither compromise nor mercy; either a man was loyal to the revolution or he was an enemy of the revolution, and if he was suspect he was more than likely to be considered an enemy. Day after day, crude carts trundled through the streets of Paris, their big wooden wheels groaning and squeaking, their bellies bulging with new victims for the guillotine. And day after day the big knife was wound up its scaffold and then released to fall upon another neck. From the king's wife to a tavern keeper, to a simpering duke, to a midwife who had sheltered him. This was revolution in a way Paine had never dreamed of, not tall farmers who had always known that freedom was a part of their lives, but frightened little men who saw freedom for the first time in a thousand years, and were going to kill, kill, kill anything that stood in the way of its accomplishment. A dark cloud over Paris as the winter of 1793-1794 set in, a bloodstained cloud. Robespierre had to be a strong man.

And as the heads rolled, there died those friends of Paine's who had made up the party of the Plain, or the Girondins. Traitorous, or deceived, or weak, or without understanding, or frightened, or brave, or cowardly, or righteous in the only way they knew, they all died, Roland and his wife, Condorcet, Brissot, Petion, Lebrun, Vergniaud, Buzot—all of them, all under the knife that was the dark door at the end of a dark lane into which liberty had wandered. Long live the Republic—and the Republic died too. Paris was a city of death.

During this time, Paine still attended the Convention. He had to; he had to make reason out of this dark thing that was happening, or else he could not live. What happened to good, simple men? What moved them? What drove them? Had they forgotten mercy, decency, goodness, or had the priests and the kings made those words so foul that they could never again have meaning? Paine had to know.

He had changed his living quarters from White's Hotel to a farmhouse in the suburbs of Paris, a big, whitewashed stone-and-wood building that practiced a bucolic deception on a world that was falling apart. In many ways, this new home reminded Paine of an English yeoman farmer's place, the bricked-in courtyard, a confusion of ducks, hens, geese, the flowers and the fruit trees and the stacked hay; again, it reminded him of Pennsylvania. He was of an age to be reminded of many things, all stacked away, layer upon layer, in his uneasy mind. With him at the farm were a few other English men and women, the same Johnson who had made the abortive suicide attempt, a Mr. and Mrs. Christie, a Mr. Adams, forlorn radicals who were radicals no longer, but had been swept aside by the current of revolution. They were poor company for Paine; their mutterings, their vague discontents, their fears were all at odds with his own terrible and personal problem.

Death mattered little to Paine. Though he hoped and prayed that it was not so, he had a feeling that most of his work was done. Things had gone beyond him; all he felt now was a dire need for rationalization, for reason in a world ruled by anarchy. Sometimes he would sit down at cards with the others, but cards were not for him. There was still a world beyond bits of pasteboard.

"I am Tom Paine," he would remember, and then he would go back to Paris and plunge once more into the current of revolution. Some things he was still fitted for, and when it came to a matter of American policy, he would quietly give to the Jacobins all the knowledge and information he had. They got little enough out of the American ambassador, Gouverneur Morris.

That the turns of fortune had made Gouverneur Morris, Paine's reactionary opponent in the old Philadelphia uprising, American ambassador to revolutionary France, was in itself something to evoke both tears and laughter. Paine thought he saw reason behind this seeming insanity. Morris, the aristocrat, was a living proof to Britain that in America the conservatives of 'eighty and 'eighty-one were again in the seat. They would play the game with England—all the way.

"We have to," they would say. "We are a tiny, new nation, barely out of our birth pangs. Another war would finish us. At any price, we must preserve peace with England—and this

French revolution—well, what have we to do with blood
baths?" So they sent Morris to France as ambassador, the
drawling, sneering Morris who had once remarked that
Paine was neither clean nor genteel, but a piece of dirt wisely
scrubbed from England's skin.

In his own way, a completely unofficial way, Paine was
America's representative, doing small and large favors for
the citizens of the land he had fought for, helping ship captains through the tangle of revolutionary customs and laws,
serving however he could serve. James Farbee, for instance,
a worthless soldier of fortune, not too bright, had been
caught in a royalist plot that was no doing of his, and now
waited for the thin steel blade to sever his head from his
body. Paine came to see him in jail and said, "For fools like
you, innocent men pay."

Farbee protested that this was none of his fault; footloose
and free and without a job at home after the war, and what
does a man do who has known nothing else but fighting
since the age of eighteen?

"And you were in the war?"

"I was, sir."

"What command?"

"Greene's, sir."

"And who was lieutenant-quartermaster?"

"Franklin."

"Captain-secretary?"

"Anderson, Grey, Chaplin, and I think, after that, Long."

"Were you in the Jerseys?"

"Jersey and Pennsylvania, sir, and then the Carolinas. My
God, sir, I was with you at Germantown, don't you remember?"

Paine, appearing before the Revolutionary Tribunal, said,
in slow, halting French, "Farbee must not die. He is a fool

and a knave, but a soldier of the revolution. Are we all saints?"

And Farbee lived, just as Michael Peabody and Clare Henderson lived because Paine pleaded for them.

But all that was aside from the main problem which obsessed him, the problem of one more book remaining for him to write, who had produced both a reason for revolution and a handbook for revolution. Sitting in the big farmhouse, he scribbled, blotted, forced his thoughts, and realized with horror and agony that his old ease, fire, and facility were gone. He would cover a sheet with writing and then tear it up. He wrote words and they were not the right words. He was old, not so much in years as in usage of his big, peasant body, in the usage of a mind that burned itself as had few minds in all human history. It is a sad and woeful thing when a man loses the use of tools that give him reason to live. He would struggle as he had never before struggled, and then, giving up for the time, go to the Convention hall and sit and listen. The throbbing heart of the revolution was here, and here he pressed his thoughts. A reason and a motif came one day when Francis Partiff arose on the floor and screamed:

"God is dethroned, and Christianity, corrupt as a priest, is banished from earth! Henceforth, reason shall rule, pure reason, incorruptible reason!" And standing there, Partiff shredded a Bible, page by page.

Paine got up and left; he walked through the streets and saw a cart with four bodies for the knife. He came out by the river and saw a red sun setting over the old roofs of ancient Paris. God had died; Paine walked more and more slowly, and then the sun was gone, leaving nothing but the reflected goodness in the sky and a swallow to trace a pattern before it.

"And men, who are beginning to climb to God, to be like gods, disown him! Then there is blood on the earth, and they hate—how they hate!"

He went home and he wrote; it came more easily now, his painful script, capturing thought, building to a bolt that would be loosed on men and cry once more, "Here is Paine, the friend of man." He wrote all night long, and toward dawn, he fell asleep, his head on the paper. In the morning, when Mrs. Christie came to bring him an egg and some tea, he was like that, his big head and shoulders sprawled over the desk, his breath ruffling the foolscap upon which he had scribbled. Unwilling to disturb him, knowing how many long and silent battles he had fought with insomnia, she set down the food and quietly went out.

About noon, Paine woke, had a cup of cold tea, and went back to his writing.

The Terror came closer, a black shawl drawing night over Paris, and by ones and twos the English radicals who shared the farmhouse with Paine fled, some to Switzerland, some to the north. Mrs. Christie begged Paine to go with her and her husband, but smiling curiously, he asked, "Where would I go?"

"Home."

"And where is my home?" Paine wondered. "I made the world my village, and it's too late to undo that."

"And soon they will come for you with the cart."

Paine shrugged. "If they think it necessary for me to die that the revolution may go on—" He shrugged again.

He was the only lodger left in the big farmhouse. His only companion was the landlord. And then the soldiers of the Republic came for the small, mustached Frenchman who owned the place, Georgeit, his name, with the dread warrant.

"But, Monsieur Paine, tell them," the landlord pleaded. "Tell them I have neither schemed nor plotted."

"It is no use to tell them. They do what they have to do. Go with them, my friend; there is nothing else to do and no other way. Go with them—"

And then Paine was entirely and completely alone, alone and unafraid, sitting at his desk and writing a thing which he proposed to call *The Age of Reason*.

"Let me write in letters of fire, for I am unafraid. To-morrow I will die, or the next day. There is so much death that I have become a part of it, and that way I have lost my fear. They told me to run away, but where can Paine go? To America? They have no use for an old revolutionist in America today—indeed, I do not know that they would recognize me in America. The tall man from Mt. Vernon is not the comrade in arms that I once knew; he has forgotten how we marched down through Jersey. To England? A hundred years from now they will welcome me in the land where I was born. My work is in France and France must be the savior of the world, and if they take Paine's life, what is the loss?"

The Age of Reason, written in large letters, and underlined three times. An offering for the new world, for the brave, credulous, frightened new world, which had come out of his hands as much as out of any other's. The new world had renounced God, and thereby, to Paine's way of thinking, they had renounced the reason for man to exist. Man is a part of God, or else he is a beast; and beasts know love and fear and hate and hunger—but not exultation. As Paine saw it now, man's history was a vision of godliness. From the deep, dark morass he had come, from the jungles and the lonely mountains and the windswept steppes, and always his way had been the way of the seeker. He made civilization and he made a morality and he made a pact of brotherhood. One day, he ceased to kill the aged and venerated them, ceased to kill the sick and healed them, ceased to kill the lost and showed them how to find themselves. He had a dream and a vision, and Isaiah was one of his number, as was Jesus of Nazareth. He offered a hand, saying, Thou art my brother, and do I not know thee? And he began to see God, like going up a ladder, rung after rung, always closer to a something that had been waiting eternally. First wooden images, then marble ones, the sun and the stars, and then a just, unseen singleness, and then an unseen one of love and mercy, and then a gentle Jew nailed onto a cross and dying in pain. Man does not stop; he will be free and the brotherhood world wide, and a musket is fired in a Massachusetts village—

And now the revolution, gone down an uncharted road, sick of an organized, venal, preying church, had embraced the godlessness of nothing and nowhere. So Paine told himself, "I will write one more book and tell them what I know of a God that has not failed me." And he began:

"It has been my intention, for several years past, to publish my thoughts upon religion; I am well aware of the difficulties that attend the subject, and, from that consideration, had reserved it to a more advanced period of life. I intend it to be the last offering I shall make to my fellow citizens of all nations, and that at a time when the purity of the motive that induced me to it, could not admit of a question, even by those who might disapprove the work.

"The circumstance that has now taken place in France of the total abolition of the whole national order of the priesthood, and of everything appertaining to compulsive systems of religion, and compulsive articles of faith, has not only precipitated my intention, but rendered a work of this kind exceedingly necessary, lest, in the general wreck of superstition, of false systems of government, and false theology, we lose sight of morality, of humanity, and of the theology that is true.

"As several of my colleagues, and others of my fellow citizens of France, have given me the example of making their voluntary and individual profession of faith, I also will make mine; and I do this with all that sincerity and frankness with which the mind of man communicates with itself.

"I believe in one God, and no more; and I hope for happiness beyond this life.

"I believe the equality of man; and I believe that religious duties consist in doing justice, loving mercy, and endeavoring to make our fellow creatures happy.

"But, lest it should be supposed that I believe many other things in addition to these, I shall, in the progress of this work, declare the things I do not believe and my reasons for not believing them.

"I do not believe in the creed professed by the Jewish church, by the Roman church, by the Greek church, by the Turkish church, by the Protestant church, nor by any church that I know of. My own mind is my own church.

"All national institutions of churches, whether Jewish, Christian or Turkish, appear to me no other than human inventions, set up to terrify and enslave mankind, and monopolize power and profit."

That way, there was a beginning; he put down what he believed, what he did not believe, and then he labored, day after day, in the old, deserted farmhouse. He was not fashioning a creed; men had done that already, as much by acts as by words. Christ on a cross had fashioned it and so had a rustic boy dying on a village green in New England. So had a thousand and a hundred thousand others. It remained only for him to formulate it and put it in place as the last work in his encyclopedia of revolution.

During those quiet days when he worked on *The Age of Reason*, he did not go into old Paris very often. Once to seek for a Bible written in English; Bibles there were in plenty, but all in French, and for the life of him he could not lay hands on a King James version. That made it harder for him, having to work on out of his memory, seeking back to all the times in his childhood when he had read certain passages over and over, quoting as he worked, sometimes correctly, sometimes incorrectly. The Bible was necessary, for in writing down a faith that could be accepted by a reasonable man, a gentle man, a good man, he had to tear apart, boldly and ruthlessly, the whole fabric of superstition that had been woven through the ages.

Often he was tempted to send to England for the work he needed, but the passage of even a piece of mail was long and uncertain, and Paine was driven by a deadly sense of urgency. No one, living in or about Paris as the year of 1793 drew to a close, could forget the pall of The Terror. It had lost meaning and reason, and struck about as wildly as a maddened beast. First it had been the *right*, but now Jacobins of the extreme left joined the procession to the guillotine. What Paine had feared most was coming about, the dictatorship of violence gone amuck.

On one of his trips into Paris, Paine looked up an old acquaintance of his, Joel Barlow, whom he had helped once when Barlow was in legal difficulties with a French court.

"Whatever happens," Paine said, "I don't care too much, but I've been working on a manuscript that will soon be

finished and that means a great deal to me. If they come for
me, can I entrust the manuscript to you?"

"Gladly," Barlow nodded, and then begged Paine to leave
for America.

"In good time," Paine nodded. "When my work in France
is over."

He had finished his book; his credo was down on paper,
and he felt a complete and wonderful sense of relief, the
feeling of a man washed clean and rested. He had struck a
blow at atheism, and he had—or so he believed—given the
people of France and of the world a rational creed to sustain
them through the years of revolution that he saw ahead. He
had proclaimed God in all that man saw, in the perfect sym-
metry of a leaf, in a rosy sunset, in a million stars cast like
a hood in the night, in the earth, in the sea, in all creation.
He told them not to look for cheap, tawdry miracles, when
they themselves and the world they lived in were the greatest of all miracles.

He told them to believe in God because they and the
world they inhabited were the strongest proof of God. God's
work was creation; His bible and proof were creation. It
was a blazing, living, signed document, and it required neither superstitions nor horror tales to support it. It was Tom
Paine to France, saying, "If you choose atheism now, I, at
least, have done my part."

On one of his short trips to Paris, he had gone to the
Convention hall and told the doorkeeper in very bad French,
"Deputy Thomas Paine, representing Calais," and the doorkeeper stared as if he had seen a ghost. And others stared;
all over the hall brows raised and necks craned as they turned
to look at him.

There was only one of the old radical group of foreign expatriates left in the hall, Anacharsis Clootz, the Prussian, one of the extreme left, a man a hundred years ahead of his time, a socialist before there was socialism, a little mad, a great deal brilliant, unafraid, vehemently outspoken, much like Paine and very much unlike him. Until now, they had worked together occasionally, but not easily; Paine was a republican, an advocate of democracy; Clootz was the advocate of a social conception, the theory of which hardly existed. He waved at Paine now, and afterwards, leaving the hall, got close to him and called:

"Hello there, my old friend, where have you been?"

"Writing."

"They all write before they go to the Madam Guillotine. And what nonsense this time?"

"Gods and men."

Clootz was a militant atheist; he held his stomach now, roaring with laughter and calling after Paine, "We will discuss that, no?"

They were to discuss it soon enough.

His time had about run out; he had desired a reprieve, not out of any great desire to go on living a life that for all practical purposes was over, but because, as so often before, he had something which he felt he must put down on paper. But now that it was done, he went to meet his fate almost eagerly. They would not have to seek him; he was no recluse, and he had never fled from a judgment. Already, he had been too long alone in the big farmhouse; that was not for Paine; for Paine was the feel of his fellow men, their nearness, their voices and their smiles and their good intimacies. So he packed together the few things he had, the finished manuscript, some other papers, a book or two and some shirts and underclothes—not a great deal, but he had never been one for worldly possessions. If a man makes the world his castle, he does not seek to furnish it.

He returned to Paris and White's Hotel, to raised brows and breath softly drawn in. "Still here, Paine?"

"Still here."

And such whispered comments as, "Well, there's no fool like an old fool."

And behind his back, slick, a finger across a throat—"If he wants to, that's his own affair."

He ordered a brandy, he proposed a toast, "To the Republic of France, forever, gentlemen!" And no one knew whether to laugh or to deride.

On Christmas Day, a motion was put forward in the hall to exclude all foreigners from seats in the Convention. There were only two foreigners left, Paine and Clootz, and it was at them that the move was directed. Paine had seen this coming; he knew it when he returned to the city, when he made the toast to the Republic, when he finally went to bed to sleep what might be his last night as a free man. He was not afraid; he wanted it to come quickly; no longer a deputy of France, he wanted the surge of the revolution to overtake him, to devour him if it must.

And in the early dawn, it came.

Thus—there were two agents of the Committee of General Security pounding on the door of his room and unrolling their imposing warrant when he came in his nightshirt to let them in.

"For Citizen Paine! And you, monsieur, are Citizen Paine?"

"I am," he smiled. "Come in, gentlemen."

The two agents were followed by one corporal and four

privates. The corporal took his place at the foot of Paine's bed, after saluting, the privates on either side.

"Permit me to dress," Paine said. The corporal graciously nodded and the two agents set about searching the room. Paine poured them each a brandy, and the privates stared intently at nothing at all. "Excellent brandy," the agents admitted, and went on with their searching.

When he was dressed, Paine asked, "I would like to know —the charge—"

"Monsieur Merson," one of the agents introduced himself, a small tribute to the brandy, and read from the warrant, "Conspiring against the Republic."

"Conspiring against the Republic," Paine repeated, softly and tiredly. "Citizen Paine is under arrest for conspiracy. He sits alone in an empty farmhouse and broods about God, and thereby the Republic is endangered. I wonder whether the shortest thing in the world is not the memory of men." He had spoken in English; when the agents raised their brows, he shook his head. "Nothing, nothing—I have some papers at the Britain House, may we go there and get them?" pouring another brandy for each.

"Not entirely in order," Merson shrugged. "But when one arrests a citizen one admires, so reluctantly, one may make an exception."

At the Britain House, Barlow was waiting, and Paine gave him the manuscript of *The Age of Reason*.

"I wish to God you had left France," Barlow said.

"And I may, sooner than I expected," Paine answered ruefully. "Barlow, this thing I wrote may be trash, but to me it's very dear—in the loose talk of an old man, the finish of a life. If I go to the guillotine, try to have it published. I have some friends in America; the printers in Philadelphia would do me another turn, for the sake of old times. There's

Jefferson and Washington—I think they remember me. If you have to, play on their feelings, tell them, recall to them an old soldier in the times that tried men's souls."

"Don't be a damn fool," Barlow muttered.

M. Merson said, "Please, citizen, I have been good enough to allow you pass on your book and gullible enough to come here and meet your friend. But now we must go."

"Where are you taking him?" Barlow demanded.

"To the Luxembourg, for the time."

On their way to the prison, they stopped off long enough to arrest Anacharsis Clootz, and then, with soldiers on either side, the two ex-deputies were marched through the streets. Clootz was bubbling with suppressed mirth; there was something diabolical in the way he regarded this last march. "So we go, friend Paine," he chuckled, "you at one end of the long bar of revolution, I on the other, and in the end it makes no difference to the good Lady Guillotine. She will go chop, once, twice, and then it will be a finish to Paine and Clootz—and to what else, old friend? Who can tell?"

"But why? They accuse me of being a traitor to the Republic, a charge I don't have to answer. The name of Paine is answer enough. But of what do they accuse you?"

Clootz let go with a furious burst of laughter. "You are an old man, Paine, so even the remarkably simple becomes greatly involved. You are a republican, and I am, to coin a phrase for our times, a proletarian. You believe in the democratic method through representation, and I believe in the same method through the will of the masses. You say, let the people rule; I say the same thing; we are after the same thing, only in different ways. I believe that your way is hopeless, part of the past; but otherwise we are the same, and the dictatorship, which this Republic of France is fast becoming, does not want us. Therefore, chop, chop—let the good Lady Guillotine take care of everything."

They continued toward the prison, and for a while Clootz was silent, his bushy brows puckered intently, and to Paine it seemed that the German had finally realized his destination and his fate. But suddenly Clootz swung on him and roared,

"What is this nonsense you write, Paine, about the creation being the Bible of God?"

"A simple fact which I believe."

"Which you believe!" Clootz snorted, stopping the march and turning on Paine, arms akimbo. "You repudiate organized religion and substitute mystical rationalization! My friend, Paine, you shock me. With you I spend some of my last precious hours. On every hand people in the streets turn to stare at us and whisper to each other, There are Paine and Clootz on their way to the guillotine. These good soldiers, these two agents of what calls itself the Republic of France, will go home to their soup and their wives with the news that they marched the last march with the two greatest minds of the eighteenth century. And you rationalize about the creation being the Bible of God. What creation?"

"Of course, it happened!" Paine snapped. "Atheism, the great creed of chance! Like a game of cards, everything just fell together until it fitted nicely!"

"And why not? Where is reason, but in our minds? Where is godliness, but in the people? Where is mercy, but in the masses? A thing becomes reasonable because we make it reasonable, and we are not reaching toward God, but toward goodness, a formulation of the people, a concept of small, suffering men—"

M. Merson interrupted, "Please, please, citizens, we are on our way to the Luxembourg jail. I pray you not to argue,

for it is unseemly in men going our way." And they continued on their way, Clootz roaring his theories at the top
of his lungs.

It had been the Palace of Luxembourg before the revolution; now it was the house of arrest, the last stop. It stood
in the famous old gardens where all was beauty, so that the
many who went to the guillotine could bring a good last
memory with them, and in no place was horror and warmth
so neatly and terribly combined. Great rooms, high ceilings,
rugs and tapestries and gilt chairs, and death. If you sat with
your friends and mused of things that were far away, large
things and beautiful, such as men in prison bring to life with
words, the green hills of Pennsylvania, the white cliffs of
Dover, the moors of the north country, the Palisades on a
cold, windy winter day, a storm at sea or a sunrise at sea;
and musing upon those things heard a series of piercing
shrieks, moans and groans and fervent calling upon God, you
pretended not to notice—for it is saddest of all things to
contemplate human beings going to their deaths. But you
thought to yourself, the duchess, perhaps—or the wife of the
little man who kept a tobacco shop on the Rue St. Denis—
or the quiet woman in black who has no identity at all.
You kept your quarters clean even if you had never kept
quarters clean before, for you acquired at the threshold of
the grave a fastidious sense of delicacy. You acquired hu-
mility, whether you were a count or a butcher, for here were
all classes living in the most incredible little democracy the
world had ever known. When you wept, you tried not to
show your tears to others, for early in your stay at the Luxembourg you saw the quiet contagion of tears, twenty persons
in a room where one began to weep, and then another, and
then another—and then all.

You came to admire the French if you had never admired them before, the way they faced death, the way they could joke about it, the way with a simple, expressive shrug of their shoulders they could divest it of all importance. You found a people from chimney sweep to duke so wonderfully civilized that even while you were dying because a revolution had gone amuck, you never for once doubted that in France was the salvation of mankind. You came to know M. Benoît, the jailor, who would sometimes say, with a deprecatory smile, "I must have a large heart— How do I know, monsieur?—because whenever one of my charges goes away, a part of my heart goes with him. You who are here die once—and how many times do I die? A hundred? A thousand? Why don't I go away, monsieur? Who would replace me? I am not a saint, but not a villain."

You heard people say, "It is The Terror. It is the war." Not complainingly, but with an acceptance of the fact that explained a little how this strange, sunny land had once lived through a hundred-year war that had desolated three quarters of it.

You would be with a group, and a door would open, and there would be a new one among you, Benoît leading him in and asking apologetically, "There will be some friends of yours, perhaps? You must make your best, and I will do my part," and turning around you would recognize him. Others recognize him too, some with bewilderment, some with a trace of satisfaction, but they all greet him as if he were coming to a club and not to a last stopping place.

Your old, good friend has learned that tomorrow it will be his turn, and he asks you to take a walk with him in the garden. Arm in arm, you stroll around the court, around and around, never once mentioning that this is the last walk on the last cold, winter afternoon, and looking at the gray winter sky, you realize the beauty of what was never beautiful before. The snow begins to fall, and your friend lays the palm of his hand against the melting flakes and reminds you that here is a great wonder of existence, so many snowstorms, so many flakes, so many countless millions of them, and yet all different, never two the same. "A wonder of infinity for us who delude ourselves with our greatness."

Or the mother of the boy, Benjamin, comes to you with word that they are taking him, he who is only seventeen. "A child, a baby, an innocent," she pleads with you. "Yesterday, I nursed him at my breast, just yesterday. What could he have done to deserve death?"

You don't know, and you try, with the foolish, blundering ways of a man, to comfort the mother. And then you go in to the boy, who, looking at you so trustingly, asks with his eyes for you to clear away the great mystery of death.

And so time passes, and presently there is no world at all except the Luxembourg Prison.

In the beginning, Paine had hope. He did not want to die; no one wants to die, and in this case, Paine had committed no crime, had indulged in no act of treason, and had consistently expressed his faith in both the Republic and the revolution. It was true that he had voted with and consorted with a party now overthrown and discredited, but even in that situation his motives had never been suspect, and he had been deliberately acquitted when the others went to the scaffold. Why then should he be held in prison? Treason? If there were a thousand men who hated Paine, accusing him of almost every crime known to man, they at least left treason out of the roster. In his fidelity to what he believed, he had never faltered.

Nor could he accept his fate with the laughing abandon,

shown first by Clootz and later by Danton. Well enough for them to find this whole business of mankind so amusing that death under the guillotine seemed the final jest in a ridiculous comedy. Paine had always loved life; the simple fact of living was an adventure, each new face presented to him an added bit of happiness. He was gregarious to an extreme, not merely loving his fellow men, but feeling a passionate need for them, without which life could not be endured. He had a sense of property which, not fixing itself on some little bit of acreage, had embraced the whole world.

So in the beginning he had hope, and he fought for his freedom. Not only was he a citizen of France; first and foremost, he was a citizen of America; he had weaned a piece of that land, he had nursed it and seen it out of its swaddling clothes. Therefore, he could, without shame or conscience, call on America in this hour of his need.

As simple as that; he got word to his friends, Barlow and a few others, to put pressure on Morris, the ambassador, and have him obtain Paine's release. And it was as simple as that, for the only nation in all the world revolutionary France could look to for friendship was America.

It was a situation to delight Morris's heart. There was a time in Philadelphia when the people rose up against a small group that would have turned the American revolution to their own ends; and the leader of the people was Paine, and one of the small group was Gouverneur Morris. There was a time when a revolutionary tribunal was set up in Philadelphia, and one of those who sat in the tribunal was Tom Paine, and one of those it passed judgment upon was Gouverneur Morris. "So slowly do the wheels of fate turn," Morris mused, "but so aptly." How many years had he waited for this moment—twelve? thirteen? A man forgets the years, but some things a man does not forget. In this land of shopkeepers and pigs, Paine and Clootz had walked to jail through the streets of Paris, arguing aloud their respective modes of atheism; yes, Morris had heard of that. What a glorious opportunity when a man can avenge his own feud and serve God at the same time. As brief insurance, Morris wrote to Jefferson, who represented all that was left in America of the revolution, the people and the ideals which made it:

". . . I must mention, that Thomas Paine is in prison, where he amuses himself with publishing a pamphlet against Jesus Christ. I do not recollect whether I mentioned to you, that he would have been executed along with the rest of the Brissotines, if the adverse party had not viewed him with contempt. I incline to think that, if he is quiet in prison, he may have the good luck to be forgotten. Whereas, should he be brought much into notice, the long suspended ax might fall on him. I believe he thinks, that I ought to claim him as an American citizen; but, considering his birth, his naturalization in this country, and the place he filled, I doubt much the right, and I am sure that the claim would be, for the present at least, inexpedient and ineffectual. . . ."

That done, Morris proceeded, with a clear conscience, to serve both his God and his country. The first step was to have Paine guillotined, which would be a service to the Almighty, and the second to break relations with France for that very thing, which would turn the service of the Almighty to the ends of the Hamiltonian party in America. To Barlow, Morris said:

"Paine is out of my hands entirely, a citizen of France, you know."

"But a citizen of America first!"

"I prefer to believe that Americans are not his ilk. I prefer to cherish some small respect for my native land. . . ."

And to Robespierre, "Really, sir, I would not stand in your way if Paine's execution were necessary to the welfare of the French Republic."

"And you might not be displeased," Robespierre said keenly.

"One doesn't commit oneself on such matters."

"Yet if Paine goes to the guillotine," Robespierre speculated, measuring Morris with his small, bright, merciless eyes, "there might be some displeasure in certain sections of your land. The militia, for instance, who fought with Paine, might remember him and object to his death; and Jefferson might remember that Paine once wrote a book called *Common Sense*."

"I assure you, sir, that neither the militia of a war that was over ten years ago nor Thomas Jefferson exerts too much influence upon the foreign policy of President Washington's government."

"Yet even your President Washington, if he needed a reason—speaking purely theoretically, you understand—might recall that once he and Paine were comrades in arms and, recalling that, might play upon the sympathies of the American people—"

"If you insinuate—"

"I insinuate nothing," Robespierre said quietly. "It is Monsieur the American ambassador who insinuates. Meanwhile the good Lady Guillotine drinks enough. When Paine's time comes, he will taste the justice of France, and until then Monsieur the American ambassador must wait patiently. Monsieur the American ambassador must not expect the French Republic to use its tribunals for personal—"

"That is enough, sir," Morris said.

Yet all in all, he was content to wait. He had waited a long time, and what were a few weeks or months more?

To Paine, none of this was apparent, as in the Luxembourg weeks stretched into months. He heard of a petition on his behalf put forward in the Convention by Americans living in Paris, and he heard of the sneering reply the aging president of the Convention made. He heard of a correspondence between the French foreign minister and Morris, and he took it in good faith. True enough, Morris did not like him, but one does not send a man one dislikes to his death. As time went on and absolutely nothing was done about his imprisonment, Paine's hope ebbed, but it never entirely vanished.

The Terror became more terrible, and the flow of victims to the guillotine was speeded up. A dread silence settled over the Luxembourg, a tightening of restrictions, a severing of all bonds with the outside world. Weeks and months passed, and no man left the place except for a single reason.

It came time for Clootz to go, and he waved to Paine and laughed, "Now, my deistic friend, I shall see which of us is right on this question of God, while you sit here and rack your poor brains."

And Danton, going the same way to the same bloody blade, shook hands with Paine, smiling rather sadly, and murmuring, "What a foolish, foolish world, fit only for children and idiots!"

And Luzon said, softly, fervently, "Good-by, my friend Paine. You shall not want for comrades, if they have republics over there."

And Ronsin said, "You will be lonely, Paine. The whole world we knew has already passed."

Twenty one night, forty the next, over two hundred one

terrible time. The gentle Benoît was no longer jailer; a hulking, sadistic brute called Guiard became custodian of the old palace; he closed off the courtyard and denied the prisoners a little air and a little sky before they met their deaths. He told them:

"Speak, and you are overheard. Plot, and I know what you are plotting. Guiard never sleeps."

In a fashion, it was true; he had the place filled with his spies, and a word was enough to send a man to the guillotine.

In this hellishness, Paine became something more than a man; he became a spirit and a faith; he became consolation and redemption. He knew when to smile—and a smile was the only thing on earth these poor devils could be given. He knew the few words that could help a man go to his death; he knew a phrase to console a mother. He was tireless, without fear, without hesitation. Gaunt, his health failing, nevertheless the mere sight of his big, angular figure entering a room was enough to cheer the occupants. "It is Monsieur Paine—come in, come in." He had a vast fund of stories, the drawling, American frontier jokes, which translated into his very bad French made almost no sense at all, but which were funny and pointless enough to send the poor devils who heard them into aching laughter. And he knew when to call up mirth; he knew when to be silent, when his mere presence was enough, when a word was enough.

And man after man, woman after woman, going to meet their death, said, "Send for Citizen Paine."

He lay in his bare room; he waxed hot and cold with fever; time lost meaning for him and disappeared. The fever came and receded, like undulating waves of fire, and he lived in a nightmarish world, populated by saints and devils. Vaguely he sensed that men were entering and leaving;

screams sometimes made him wonder where he was, and in a moment of clarity, he heard a man say:

"This wretch is dying."

And it mattered little or not at all, for the fever always returned, burning him, chilling him, burning him again.

Then, after a long, long time, sanity returned. He asked what month it was.

"July—"

And he counted, "January, February, March—"

"I am still in the Luxembourg?"

"Quite true, citizen, but matters have changed. Robespierre is dead. St. Just is dead. Take heart, citizen. The Terror is over."

"So The Terror is over," Paine sighed, and that night he slept without dreams.

It is difficult to regain one's strength in prison, even if one does not live in hourly fear of death. Paine, looking in a glass again, found a gray-haired stranger confronting him, a sunken face that was etched all over with lines and wrinkles. It made him smile, so much a stranger was the image, and the smile that the mirror returned him was hollow and mocking.

The beast, Guiard, had passed on with the downfall of Robespierre's government, and Arden, the new jailer, allowed the prisoners the freedom of the courtyard. Paine could walk again in the blessed sunlight; it was summer, and he could smell the flowers and watch the strollers in the gardens and mark the little clouds as they scudded overhead. The whole air of the Luxembourg had changed; it was still a prison, but it was not a death house. People left, again by the tens and twenties, but now they passed through the gates to freedom.

For the time being, Paine had little to do but to think—to contemplate the events of the past six months, the strange silence which had abandoned him during that time when the Luxembourg was a place of horror. Why had Morris made no effort to secure his freedom? he asked himself. Why had the American nation remained completely passive? Did it mean nothing to George Washington that Paine was in prison, perhaps to be guillotined any day? The whole attitude of Washington was incomprehensible. Why had he never really expressed his thanks to Paine for inscribing to him *The Rights of Man?* Had he forgotten that the country he presided over now was born out of revolution?

During the long days Paine spent recuperating from his sickness he brooded long and often over what had happened to America during these past years. Most difficult of all was to believe ill of that man who had seemed to him, for so many years, better and truer than any other man he had known, George Washington.

And then there was a ray of hope. Gouverneur Morris was no longer minister to France; James Monroe, a Jeffersonian democrat, had replaced him. Eagerly, Paine waited for Monroe's arrival, and once he was installed, sent him a long memorial, pleading his case and begging Monroe to make some effort to obtain his freedom. Monroe answered with a cheerful and hopeful reply, that he would work on the case and that Paine could expect liberation soon.

Yet it didn't come; the summer was over and another winter began, and almost all the other prisoners who had been with Paine in the Luxembourg had been freed; but he remained. It was fever again, sores developing in his side, his big, strong body finally crumbling under ten long months of imprisonment. His hand barely able to hold a pen, he wrote to Monroe again.

Barlow came to see him, and looking at the American with dulled eyes, Paine said barely a word.

"Paine?"

"It was never the dying I minded," Paine whispered. "But to have it drawn out like this is more than I can bear."

Then Monroe wrote to the Committee of General Security, "The services which he [Paine] rendered them [the people of America] in their struggle for liberty have made an impression of gratitude which will never be erased, whilst they continue to merit the character of a just and generous people. He is now in prison, languishing under a disease, and which must be increased by his confinement. Permit me, then, to call your attention to his situation, and to require that you will hasten his trial in case there be any charge against him, and if there be none, you will cause him to be set at liberty."

And it was done; in November, 1794, Tom Paine was released from Luxembourg Palace, not the man who had entered, but one sick and old and gray-haired.

14

NAPOLEON BONAPARTE

Paine had been living with the Monroes, gaining back his strength so slowly that again and again he despaired of ever being more than an invalid. No one expected him to live; they were so certain he would die that already news of his death had been sent across the ocean to America.

Yet he did not die. His strong, leathery body could absorb a fearful amount of punishment, and presently he was well enough to ask for the manuscript of *The Age of Reason*.

He read it through with delight; in parts, it was lacking, but in others it was very good, fiery, a ringing memory of his old self. He would have to add to it, but meanwhile he would have this section published. Let the atheists read it and find something worth believing in.

Meanwhile his thoughts turned increasingly toward America. There was not much, if anything, left for him in France; the revolution had imprisoned him, cast him out, departed from the principles he preached. In America it was different; he was not too old to fight, and back in that land he so loved he would once more fight for liberty against the strange, dark reaction that had set in with the Washington administration. Now it was winter, but when spring came again, he would be strong enough to travel.

And then the National Convention recalled him, gave him

back his seat, and made him once more a deputy of France. Monroe was delighted. "You see, Paine," he said, "that this vindicates you—this is the final confession of injustice. Once again as Citizen Paine, as leader of liberal democrats throughout the world, you can take your seat in the representative chamber of Republican France."

But for Paine, there was no triumph; he was almost frightened. The ten months in prison had done something to him, not only deprived him of bodily strength but taken away a certain resiliency of mind. Another Terror, he could not endure; another shattering of all he worked for would be worse than death.

He sat down and wrote to the Assembly:

"My intention is to accept the invitation of the Assembly. For I desire that it be known to the universe that, although I have been the victim of injustice, I do not attribute my sufferings to those who had no part in them, and that I am far from using reprisals towards even those who are the authors of them. But, as it is necessary that I return to America next spring, I desire to consult you on the situation in which I find myself, in order that my acceptation of returning to the Convention may not deprive me of the right to return to America."

But it was of that very right that they deprived him. Later, Monroe desired to send Paine to America with certain important papers. The Committee of Public Safety answered that Paine could not be spared.

So he stayed on at the Convention, old, feeble, a gray-haired man who sometimes rose and said a few words no one listened to. He felt trapped and helpless.

And then *The Age of Reason* was published in England and America.

Youth had almost returned to him as he worked alongside

the French publisher, sought with him for a good English typesetter, and breathed once again that delicious smell of wet printer's ink, that smell which evoked every dear and splendid memory he knew.

It was his confession of faith, his last work, his tribute to God and to good men. It was his stroke against atheism; it was his fervent faith in a deity that was good and merciful, and in man's ability to approach that deity without compulsion and superstition. And then it was published, a batch of copies sent to England, another batch to America, and then the ax fell.

Formerly, Satan had been one; now he became two, himself and Tom Paine. Every religious denomination joined together to attack this devil who had thrown doubt on all organized religion. Even in France, the repercussions jolted and tossed the tired old warrior. There was no understanding, no sympathy, nothing but abuse, abuse, and abuse. The servants of God conceived a vocabulary of foul names to apply to Paine, such adjectives as the world had not seen before, and as a summation it was decided that since the creation there had been no human being more wicked and more vile than Paine. To most of this, Paine did not reply; if he were wrong, it would have been different; if he were wrong they would have gone about proving him wrong and not showered him with filth. Convinced that he was right, he saw no need to go on adding to his arguments.

Yet now and again, he was driven to an answer, as for instance when Wakefield, the English Unitarian, attacked him. To him Paine wrote:

"When you have done as much service to the world by your writings, and suffered as much for them, as I have done, you will be better entitled to dictate. . . ."

He was terribly tired; sick again, he heard of the reaction in America; it was not all abuse there, as in England; some stood up for his point of view; there were still old comrades of his left, old revolutionists who had not forgotten how to think—and they were buying many copies of his book.

To Monroe, he said wearily, "I want to go home, I am so tired." Now there was a place called home; the world was his village, but now he kept thinking of the green hills and valleys of America. He was an old man in a strange land. He was the most hated—and perhaps by a few the most loved— man in all the world. For twenty years his broad shoulders had taken abuse; they were tired now.

Monroe said, "I wonder whether publication of *The Age of Reason* was wise, Paine. In America—"

"When have I been wise?" Paine cried. "Was it wise to throw my fortune with a pack of farmers the world knew defeated before ever they began to fight? Was it wise for me to cry out for independence before any of your great men at home had dared to conceive the notion? Was it wise for me to give a revolutionary credo to England and then have to flee for my life? Was it wise for me to spend ten months under the shadow of the guillotine? I have been many things, but never prudent, never wise. That's for heroes and great men, not for a staymaker!"

The portrait of Paine, drawn with horns, hung on the wall of many an English home. Taverns displayed beer mugs with Paine's picture, and underneath it, "Drink with the devil." In a hundred churches on a hundred Sundays sermons were preached on Tom Paine, apostate. In London, Liverpool, Nottingham, and Sheffield, piles of Paine's books were burned, while crowds danced around the fires, screaming:

> *"Paine, Paine, damned be his name,*
> *Damned be his fame and lasting his shame,*
> *God damn Paine! God damn Paine!"*

Feverish again, he lay and brooded and thought he was going to die. He didn't care. He turned over in his mind, one by one, all the horrors he had suffered during his imprisonment, and his resentment came to center upon a single man, George Washington.

There were others, Morris and Hamilton and the whole counter-revolutionary crowd, but what other had he worshiped the way he worshiped George Washington? He remembered how Washington, the aristocrat, the wealthiest man in America, had taken the hand of Paine, the nobody. He remembered how Washington, at Valley Forge, had begged him to go and plead his case before Congress. He remembered that he, Paine, had written, "The names of Washington and Fabius will run parallel to eternity."

So it was not the others who mattered, but George Washington; the others had not betrayed him, he had no claim on them. Washington it was who sent the contemptuous Morris as ambassador to Republican France; Washington had sent Jay to England to smear the honor of America; Washington had ignored *The Rights of Man*, dedicated to him, the key to the Bastille, presented to him; Washington had turned his back on the people and on democracy.

Sick as he was, tired as he was, he could not seek for a true perspective. He did not know what Washington had been told of him, nor did he care, but desired only to lash out at this man who, as Paine saw it, had betrayed both a friend and a cause. And believing he was going to die, he put into a letter his rage against a man whom he had once loved more than any other on earth.

Monroe begged him not to send it. "It will accomplish nothing," Monroe pleaded. "Believe me, it will accomplish nothing and gain for you only more enemies. How many years is it since you left America? Washington is only a man, and men forget."

"I haven't forgotten," Paine said.

For a time he held the letter, then he sent it, to be made public.

Paine continued to attend the Convention as a delegate from Calais. When the Thermidorians put down the popular uprising by force of arms and denied the people a voice in the new government, demanding property qualifications for the right to vote, a feeble old man stood up in the Convention and faced them. Even now Paine could vividly recall the torture of his abscessed side as he stood there in front of rank after rank of hostile faces. No screaming gallery with food wrapped in paper, eating as they applauded or hissed, no fervent radicals demanding death for those who opposed the people's will, but rather well-fed, stolid legislators who made a good thing out of the decadent remains of what had once been a movement for the freedom of man.

They looked at Paine and they whispered to each other, "Has the old fool no sense at all? Isn't ten months in the Luxembourg enough? Or must we send him back there for good?"

"What is he up to now?"

"Franchise."

"Yes, he wants them to vote. Let every blessed beggar vote, and the judgment day will come."

"Make a move to block it."

Someone else said wearily, "Let him speak. No one is listening."

And he spoke of franchise, of the right of every human being to vote. He had a knack of making enemies; he had a knack of always saying the wrong thing at the wrong time; he had a knack of making people hate Paine as they had never hated anyone else. Now amid the hundred voices crying out against him, one said:

"Is it difficult to tolerate that man who has never manifested the least degree of intolerance to anyone?"

No, he had never lost faith; he had not abandoned democracy, it had abandoned him—the Thermidors, then the Directory, the whole gradual and complete collapse of the revolution.

He began to run down like a watch; he stopped functioning in the only way he was fitted to function, as a revolutionist. Nothing but that could have made him so feeble and purposeless, not the hatred stirred up by *The Age of Reason*, not his sickness, not the silence of his old comrades in America, but simply the fact that he had ceased to fulfill his purpose.

He wrote a little; he was a writer and until he died, he would fumble with a pen. He remembered old Ben Franklin who had been a philosopher and a scientist until the day of his death, and Paine thought he too would dabble with philosophy and science, little machines, models, gadgets that were ingenious enough but meant nothing more than the chattering of a voice that had once roared out firm and strong, and since the voice could not be completely silenced it took these small, futile directions.

And thereby, he went to pieces. Forgotten—a new age was dawning, the nineteenth century. Had a fool once said, "Give me seven years and I will write a *Common Sense* for every nation in Europe"? That too was forgotten. The wave which

he started, the upsurge of the common man, would never disappear, but it would undulate, sinking now into obscurity,
coming up again in a spurt of fresh power. For him, for
Thomas Paine, revolutionist, that was no consolation; he
had failed, and the powers of darkness were rising.

He, who had never been meticulous about his appearance,
now completely neglected it. He shaved once a week, sometimes less often. He wore dirty linen and old felt slippers
out of which his toes poked forlornly. He shuffled back and
forth in the confines of his littered chamber, and sometimes
he would stand, head poised, as if trying to recall something
he had recently forgotten.

What had he forgotten? That the bells were ringing at
Lexington?

Liquor was an old friend; it was a friend when other
friends were gone. Let the teeto alers cry out against it, his
body was his own; when it was good and strong and vigorous,
he had used it unsparingly and not for himself; now it was
old and worn out and sick, and if he drank to ease the pain
and the loneliness, that was his business and no one else's.

He still had a friend or two among the plain Parisians;
good people, the French, simple people, enduring people—
civilized people. They understood such things; a man is a
man, not a god, and when they saw Paine coming down the
street, dirty, shuffling, they did not laugh or hoot at him,
but gently passed the time of the day with one who had once
been great.

"A good day, Citizen Paine."

They didn't forget so easily. If there were five heads outside the wineshop, bent over one of the small, smudged Paris
newspapers, trying to unravel the involved politics of Talleyrand, and Citizen Paine came along, they deferred to him.

"A good day, citizen—this man Talleyrand."

"I know him, only too well," Paine said.

There was nothing incongruous to them in this poor creature having been not so long ago the intimate of Talleyrand.

"He came to me for advice," Paine said. "I don't like him."

Nothing incongruous in that either; a king became a beggar and a beggar a dictator. Hadn't they lived through those times and didn't they know the broad loops the wheel of fortune made?

In the wineshop, the shopkeeper was the soul of quiet courtesy. He had sold to Danton, to Condorcet, and now he was selling to Citizen Paine. He saw glories that were not so long ago, and he tried not to see a dirty old man.

"The best, of course," he nodded, and chopped a franc he could ill afford from the price.

In that way, Citizen Thomas Paine passed out of the public life of France.

Living with the Bonnevilles was an old man called Paine, a rather ineffectual old man who puttered about at one thing and another—and sometimes would pause in the midst of what he was doing, with an absent seeking expression on his lined face. He was given to brief lapses of memory, and he was none too tidy. Sometimes out and rambling about Paris, he would come home with a bottle of brandy wrapped in newspaper under his arm, and closing his door behind him would drink half of it in an hour. Then, drunk, he would sometimes make a nuisance of himself—all of which the Bonnevilles put up with very patiently. When asked why by a curious neighbor, they would answer, very simply:

"You see, he is a great man, one of the greatest men this world has ever known. But the world is a quick place, and you have to scurry to keep up with it. He is too old to scurry about like a hare, and therefore the world has forgotten him. But we have not forgotten him."

Nicholas de Bonneville was a newspaper editor, a liberal, and a republican. His wife was a good-natured young woman who believed ardently in whatever her husband believed in. When he told her of Tom Paine's greatness, she nodded and agreed. She came of country folk, and had the peasant's tolerance for the whims of the aged, and because of that and because of what her husband told her, she put up with this untidy old man whose room was a litter of newspapers, books, little mechanical contrivances, empty brandy bottles, and numerous manuscripts, some of which occasionally appeared in her husband's newspaper.

One morning, in the fall of 1797, a short, pudgy stranger appeared at the Bonnevilles' front door and asked for Citizen Thomas Paine. At first Madame Bonneville stared at him suspiciously, then, recognizing him, she broke into excited welcome, ushered him into her parlor, offered him a glass of wine which he refused, blundered here and there and everywhere in her nervousness, and finally clattered upstairs to call Citizen Paine.

Paine, laboriously working at a manuscript, raised his brows as she burst in and asked whether or not the house was burning down. Ignoring this bit of facetiousness on the part of her lodger, she said breathlessly:

"Monsieur, Bonaparte is downstairs!"

"Who?"

"Listen to me, listen very carefully, Monsieur. Napoleon Bonaparte is sitting downstairs in my parlor at this very moment, waiting to speak with Citizen Thomas Paine. Do you understand me? He has come here, alone, for no other purpose than to speak with Citizen Thomas Paine!"

"Of course, I understand you," Paine growled. "Stop shouting; go downstairs and tell him to go away."

"What? Monsieur, surely you misunderstand me. I said—"

"I know what you said. Go down and tell him I have no time for brigands and evil men."

"No, no, no, no," Madame Bonneville sighed. "No, no, this you cannot do here under my roof. I have put up with many things, with dirt and drunkenness and noisiness, but I will not see a great general of France who has come to my house turned away."

"I pay my rent and keep," Paine muttered.

"No, Monsieur, it is not a question of rent, not if you paid double what you do. You will see Bonaparte or—"

"Very well, I will see him," Paine snorted. "Bring him up here."

"Here? In this?"

"And what's wrong with this? I live here, don't I?"

"No. no, no, no, Monsieur—you will come down to my parlor."

Paine shrugged. "Then down to your parlor," he agreed, and followed her downstairs. As they came into the parlor, Bonaparte rose and bowed, and Paine was struck immediately with the insignificance of the man, so short, so pudgy in body yet so lean in face, a shopkeeper possibly, but not the great general, not the warrior, not the diabolical genius who was shredding away the last remnants of the French Republic and the hopes and prayers of all men of good will.

"How sad it is," the old man thought, "that the great heroes and great villains of the world do not fulfill themselves physically!"

"You are Citizen Paine," Napoleon said. "I am Bonaparte—I have looked forward to this day, eagerly, hopefully. It is not often given us to meet the great ones of the ages

They pass away, and we must content ourselves with the legends. But I stand face to face with the greatest of all legends—Citizen Paine!"

That was not what Paine had expected; that broke through his armor, his defense, his calculated hatred for a man who represented all that he deemed evil. He was old; he was lonely; he was tired of being vilified; and this was a tribute.

He said, "Thank you, General."

"Not General, Citizen Bonaparte to Citizen Paine. My friend, sit down, if it pleases you." He had a way of command, even in things he asked, such as the simple matter of courtesy. Paine sank into a chair, but Napoleon paced back and forth, his head forward, his hands clenched behind him in a gesture that was already part of him.

"Citizen Paine," Napoleon said, "whatever you have thought of me, here is what I have been thinking of you— that a statue of gold should be erected to you in every city on the face of this earth, that your work should be enshrined—enshrined, I say. Don't I know? Have I not read *Common Sense, The Rights of Man, The Age of Reason?* Read them—reread them, I tell you! I sleep with *The Rights of Man* under my pillow, so that if I spend a night in wakefulness, insomnia shall not rob me but become instead a privilege. You and I are the only republicans, the only men with vision enough to look beyond the stars! A United States of the World?—I agree with you. I say an end to autocracy, an end to dictatorship! I take up your torch!"

Bewildered, Paine could only sit there and stare at the little man. What do words mean? Had he been mistaken? Does utopia come out of such blustering and through no other manner? He didn't know; his head was whirling. Perhaps he had listened only to the lies that were spoken about Bonaparte; they told lies about Paine too.

"I need you," Napoleon said. "We are both dedicated to mankind, to Republican France, and if we work together who can say to what lengths the dreams of Citizen Paine and Citizen Bonaparte may not go? Soon I will have a military council, and if you will sit there, I will be both honored and rewarded."

The old man was staring at him.

"You agree then?" Bonaparte smiled; his smile could be very winning.

"I will think of it," Paine nodded. "I will think of it."

After Napoleon had gone, Paine went up to his room, shaking off Madame Bonneville who would have a first-hand account of every word that had been spoken. He wanted to be alone; he wanted to think back and see what had brought him to this. In his room, he saw himself very plainly, the trash and dirt all about him, the old, stained dressing gown that he wore, the grime under his nails, the disarray of his gray hair. He found a comb and began to draw it through his thinning strands, musing all the while on these last years in Republican France.

Would he meet with Bonaparte? "Why not?" he asked himself. "Didn't I go back to the Convention again? I have not abandoned men; they have abandoned me and my principles. If the only hope left is Bonaparte, then I will go to him."

Hope had returned, a future had returned, and once more he was Thomas Paine, champion of mankind. He was going to sit at a military council with Bonaparte. After he had shaved, he looked in his mirror and said:

"Ten years younger—a man is as young as he feels. When Franklin was my age, the revolution had not yet started.

They will say of Paine that his life began at sixty, that he taught the world that the mind does not grow old."

He had money, for his books were selling well, and he stuffed his wallet greedily. The devil with the future. First clothes, and then the hairdresser; a man does not go to the hairdresser in rags.

At the tailor's, a brow was raised until he snapped angrily, "I am Citizen Paine, damn you! Enough of that and show me your styles."

"Something special, perhaps? Something for an occasion?"

"Something for a military council," he said, as offhand as he could. "Bonaparte will be there."

And then a hurry and a scurry, clerks running from all over the place.

"Something simple, black, I think."

"Naturally, black, citizen. One recognizes that for such an occasion a black worsted, in keeping with your background, and perhaps a touch of satin to add dignity—"

He bought shirts and shoes and stockings; the generals of France would not sneer at Tom Paine. Then, clothed in his fine new raiment, he went to the hairdresser. There were no secrets from a Parisian hairdresser. "I look too old, much too old," Paine said. "When a man still has work to do and people to meet, important people, he desires to make a certain impression."

The years can't be bounced off so fatuously, and when Paine came back to the Bonneville house, the reaction had set in. He sat in the parlor in his new clothes, staring at the place Bonaparte had occupied, the pudgy little man with the thin face, the commanding voice, the savior of mankind—

Bonneville came in, glanced at Paine, raised a brow but politely refrained from any comment.

"Tricked out like a popinjay," Paine smiled, a note of dejection in his voice. "Do you like it, Nicholas?"

"Very much," Bonneville nodded.

"Necessary," Paine shrugged. "I am embarking on a new career. When everything else is done and gone, the great Napoleon Bonaparte visits me, makes me his confidant, and informs me that he sleeps each night with a copy of *The Rights of Man* under his pillow. Either his pillow is too low, or I have been mistaken in the man." Paine leaned back in the chair, closing his eyes for a moment or two, then whispered:

"Nicholas, I am afraid. This is my last hope. What if it fails?"

As he entered the room where the council was being held, the military men, the engineers, admirals, generals, and political advisors who made up the group, each rose and bowed under the watchful eye of Bonaparte, who said again and again, very ingratiatingly:

"Here is Citizen Paine, messieurs, of whom you have heard. If you saw me with a book in my hands during one of our passages in arms, you may be sure that it was something Citizen Paine wrote. I introduce him as the first republican."

They were all very happy to meet Citizen Paine. Some he knew; most he had heard of, Bonaparte's generals and advisors, some of them intriguers, others open-faced men who had started off in the blue smock of the national militia in those dim, distant days of the Republic, and now were faintly troubled—though vastly impressed—by the heights to which they had risen. Some had been confidants of Robespierre and looked at Paine none too kindly; others dated from the Girondin times. It was only in events, not in years, that those periods were so ancient; almost entirely, the men at the council were young, Paine standing awkwardly among them like a fragment of the past.

It was the first time he had been in a group of French leaders and felt such a biting, incisive insularity. Heretofore, France and the world could be identified; Paris was civilization, and the revolution excluded nobody. Even during the worst of The Terror, when the revolution lashed out so frantically, it did so to defend itself, not to make itself exclusive. And in the beginning, many, many foreigners had sat in the National Convention along with native Frenchmen. The light-haired, stolid-faced, grim and tired Polish radicals had come to Paris after fighting alongside the Americans in the Revolution; British exiles, too, had come by the hundreds, Prussians who loathed what Prussia had come to stand for, Italians who dreamed of a free Italy, Spaniards who dreamed of a free Spain; they had all come to a rendezvous at Paris, because Paris was the heart and soul of the revolution, and the Parisians had welcomed them.

But here that was gone; this was a narrow, close gathering, and the terms used were entirely terms of military conquest. Enough of such drivel as freedom and liberty and fraternity and equality; this was Bonaparte.

When they said, "Most pleased to greet you, Citizen Paine," he knew they were thinking, "How useful will this Englishman be?"

When he spoke—and his French was still execrable, for all the years he had spent in France—they could not keep their lips from curling at his accent; and when they, in turn, said something which they did not wish him to understand, they lapsed into their quick, flashing patois, a rippling flow of sound that was utterly meaningless to Paine.

Finally, they were all assembled, and the council came to order. The men were seated in the form of a horseshoe, at the open end of which Napoleon stood behind a small table. There was a chair for him, but not once during the council did he sit down. Most of the time he paced back and forth, as if consumed by a nervous energy which would give him no rest. When he spoke, his head poked forward like a bird's and sometimes he would fling an arm at the man to whom he was speaking. Paine had a feeling that through all his thoughts, through all his scheming, planning, lightening-quick decisions, he was never for a moment forgetful of the fact that he was so small, so pudgy, so little physically of what a great conqueror should be. His French was not the French of the others; it rasped, it grated, it popped sometimes like rapid fire. He could be imperious, and a moment later, meek and humble; he had a black forelock which in moments of anger he shook down over his high white brow, over his eye. He could be crossed only when he asked himself to be crossed.

"We speak not of France, not of Europe, but of the world," he began.

Marcy: "And the world belongs to England."

"Does it? I presume more of the world. I presume it is not the possession of a nation of clerks and shopkeepers."

D'Arçon: "They are very good sailors."

Bonaparte: "One does not have to be a Columbus to cross the English Channel."

Gabreou: "That, sir, makes it a question of transport and potentials. I have no doubt that with the continent of Europe at our backs, we can outbuild them ten to one. If it is merely a question of putting an army ashore on the coast of England, we should not regard that as an obstacle, but rather as a problem."

Bonaparte: "Then as a problem?"

Gabreou: "It can be solved, naturally."

D'Arçon: "I am sorry, sir, if I do not see it that way. At least all our first brigades will be cut to pieces unless we raise some sort of diversion among the people. The manpower of France is not limitless, and there is no operation so difficult as a landing against a defended line of coast."

Bonaparte: "We have with us that illustrious republican, Citizen Paine. Already, I think, I have made it clear to him that our whole movement is a continuation of the revolution. Citizen Paine has had signal success with the revolutionary cause in England. We may presume that had not the liberal party abandoned him to the Tories, he would have been successful. What do you say, Citizen Paine, to a popular uprising in England?"

Paine: "There is no doubt that the British people have grievances enough against their rulers."

Bonaparte: "Then they will aid a French army? They will not resist?"

Paine (*very quietly*): "I think they will resist, sir. I think they will cut your army to pieces. I think that if you invade England, not a man of the invading force will return to France."

Bonaparte: "Are you trying to make a fool of me, citizen?"

Paine (*uncertainly*): "I don't know—it is so many years since I have been in England. I did not think, coming here, that it would be a question of military invasion."

D'Arçon: "Did Citizen Paine imagine that we proposed to invade England without weapons?"

Paine (*very uncertainly*): "I didn't know—I thought that the revolution would be reaffirmed. The English people are disaffected and mistreated, but that would not matter in the case of invasion."

Bonaparte: "And why would that not matter?"

Paine: "Because, my general, it must be understood that in England there are two things, the people and the empire. The empire can be destroyed, but the people cannot be conquered. Force would only unify them, and if you were to land an army on their shores they would forget that they work for sixpence a day and remember only that they are Englishmen. The revolution must come from within them, not with invasion. With the empire, it is another matter."

Bonaparte (*very evenly and coldly*): "And how is it another matter with the empire, Citizen Paine?"

Paine (*wavering, but his voice gaining in strength as he speaks*): "The empire is vulnerable. Make peace, promote franchise, reassert the principles of the Republic and proclaim them throughout Europe, cry out for the rights of man, win back the glory of Republican France and ally yourself with Republican America. What is the empire? Commerce? Then proclaim the freedom of the seas and enforce it; America will join you; abolish duties and open the ports, and see how long Britain can compete with you. Is the empire subjugation? Then glorify France, establish old-age pensions, lower the working hours, raise the pay of the poor, and proclaim the revolution far and wide. Then the English people will rise up and join you. England can't be conquered, but she can be won."

There was a silence after that, a silence so deep and ominous that Paine felt sick and afraid. From the old sores, there was heat and fire as he felt his way back to his chair. This end, this last frail hope was over. This was the outcome of all he had lived for, invasion of the green shores of England, death and destruction to all the small men and women he had once promised to lead from the abyss into bright sunlight.

And Gabreou, rising, sneered, "Citizen Paine, I presume, talks as an Englishman?"

There was one spark left; groping to his feet, Paine whispered, "Ask that of the dead, not of the living. Ask the people of three nations whether Paine ever spoke other than for humanity."

And Bonaparte said, "That is enough, Monsieur Paine."

15

"BUT NO MAN KNOWETH OF HIS SEPULCHRE . . ."

I<small>T WAS</small> a long passage, but not a bad one; even for the time, it was long, fifty-four days now and still no landfall. The experienced travelers said, no, that was nothing at all; a bad voyage was a hundred days; ships were better now in this year of 1802; you didn't call a voyage bad until the drinking water went bad, and, God willing, there would be a landfall tomorrow's dawn.

Tomorrow's dawn found half the passengers clustered on the foredeck, each wanting to have first sight of the good, green country called America; and the same thing happened on the next day and the next, each time more passengers crowding the dipping prow until at last land was sighted.

Among the passengers was the old man, Paine, standing silently at the rail, peering ahead, trembling a little, and nodding when the captain said, in a rich, down-east twang:

"Looks good, the old country, aye, Mr. Paine?"

"Yes—"

"A leetle bit changed, but not so much that you won't recognize it."

"It's been a long time."

"Well, that's the way. A man may have an itch to travel, but he's mighty glad to get home in the end." Above, they were making sail, and as a loose rope whipped by, the captain roared up, "Look lively there, you confounded lubbers!" And then to Paine, "We'll make Baltimore close enough, just a day or two. You'll be going on to Washington?"

"I had planned to," Paine nodded. His voice was somewhat hesitant as he said, "I will want to see my old friend, Mr. Jefferson. It's been a long time—"

"There you are," the captain laughed, raising his voice enough to make sure that those standing by overheard him talking so familiarly with a friend of the President of the United States. Privately, he had little enough sympathy with this old rascal, although Paine was in no way so repulsive as he had been pictured. He was said to be the enemy of Christianity. The captain was a religious man and didn't hold with that sort of thing, but still it never hurt to put in the right word at the right place.

"There you are," he laughed. "I go home to the missus, and you go off to dinner with the president."

And it was time enough, Paine thought to himself, that he had come home. A man wants to die in a friendly place; he wants to have a friend or two about him. The world is too big—a man wants to have just a little corner of it when he's old and tired. They might hate him, laugh at him, abuse him everywhere else on earth; but America would not forget. The times that tried men's souls were not so long ago that they should have any real reason for forgetfulness. Washington was dead, but most of the others were still alive. They would remember old Common Sense.

They hadn't wanted much to do with him on shipboard, and that was just as well; break clean; his work was done

Napoleon was the master of Europe, and all Paine wanted now was to go home and forget.

He came into the president's house, and the colored doorman announced, "Mr. Paine to see the president," and it was too much a dream. He felt like an old man in front of Tom Jefferson, although there was only six years' difference in their ages; Paine felt used up and purposeless before the tall, straight, handsome person who was President of the United States. Jefferson was at the height of his power and glory; the second phase of the revolution, they called it when he won the election, the dawn of the day of the common man. And Paine was used up and finished.

But Jefferson, striding forward, offering his hand and smiling, said, "Tom, Tom, you're a sight for old eyes. So the wars are over, and you've come home! It's the turn of the wheel, Tom; it's a sign that fortune is smiling when old comrades come together again."

Paine could say nothing; he smiled and then he began to cry, and then Jefferson was tactful enough to leave him alone. The old man sat in the reception room of the new presidential house, crying maudlin tears, taking snuff with a trembling hand, and then crying again.

He was all right when Jefferson came back; he was wandering through the two front rooms, peering at the old furniture and standing back to look at the oil portraits of men he had once known and fought by.

"It's new," Jefferson explained. "The whole city is new. I like to think that someday it will be one of the great capitals of the world."

"It will be," Paine said solemnly.

"You'll stay for dinner, of course?"

"The president is a busy man—"

"That's nonsense, and you'll stay for dinner, Tom. We have a lot to talk about."

Paine was eager to stay. All during the trip across, he had been speculating upon how Jefferson would welcome him. Even now the two Toms were grouped together as the world's foremost democrats, and it would be strange indeed if there was not some place for him in the Jefferson administration, even a very small place, such as secretary to the British or French legation, or perhaps one of the lesser cabinet ministers. That would be better, for it would permit him to spend his last years in America, and how could Jefferson evade the responsibility? Didn't he show immediately that he remembered the old times? A little work, a little honor, a little respect, and he would be able to die content.

It was good to be home.

At dinner, Jefferson beat all around the subject before he came directly to it. Talking about old times, he picked up one memory after another, and it soon became apparent to Paine that he was handling them uneasily; Jefferson was not a man to play hob with his own conscience; he lived by words and ideals, not by actions. He said to Paine:

"It's not that we ever differed. Our ends were always the same."

And Paine, eagerly, "That was a consolation in the worst times. If things were black, they were never so black but that I was able to tell myself, There's one man in the world who understands and believes."

When coffee and brandy were served, Jefferson shifted the conversation to Paine's experiences in Europe. But the old man was not anxious to bring back memories of a great hope that had died. It seemed incredibly banal of the presi-

dent to ask so curiously of those gallant men who had gone
forth from the Luxembourg to meet their deaths, Clootz,
Danton, Condorcet. Of Marat's murder by Charlotte
Corday, Paine would say nothing at all.

"Done with," he shrugged. "Now it's Napoleon. There's
nothing of the republic left."

"And will the French support him? I can hardly believe
that."

"They'll support him. They are good people, but now the
whole world is ranged against them. What else can they do?"

"I gather you intend to devote yourself to writing," Jefferson said, and could not help, adding, "The administration
will be glad for your support."

"One does not make revolutions at my age," Paine smiled.

"No—no, naturally. A long life, well filled, a battle well
fought, you might say. So much of what we have, we owe to
you; so much of what was done, Paine did. And now a comfortable old age."

"Old age?"

"Only in a manner of speaking. We are none of us so
young as we were, Thomas."

Holding out a hand that trembled in spite of himself,
Paine said defensively, "The machine runs down, but my
mind isn't old. Did they accuse Franklin of being an old
man? I have no family—"

"The farm?" Jefferson speculated, referring to the piece
of property at New Rochelle that Congress had granted
Paine after the war.

"I'm not a farmer. A man wants work, he doesn't want
to be laid on the shelf like a piece of old goods." That was
as near as he could come to asking Jefferson. Well, he understood a little of what the president was thinking, but an old
man becomes irritable, wrapped up in the few years that are

left to him. Jefferson stared moodily at the backs of his hands and said words to the effect of a president not being his own master, of a new, democratic administration having to start with an uphill fight, of a political alignment that was most complicated. He would never want anything to come between him and Paine; they were too much old, good friends for misunderstanding.

"I see," Paine nodded.

Jefferson said morosely, "You will find you have your enemies here, Thomas. The letter you addressed to Washington—"

"I won't talk of him," Paine growled.

"No, I'm not condoning him. But understand his position, nursing a babe of a state, in no way united, England prodding us and prodding us, and all of us knowing that another war would destroy us. You were in France—"

"Waiting for the guillotine!"

"I know, Thomas. But Washington was a strange man, not brilliant, not discerning; his heart was hurt, and there was a layer of rock over it. You think of the glory and the shouting, but what was that to a man who never in his life had anything he really wanted? He saw his duty, and he tried to perform it—"

"Even if it meant condemning me to death."

"Even if it meant that," Jefferson admitted.

There was a while of silence, and then the president mentioned *The Age of Reason.* He pointed out that the whole administration had been attacked as atheistic. Paine was tired now; seeing how things were, he wanted to get it over with and go.

"If you were to enter the government," Jefferson finally added, "it would be just the wedge our enemies are seeking."

Paine smiled and nodded.

"Perhaps in a year or two," Jefferson said.

In a hotel: "Paine? This is a godly house. We want no part of Paine."

In the street: "There goes the old beast."

In a tavern: "Drink with the devil, boys. Antichrist is here!"

And the children, flinging mud and rocks: "Damned old devil! Damned old devil!"

A woman: "You filthy old beast—you filthy, filthy old beast!"

A crowd: "A rope and a tree, and let's get it over with!"

Paine was home.

He went to visit his old friend Kirkbride at Bordentown. Kirkbride had written that he would be happy—most happy —to see Paine, and when Paine had speculated that perhaps a visit there would do harm to Kirkbride's reputation, Kirkbride waved the objection aside and begged him to come. Paine still owned the small piece of property at Bordentown, and of late a new, tremulous fear of poverty had taken hold of him. He thought he would look the land over and see whether it was worth selling.

It was good to be back in Bordentown. Word had gone about the Jersey countryside that Paine would be at Kirkbride's, and any plans the people might have had for abuse and demonstration were nipped when a dozen veterans gathered to pay their respects to their old comrade. Not the leaders, these, not politicians, but brown-skinned dirt farmers, light-eyed, slow-speaking men in their forties and fifties and sixties who had not flown high enough to leave all their memories behind them. Religious, they were, but not so religious that they excluded belief in God and men from their creed.

Gathered in a half-circle around the roaring fire, they paid a drawling tribute to their friend, and they gave Paine the last evening he would want to remember. Speech was slow and hard in coming to these men; their farms far apart, such gatherings were a rare occasion, and it took a good many rounds of old-fashioned flip before their tongues were loosened. Then, like careful masons, treasuring cement in a land where no more mortar could be had, they re-created scene after scene, passing the telling of a tale from one to another, not jealously but calculatingly, as one does with a good thing. They recalled the composition of the first *Crisis* paper, lingering over such details as the drum Paine had used as a desk.

"Pot-bellied—"

"Rib drum, I think."

"Now reckon it out, that was a right fancy drum with brass fittings. Johnny Hopper's, it was." They passed on to talk about how Johnny Hopper, the little drummer boy, had died at Brandywine, aged sixteen. "Poor damned little tyke." Then, from him, one old face after another was brought back. It shocked Paine to know how many were dead. Had a whole era, a whole age passed away? It was a roll-call from beyond the grave, Greene, Roberdeau, Putnam, Hamilton, name after name. "Disbanded," someone said.

But for all the talk of what had been and was no more, it was a good night for Paine, a sweet, warm night, a night to be remembered on such an occasion when as later, after leaving Bordentown, he passed through Trenton on his way to New York and changed coaches there. He never concealed his identity; he was Mr. Paine, and proud of it, but the pick-up coach driver told him:

"Damned if you'll ride in my stage."

At which Paine bowed his head and said quietly, "Very well, I'll wait for the next."

Between coaches, a gang of teen-age hoodlums gathered. It was amusing to kick the old man's luggage around, and then to clout him over the back with a stick or a lump of mud when he went to get it. And the best part of it was that grown folks stood about and laughed and cried, "Go to it! Give the old devil what he deserves!" Better fun to spit in his face as he lost his temper, to jolt him with hip or shoulder, to dance just out of his reach, screaming, "There ain't no God! Paine says so! There ain't no God!" Best fun of all when Jed Higgens tripped him and sent him face down in the mud; and then, while he lay there, whimpering like the old coward he was, Jed opened his grip, threw out half the clothes, and stuffed it with the empty whisky bottles that littered the station.

It might have gone on for a pleasurable long time, had not Mark Freeburg come along. Mark had only one arm; he had lost the other in the war, but the one was strong enough to send the young blades running and help the old man to his feet.

He stayed a while in New York, before going on to the farm at New Rochelle. His side was troubling him again, and his hands trembled worse than ever. He didn't mind discomfort in other parts of his body, but if he could not control his hands, how could he write? And writing was the only thing left to him. In addition to that, the long arm of Napoleon reached across the Atlantic and touched him. Bonneville was in trouble with the new government; his paper had closed down, and he was afraid for his wife and children. Now he could not leave the country himself, but couldn't Paine make some provision for Madame Bonneville and the children? Perhaps she could keep house for Paine? In France, under Napoleon, there was nothing left for a man who loved freedom, and it was said that Paine was a great man in America—

Yes, Paine wrote, he would do something.

So to add to other things, there was a woman and three small children on his hands.

It was all much too involved for him; his head ached with the strain of it, so many things to do, so many matters to attend to. Jefferson was running for the presidency again, and Paine, after a pet of childish rage, fought the issue out with himself and decided to support the president. Writing articles and pleas—but his hands shook so. Then the Bonnevilles came, and he shipped them off to the place in Bordentown. Too old to be bothered with children. He would forget something, and then walk round and round his little New York room, trying to recall what he had forgotten, and then go out into the street in slippers and dressing-gown, realizing what he had done only when the laughter and jeers of people woke him to it. There were the fits of depression when the brandy bottle was his only solace, and he drank until the glass slipped from his trembling fingers.

Then Madame Bonneville returned from Bordentown, bored, after so many years in Paris, by life in a rustic village where no one could speak a word of French. She took rooms in New York, and when Paine protested that after all he had given her a house, and that he was not wealthy enough to pay for an apartment too, she said:

"And who took care of you in Paris?"

He was old enough to be bullied now; he wanted peace; he was not too certain in his mind any more about what debts he owed to what people.

He tried to live alone on the New Rochelle place, but it was peopled with ghosts. When he lit a fire at night, to the accompaniment of brightly beating drums and shrill fifes, the past came marching out of the flames, ragged continentals with their long firelocks over their shoulders, shouting forlornly, Hello there, old Common Sense! It was more than he could stand; he didn't want memories. He flung dishes at them and begged them, "Leave me alone, leave me alone!"

He had a stroke and tumbled down the narrow flight of stairs in the house. Crying softly, he lay at the bottom, not quite sure what had happened to him, calling aloud for help when he found he could not use his hands. There was no help; no one heard his cries. He lay on the floor until he had enough strength to climb into bed, and he lay there for a horrible week during which he somehow managed to keep alive.

Then he was afraid to be alone, and he got Madame Bonneville to come and keep house for him. She was little enough use; three children that ran like rabbits kept her in perpetual fear that they would be lost in the woods and kidnaped by Indians. Paine could not explain to her that there had been no Indians near New Rochelle for a hundred years. She was convinced; she alternated her fear with mournful longings for Paris, and to the sick old man she was more of a nuisance than a help.

"Go back to New York," he finally told her. "I will take care of the bills."

She had talked him into leaving a legacy for her and the children, and now she reminded him of it.

"It will be done, it will be done," he said.

But he couldn't be alone. He wasn't afraid to die, but he feared the terrible, paralyzing effect of a stroke, and the doctor had assured him that it would come back sooner or later. So he found a hired man, named Derrick, who would work for him.

Derrick was jealously religious; religion was all his, his personal, dread possession. With the angels behind him, he came to work for the devil, his long, horse-like face wary and determined. He could do nothing well, not plow a furrow, not cut a tree, not split a rail, but that didn't matter for his chief occupation here was watching Tom Paine, stealing manuscripts he imagined were written in consort with the devil, burning them, carrying tales, making remarks about his employer. He also stole his employer's whisky and was frequently drunk.

At last, Paine discharged him; it was better to be alone. A few days later, Derrick returned, crawled up to a window where Paine was sitting, and let go with a large-bore musket, buckshot-loaded. He was drunk enough to miss the old man, but he shattered the window and filled the wall beyond with shot.

On his part, Paine was sorry that Derrick had missed. Better to have gone that way, quickly and painlessly, than to linger on here in an empty house. In the village, Derrick boasted about his feat until they were forced to arrest him, but Paine would not press any charges.

The old man feared the occasional trips he had to make into the village of New Rochelle. Not a mother had neglected to tell her child that Paine and the devil were in league, and when the thin-faced, bent old man came shuffling into town, he would attract as many children of all ages as the pied piper. It did not matter that he tried to be good to them, that he never chased them from his orchards, that he sometimes filled his pockets with candy in an attempt to bribe them away from their torments; that was to no avail, for what other game presented such fascinating possibilities as baiting old Tom Paine? Throw enough mud, rocks, and sticks at him and you could get him to lose his temper, and then you could lead him a merry chase. And there were wonderful rhymes you could sing as you danced out of reach, such as:

> *"Benedict Arnold and Simon Girty,*
> *They were false to flag and country,*
> *But compared to Paine they weren't bad,*
> *He played false with Washington and Gad."*

or

> *"Make a revolution, blood and flame,*
> *I'm the one who does it, my name is Paine.*
> *I should have gone to the guillotine,*
> *Too bad I didn't—I'm just too mean."*

And never a grown-up to reprimand you, but only to say, "Give it to him, give it to him," as they smoked their pipes and looked on.

In New Rochelle, there was no hope of an old comrade coming to his aid. This was Tory country during the war, and fiercely anti-Jefferson now, as most of Westchester County was. The villagers had not fought in the war; their neutrality swayed the comfortable way, and they gave all the aid they could to the British and to the Tory counter-revolutionaries called Rogers' Rangers. That they had not forgotten the war was proven to Paine when he came into town to vote in the 1806 election.

The election supervisors were a small Tory clique, and

when they saw Paine shuffling into town on registration day, the crowd of children buzzing at his heels, they looked at each other and nodded and smiled. Paine walked more proudly than usual; everything else gone, he could still cast a vote for principles he believed in. A mild function, an anonymous function, crosses on a piece of paper, but nevertheless the representation that he had made the guiding function of his life.

Standing on line, he closed his ears to the coarse remarks flung at him, and when finally his turn came said strongly: "Thomas Paine, sir!"

"And what do you want here?"

"This is the board of elections, isn't it? I'm here to register."

They smiled at each other, and told him, "Only citizens vote."

Paine shook his head. "I am Thomas Paine," he repeated, his twisted eyes wrinkled querulously.

"So we are given to understand. However, you are not a citizen of the United States of America."

The old man shook his head, bewilderment making him cringe into his years. Everyone laughed at the thought that this trembling old man was the murderous revolutionist, the diabolical antichrist. See how dirty he is, snuff stains all over his shirt, his stockings wrinkled and down at the knees, his hands shaking so! Patiently, the chief supervisor explained to him:

"We do not register foreigners, only citizens. You have no right to vote and you are holding up the line."

Reaching back into his memory for quiet legal arguments, for reason in a thing so obvious, for some clarification of this horrible mistake, the old man said haltingly, "But Congress gave citizenship to all soldiers of the revolution—"

"You were never a soldier of the revolution," the supervisor smiled.

"But I am Paine, Thomas Paine, don't you understand?"

"I will thank you to go, and make no further disturbance."

"But I must vote—I must vote. Don't you understand that I must vote. It is my right."

The crowd roared with laughter, and the supervisor, still patient, pointed out, "Neither Gouverneur Morris nor General Washington considered you an American citizen. Are we to go over their heads? Really, sir—"

"I won't stand such injustice!" the old man cried shrilly. "I'll prosecute you!"

"Call the constable," the supervisor said, his patience gone now. "We still have room in jail for an old rascal."

"Jail—not jail," the old man whispered, broken now. "Not jail any more."

And with that, he turned away and shuffled back along the street, the children dancing about him once more.

He had enough of New Rochelle—let the farm go to the devil. There was nothing left, nothing at all, and the only thing he wanted now was to die. Let it come quickly; let it be over with; this world was a strange place that he did not know at all, and he was a frightened, sick old man.

He went back to New York, and life prolonged itself, and he moved from one miserable lodging house to another. He drank too much; he took too much snuff, and about his appearance he cared nothing at all. A dirty old man, an unshaven old man—what did it matter? He had not even enough spirit left to shake a stick at the ever-present, tormenting children.

He sometimes asked himself, plaintively, "Is this God's

revenge?" He, for whom values had always been firm as iron, found them shifting and relaxing now. "Have I done wrong to believe in Him in an unbelieving world? Have I done wrong in saying that His name must not be profaned, that He is the top of all man's aspirations?"

Sometimes, briefly, a spark of the old Paine appeared, as when a man called Fraser forged a recantation of the so-called heresies in *The Age of Reason*. Then the old man challenged him and brought him to law. Paine might decay and die, but recant?—and on the one work for which he had suffered most, his plea for a gentle, reasonable worship of the Almighty. Never that, not even from this dirty old man who had only one thing left, his name. Fraser was not much among Paine's enemies; he confessed and pleaded for mercy, and the old man said,

". . . write no more concerning Thomas Paine. I am satisfied with your acknowledgment—try something more worthy of a man."

But the sparks were fewer now. A stroke felled him again, and he lay on the broken ruin of a whisky bottle until he was found.

He was dying, and he knew it, and it occurred to him that he would not lie anywhere but in some nameless field of beggars. To Willett Hicks, a liberal Quaker preacher, he said, "Let me lie in the Quaker burial-ground," adding plaintively, "I have never done anything unbecoming of a Quaker. They will do what they want with me when I am dead; they'll deny me a little bit of ground."

Hicks said he didn't think it was possible. One man might be sympathetic to Paine, but refer the matter to a committee, and it was doomed to failure.

"Just one small favor after I am dead," Paine pleaded.
"My father was a good Quaker, and so was my mother. I
never asked anything of the Quakers until now. In the name
of charity—"

Hicks said he would try, but it turned out as he had
anticipated. The Quakers denied Paine burial, and so did
various other sects whom Hicks sounded out. When
Madame Bonneville came to visit him, Paine complained
to her:

"They deny me even a little bit of ground. They will
strew my bones all over, like rubbish."

He was not a bad old man, Madame Bonneville thought,
for all his faults and such stubborn insanity as not wanting
to come down from his room to see the great Bonaparte.
Why didn't they leave him alone and stop tormenting him?

"You will be buried on your own farm," she said.

"It's good earth," he reflected, trying to gather his
thoughts. "American earth—that would be all right. But the
land will be sold; they'll dig up my bones and sell them."

"The land won't be sold," Madame Bonneville told him,
thinking that anything you told an old man who was dying
to comfort him was a blessing.

There was nothing but pain now—in his side where it had
become infected during his stay in the Luxembourg, in his
head, everywhere. A man dies so slowly. Madame Bonneville got him a nurse, but the nurse was a deeply religious
woman and let it be known all about that Tom Paine was
living his last hours. Thus began a pilgrimage; for what a
splendid thing it would be to hear Paine denounce *The Age
of Reason* on his deathbed!

One and all they came, Catholics, Methodists, Congregationalists, Lutherans, Quakers, Presbyterians—they had not

read his book, yet they came to fight the book and the devil.

"Renounce it! Renounce God and goodness and hope, for you are dying! Renounce mankind!"

Ministers, priests, pastors, fathers, nuns—they crept into his room, aided by the nurse, who had been divinely placed in this holy position. The old warrior was dying, and what had they or anyone to fear! The horns of the angels had pealed over Concord and Lexington, but here was only the rustle of stiff, black garments. If he called weakly for aid, his comrades could not hear him, for they were dead or far away, crossing the mountains and the plains, driving their oxen and their covered wagons, going to make the land and the world that was the dream, the handwork, and the suffering of Tom Paine. The ones in black crouched over him; they darkened and pushed away the little sunlight. They screamed, "Recant!" Ladies came to do their bit of good, dressed in proper ebony. Even the doctor, bending low, prodded him, "Mr. Paine, do you hear me? There is still time, there is still hope. Do you wish to believe that Jesus Christ is the Son of God?"

"Do you wish to believe?"

"Do you recant?"

"Do you renounce?"

"You are a dirty old man, you are all alone. Give up, give up!"

If there was a moment of peace, as there was bound to be, early in the morning and late at night, the nurse read in ringing tones from the Bible. This was a crusade; come, all ye faithful!

And then he no longer heard their voices, their prodding, their torments, their pleas that he should be weak, he whose strength was the strength of storied heroes, of the gods of old. He had peace; he had his comrades by his side; he stood among the men of good will, those who came before him and those who came after him.

Such was the funeral procession which accompanied his body to the farm at New Rochelle: Madame Bonneville, her children, two Negroes, and the Quaker preacher, Willett Hicks, those seven and no more. But it was enough; it was the whole world.

At one point during their journey up to Westchester, the driver stopped the coach to rest the horses, and a bystander called out to Hicks:

"Whose funeral?"

"Tom Paine's."

"Well," the stranger grinned, "if there is such a business as purgatory, he'll get his share before the devil lets go of him."

"On that score," Hicks mused, "I would sooner take my chance with Tom Paine than with any man in New York."

A few of the townsfolk had gathered to watch the burial. They snickered at the few words Hicks said over the grave. The coachman was grateful for the fine June day; he didn't often get a ride out into the country. Hicks asked Madame Bonneville whether there was any provision in the will for a tombstone, and she said, yes, she would have it put up as soon as it could be cut. She also intended to plant some willows and cypresses around the grave, it looked so bare. She showed Hicks the slip of paper upon which Paine had written his own epitaph:

"Thomas Paine, Author of *Common Sense*."

"That's enough," Hicks said. "That's enough for any man. How old was he?"

"Seventy-two, I think."

It was the eighth of June, 1809.

But it was not enough for the good people of New Rochelle that he had been buried in unhallowed ground. They invaded the farm and ripped the branches from the trees Madame Bonneville had planted, and sold them for souvenirs. They hacked pieces off the tombstone; they pulled up the few flowers that had grown.

Ten years later, a man named William Cobbett had a scheme. He dug up Paine's bones and took them to England, intending to exhibit them in various cities. But the British government refused to permit this last, crowning infamy, and the bones disappeared somewhere in England.

So today, no one knows where Paine lies, and that, perhaps, is best, for the world was his village.

THE END